Lelia Hardin Bugg

Orchids: a novel

Lelia Hardin Bugg

Orchids: a novel

ISBN/EAN: 9783741157813

Manufactured in Europe, USA, Canada, Australia, Japa

Cover: Foto ©Andreas Hilbeck / pixelio.de

Manufactured and distributed by brebook publishing software (www.brebook.com)

Lelia Hardin Bugg

Orchids: a novel

THE OHIO STATE
UNIVERSITY
LIBRARIES

WILLIAM CHARVAT
American Fiction Collection
The Ohio State University Libraries

ORCHIDS.

A NOVEL

BY

LELIA HARDIN BUGG.

SECOND EDITION.

ST. LOUIS, MO. 1898.
Published by B. HERDER,
17 South Broadway.

Copyright, 1894, by Jos. Gummersbach.

—BECKTOLD—
PRINTING AND BOOK MFG. CO.
ST. LOUIS, MO.

I.

FROM a window in the Senior Girls' Dormitory, Marguerite Clayton with the uneasy enjoyment attached to forbidden fruit, gazed at the Panorama of Paris outlined against the wintry horizon. She knew perfectly what a well regulated pupil ought to be doing at that hour in one of the oldest and most conservative convents in France. Her companions were enjoying their holiday in the proper and prescribed way. Some of them were walking demurely up and down the glass-covered court; some were seated in the recreation hall, reading the mild French tales written to order for the youthful feminine mind; her compatriots were studying the French classics—revised and annotated by a learned French abbé for the especial benefit of the large and rapidly growing contingent of American girls being educated at the French convents.

It was this knowledge which caused Marguerite to start guiltily at the sound of quick footsteps coming down the corridor, leading to the south wing which had recently been added; this contained a series of apartements arranged to accommodate the parlor boarders, and represented the latest concession made by a foreign country, in the person of the Mother Superior, to the conquering Americans.

"Oh, is that you Edith! You gave me such a start—I thought it was Madame Duval," exclaimed Marguerite.

"And what you be doing up here; why not you

down ze stair with ze rest of ze yong ladee?" answered Edith Kingman, mimicking the tones of the sorely tried General Mistress, when speaking English with her American pupils. Resuming the accents of Edith Kingman she added; "You'll be doomed for a hundred lines of Telemach if you don't take care."

Edith often presumed on her one year's advance in age, and her leagues of advancement in experience to give advice to her friend which her own position as a parlor boarder did not render incumbent upon herself to follow.

"Oh, I like to be by myself sometimes, and besides to-day I had a great many things to think about," answered Marguerite, trying to assume the dignity of a grown-up person.

"And what weighty affair of state, or estate, or state of life have you to think of to-day more than any other day?" replied Edith, unsuccessfully controling a tendency to smile.

"Oh, nothing really new, I suppose, only some days the thoughts all come together, and on others I don't think of anything but my lessons, and having a good time."

"Especially the good time."

"In the first place to-day is the anniversary of my coming to the convent," continued Marguerite ignoring the aspersion cast on her love of study.

"To-day just seven years ago I got here; do you remember it Edith?"

"Well I should think I do. I remember Madame Florac taking me away from a game of Parchesi, and I was winning too, to go entertain a newly arrived youngster from the States. I thought it was a shame that I should be called upon for every home-sick American who chose to seek the mines of wisdom on French soil."

"You felt proud to think you were so important."

"At any rate, I should have openly rebelled then and there, had I known that you were destined to usurp my place so completely with Madame Florac. There you sat in the gloomy elegance of the guests' drawing-room biting your lips to keep back the tears — that room always does have a depressing effect—and gazing at the portrait of Louis Quinze with the intensity of an old Royalist. I remember thinking what a puny little thing you were, to be ten years old. I was at least a head taller then, but you have caught up with me now."

"I suppose I was made up of eyes and legs and curiosity, as our own Mr. Warner says of little girls: I know I had my full share of curiosity anyhow," put in Marguerite, with all the eager pleasure of a girl talking over her first experience at boarding school."

"You had plenty of things to exercise your curiosity about. I wanted to laugh, only I didn't dare, when you asked with the airs of a young princess, to have a bath prepared, and to be shown to your room. And then your look of disgusted bewilderment when Madame said she would see about the bath, and told me to take you to the dormitory and have Sister Gabriele show you to your cell. I suppose you thought it would be like the cells in a jail, didn't you?"

"I don't remember what I thought; I only know

that I was utterly and completely, and abjectly miserable."

"Utterly is enough."

"I thought my heart would break when I came, and now I think it will break when I leave."

"Fractures are easily mended in the young; fractured hearts follow the same rule I daresay. But it does seem strange that you have never been home in all these years."

"Ah, yes, Edith and you don't know how many pangs of conscience I have had about it. Poor papa wished me to go just the vacation before he died. He intended to come over himself and have me spend a fortnight with him in Switzerland, but business prevented; then he wanted me to go home, and I refused. And in the autumn he died. I wonder if he knows now that I am sorry I did not go, and if he forgives me, Edith? I felt so bitter, so desolate and deserted when he sent me off here—it seemed into another world then, that all my love simply died. I thought to myself my papa doesn't care for me any more, why should I care for him. Papa was a peace-at-any-price man, and as his new wife insisted that her children and myself could not get along together—and I was a little vixen I don't deny—why of course I had to go. People all think it is dreadful to separate a mother from her children, but that it is nothing at all to separate a father from his: then there were two of them, and only one of poor little me. To crown my cup of woe, instead of coming over with me himself, papa sent me with a stranger, a chaperon supplied by Cook. It broke my heart, and I never forgave him.

Even now I try to feel sorry, and I say it over and over with my lips, but I don't really mean it. Rose and Lucy were such nice, well behaved, exceedingly proper, prunes and prisms sort of little girls, and I was—"

"And you were the pickles and porcupine sort I suppose."

"When papa asked me why I couldn't be nice and amiable like my new sisters, I fairly hated them and him too."

"Why Marguerite!" ejaculated Edith with all the emphasis of unconcealed astonishment.

"But you have conquered that feeling, surely."

"Oh yes, I suppose so. My step-mother and the girls have been to see me twice, and I spent one day in Paris with them without fighting or pulling their hair. Of course now that I am older I see things a little differently. Papa could not have been expected to remain a widower just for one little mite of a girl. If he chose to adopt his wife's children he had a perfect right to do so. I don't mind about the money, Edith, I don't want you to think that. I don't deny that I should like to be a great heiress, but that is only a minor consideration. But I did mind—it cut to the very quick—that papa made no difference at all in his will between me his own and only child, and the children of his second wife."

"It only shows how a clever woman can hoodwink the best of men," sagely interpolated Edith. "But you need not complain about the money; you will have nearly two million dollars, and that is enough to bring admirers to your feet as thick as blackberries."

"I was not thinking about admirers" answered Marguerite with rising indignation expressed in her big grey eyes. "I should like to do something great with my money, found charities and all that, like the queens and princesses of France used to do."

"Oh, I daresay."

"The first thing I am going to do is to found a poor school or a hospital or something as a memorial to mamma. Papa intended to do it but he got married again and forgot all about it. Edith, do you think I am anything like mamma? I have just been looking at her picture," Marguerite broke off impulsively, handing Edith a photograph which was lying with several others, in her lap.

The girl, thus appealed to, gazed critically at the faded picture, at the curls falling around a broad smooth forehead, at the pinched hour-glass waist, the enormous hoopskirt, the vague lines intended for eyes and mouth, and then fastening her orbs on the strait nose, answered confidently, with characteristic fondness for saying agreeable things: "Yes, I think you must be the living image of your mother. I never knew before where you got your Grecian nose."

Edith had always frankly admired her friend's nose with an admiration intensified by the knowledge that her own nose was anything but what a well appearing nose ought to be. Malicious ones pronounced it a snub, but she carried her head gracefully, and managed to convey the impression that her nose turned up from choice, and that if she lowered her head the nose would be lowered as well.

"Why, you have seen mamma's picture before, Edith."

"Yes, but I had forgotten about the nose."

"Is mine really like mamma's? I am going to see," and Marguerite jumped up from her chair, scattering her pictures on the floor for Edith to pick up, and tripped down the corridor to her cell. The cell was far more cozy than its name implied, with the November sun streaming through its one window, the little white bed at one side, a small wardrobe at its foot, the soft rugs on the stained and polished floor, and its one chair supplying the wants of the body. A little niche opposite the bed, containing a statue of Notre Dame de Lourdes, a silver crucifix and a bottle of holy water, administered to her innocent soul, whilst the pictures on the wall, — engravings of saints, photographs, sketches with her own initials in the corner, appealed to her aesthetic nature. A picture of St. Marguerite larger than the rest, hung over the commode, and this the girl hurriedly took down, and turning it around, a heavy glass mirror was revealed: she gazed intently into its depths, scanning her nose with particular attention; "Yes, I have mamma's nose" she said to herself with a gratified smile. The smile did not vanish as she looked critically and complacently into her own beautiful eyes, inherited from an Irish great-grandmother, at the even white teeth, the red lips, nor as she stood pinching her cheeks to start a wave of color over their smooth pallor, bringing her thick braids of bronze black hair across her shoulders and stretching them out to their full lenght, turning her neck to note its contour, throwing her shoulders back to make them appear broader, and indulging in a perplexing study of her figure; then she tried to get the general effect by placing the mirror on the bed and standing on the chair, but only her feet and the hem of her straight black uniform were visible, and of these she was not vain. After thus mentally photographing herself, she replaced the picture, with the mirror turned demurely to the wall, the saint with reproachful eyes looking out from the frame, and then darted back to her friend"

"Yes, Edith I think I look like my mamma, all but the eyes."

"Don't you remember your mamma at all" queried the elder girl tenderly, as one instinctively speaks of the dead.

"Sometimes I think I do, but it seems just like a dream: she died three years before we left San Francisco. It seems cruel that she should have been taken, just as papa was getting rich, after having shared poverty and hardships for so long. You know papa was very poor until he made a hit in mines; then he speculated in more mines and every thing he touched turned literally into gold. I suppose if he had lived he would have been one of the richest men in New York; but perhaps the luck would have changed and left him as poor as he was in the beginning."

"So you have luck in your family too, have you? So have we, it is on the Kingman side. I always say that as poor papa had no money to bequeath to me, I hope he has left me the Kingman luck."

"Why I thought you were rich," said Marguerite wonderingly.

"Oh no, I'm not; I haven't a red cent, my dear. All the money belongs to mamma and it barely makes a fortune in a lump; divided it would not be a fortune at all."

"Oh, well it is all the same."

"No, it is not. Mamma is young and good looking, and she may get married again. I used to think it was all the same too, but four winters ago when we were at Cannes Mrs. Goldwin from Chicago enlightened me.

'You'll be quite a belle when you come out, if your mother doesn't take it into her head to get married again,' she said to me. "I ran off to find mamma, and ask her intentions, but she had gone for a walk and did not return until dinner time; but the question wouldn't keep, so I asked her just as the soup was being served—we always dined at the table d'hote—if she were going to give me a new papa, and repeated Mrs. Goldwin's remark. Every body laughed, and I thought I had said something bright, until after dinner when mamma boxed my ears and said she would like to do the same for Mrs. Goldwin. Papa had good looks and winning ways, and mamma was grandpapa Carter's only child. Papa was a splendid theoretical financier, but mamma never gave him any chance to develop and test his theories, and when he tried them on his own account they usually ended in mortgages."

"You have traveled an awful lot, haven't you" said Marguerite who had picked up some American slang in spite of French seclusion.

"Yes, I suppose I have, considering. I have crossed the Atlantic nine times and have been in three continents."

"Three continents?" answered Marguerite with an interrogatory inflection.

"Yes, America, Europe and Africa."

"Oh, I forgot Cairo and Algiers; you never speak of anything about them but the hotels and the donkeys and the curios, and so I forgot they were not in Europe."

"Talking about Algiers," continued Edith, "I remember in our geography class it was described as having such a warm balmy climate, the paradise for invalids and all that. I told Madame Florac it wasn't true; that it was cold enough for fires and that the wind blew a regular gale when we were there, and she said I had traveled too much to ever pass a satisfactory examination in geography."

"I can hardly wait to get through school to see all the places I want to see," chimed in the younger girl. "I am going to travel a whole year and maybe two; Mr. Dalton says I may. If you would just come with me it would be perfect."

"Ah, I thought your heart would break to leave the convent, and here you can hardly wait."

"Edith you are very unkind. You know I hate to leave Madame Florac and Mother Salette and the rest, but of course I want to see the world. Perhaps I shall come back afterwards and be a parlor boarder for a long, long time. Only I don't think I should like it if you were not here."

"Just wait, Rita, we shall have high old times together in New York. You can't imagine how jolly it is because you have never seen any thing."

"And you have seen every thing. It is odd that you did not stay at school until you finished the course, and then traveled," commented Marguerite.

"Yes, I know it seems that way, but you see I am the apple of my mother's eye, and she couldn't do without me for a very long time at a stretch. When I was here studying my lessons, she was alone with her maid at some of the winter resorts; she would wake up at night, especially if she had taken coffee for dinner, it always makes her nervous, and get to thinking that perhaps I was ill or unhappy or something, and the next morning she would send for me. Then after I was with her for a while she would think—perhaps it was green tea that produced the second train of thought—that I ought to be in school. Her conscience would reproach her for neglecting my education, dear mamma's conscience has given her a great deal of concern, and back to school I would go. Occasionally she tried governesses, but that was very expensive, and mamma gets stingy spells sometimes. A governess, you know, couldn't be asked to go to the servants' table with the waiting maids, and I was too big to eat at the children's table—at least I wouldn't—and so mamma had to pay full rates for the governess besides her salary. Mrs. Goldwin suggested to mamma to have a maid who could teach me and do plain sewing, but whether mamma had a very high opinion of my brains or not she at least thought they were beyond a waiting maid's capacity to train, so the idea was not adopted."

"I should think—Mrs. Goldwin must be a queer sort of a woman."

"Oh, she was considering the expense; and I have cost mamma a lot of money, when one comes to count it all. One winter at Cannes mamma thought I ought to be taken at children's rates, because she had stayed at the hotel so much and had brought so many of her friends there; the landlord expressed his gratitude with his hand on his heart and his eyes turned heavenward so that you would have thought mamma had saved his life, but when it came to making terms he was very sorry, but mademoiselle, which was myself, had grown to be such a fine big girl it would be a pity to keep her a little child any longer, and mamma had to pay grown up folk's rates; but she was determined to get the worth of her money; she sent for a physician, the physician to various royal highnesses, by the way, pretending that I was ill, simply because I could not eat quite as much as a grown person; he charged a hundred francs for giving me a tonic, so mamma was out of pocket after all." Marguerite laughed; she was accustomed to her friend's absurdities, and knew Mrs. Kingman to be a most estimable matron without any nonsense about her, and a level head, which she assured Edith she had not inherited.

"Oh, you don't know how sensible I can be on occasion," retorted the parlor boarder.

"No, the occasion never happened to have presented itself."

The two friends enjoyed these encounters of words, for they understood each other perfectly, and their friendship had begun, so Marguerite declared, on the first instant they met, although

Edith said it was probably after a half hour had elapsed. It had grown steadily with the years of companionship at the convent, which the isolation of foreign association fostered. It had not been an uninterrupted course of true love however; open hostilities, followed by the most cutting and punctilious politeness had not been infrequent, but reconciliations ardent and sweet had always ended them. It was Marguerite who usually made the acts of contrition and Edith who did the forgiving; but then it was generally Marguerite who was in fault. If Edith talked longer to another girl than her Damon approved, there was a scene, but before bedtime Marguerite, tearful and penitent, crept into Edith's arms, and nestling a tear-stained face on her shoulder, begged to be friends again. Not but what her pride was strong, but her affections were stronger. Her temperament required some one to love, and some one to love her, and her histrionic talent in embryo always made the most of the dramatic element in the reconciliations. Edith returned her affection with a warmth in no way diminished when Madame Florac came to hold first place in her friend's regard.

"Madame is my second mother, and you are my own dear sister" was the way in which Marguerite herself disposed of the divided allegiance, and Edith accepted it good naturedly.

"Oh I do believe Madame Duval is coming" said Marguerite in a stage whisper, sinking to the floor in a little heap and burying her head, ostrich like, in Edith's lap.

II.

A light rapid footstep came through the lower door of the dormitory, paused an instant and then continued down the hall.

"That was Madame Duval. I know that cat-like tread any where. I never did like her" said Marguerite, regaining her former position by the window.

"I know you never did, but that is just one of your silly prejudices;" answered Edith, "you never had any reason for disliking her, and it shows a very unbalanced mind to dislike a person for no reason."

"Oh she is so sanctimonious, and so smooth, and so, so like a stick. And then she is always talking about her holy vocation, *hers* if you please, just as if God had particularly called her by a special angelic messenger, to the cloister."

"Why Marguerite, what *is* the matter with you to-day; is it the effects of original sin, or of those oranges you smuggled to your cell last night."

"Both."

"I thought such wickedness could only come from a deranged stomach."

"And then she is always talking about the girls of rank who have been educated here," went on Marguerite impetuously, "I have simply been bored beyond endurance by the virtues and the quarterings of the Princess Orlandorf. I can imagine her going into heaven, after a sojourn more or less prolonged in Purgatory and saying to St. Peter: We trained the young ladies belonging to the best families in France; Madame la Comtesse This, the Baroness That, the Princess de Something else, were educated at our convent; Let me pass instantly, "Monsieur le Curé says in his sermons that all are equal before God, but I am certain she does not believe him. The wealthy bourgeoise seem to be her particular aversion. I am not sure whether she counts us Americans as belonging to the lower upper classes, or the higher lower classes. She can never understand how a girl whose father is a merchant or a banker in America can associate with princesses and countesses over here."

"You at least Marguerite, cannot complain of any neglect on the score of rank. A girl with a dowry of ten million francs in her own right is not, usually, made to feel any inferiority in a European boarding school, and you have found no exception in Madame Duval. She has always been very nice to you; I wish I could say the same for your conduct towards her."

"There comes Madame Florac" exclaimed Marguerite joyfully, springing to her feet, forgetful in her gladness at seeing her "dear Mother" of the punishment discovery would involve.

"Marguerite, Edith, what are you doing here? Why are you not down stairs where you belong?" Coming swiftly down the dormitory between the rows of white curtained cells, was a tall stately nun with a patrician face, illumined and made beautiful by an expression which Marguerite, in the extravagance of her affection, had declared a seraph might envy. There were purplish rings beneath the soft blue eyes, and a marble whiteness of skin which indicated any thing but a robust constitution, but Marguerite did not remember of her ever having been ill, so she came to the comforting conclusion that the nun was stronger than she looked.

Both girls advanced to meet her; Marguerite was soon clinging to her arm in an abandon of affection, trying to exculpate herself at the same time.

"No, no I will not listen to any excuses; you have broken the rules, and you must suffer for it," said Madame Florac firmly. "This afternoon when the girls go for a walk you and Edith may take exercise in strict silence in the court; you on the right side and Edith on the left." She continued her scolding, although she did not repulse the caresses of Marguerite who was still clinging to her arm; but she showed that she meant the penance to be carried out, by repeating the order of punishment to the religieuse in charge of recreation that day.

"Isn't she lovely!" exclaimed Marguerite ecstatically, giving Edith a hug intended for Madame Florac, as the nun disappeared down the corridor leading to the monastery.

"If Madame Duval had scolded you in that way Marguerite, you would have turned the place into a regular Vesuvius" answered Edith ignoring the question.

A quarter of an hour later Madame Florac appeared at the door of the study hall where the two girls were pretending to read.

"Edith, Marguerite, I have a piece of good news

for you, but I shall keep it until this afternoon."

She did not repress a smile when Marguerite looked up with a roguish twinkle, and tossed a kiss from the tips of her slender fingers as the door closed again. She had been accused more than once by her sisters in religion of allowing too many liberties to Marguerite.

"Poor child" she said with a sigh. "I wish she were not so impulsive and so self-willed."

Madam Florac's peculiar talent, knack, gift or whatever name it was called, for managing girls had early been recognized in her religious life, and all during the years of Marguerite's stay at the convent she had been her friend, adviser, mother, regardless of any change of Superiors.

She came from a noble, but impoverished family, and when, after her school days were over and she had passed a season with an aunt in Paris, she signified her desire to enter the Order consecrated to the service of God and the salvation of aristocratic souls, the question of dowry had been waived in consideration of her worth. A dowry of brains was really more needed than one of more tangible matter, for the convent was one of the wealthiest in France, and the wealth was well invested. Madame Florac had learned English when she was a little girl from an invalid American who eked out her income by giving lessons to private pupils. This knowledge made her particularly useful in the convent, for the number of American and English girls who came there for an education was increasing every year. Marguerite and Edith had never lacked for opportunities to hear their own tongue at any time during their school life, although the parents of all the Americans had stipulated strictly that they were to speak French only.

"We already speak French better than the French do themselves" said Edith audaciously plagiarizing. "At any rate one can understand us easier."

"Yes, if the one happens to be an American." Marguerite assented.

In the afternoon the twain were faithfully performing their penances, each with a book tucked under her arm, the solitary occupants of the vast court. The other girls had all gone off under the guidance of the outdoor sister, for a ramble in the woods, after vainly uniting in a chorus of supplication for the culprits. Madame Florac opened the door, and paused with a kindly smile lurking on her lips, unseen by the two girls marching like sentinels up and down the court. They had been put on their honor in regard to silence, and both would have suffered the rack rather than have broken it. Madame Florac noted with the impersonal pride, which a nun takes in all things pertaining to her convent, that the girls carried themselves with an ease and elegance which would have done credit to any dancing master in Paris, and as her eyes dwelt on Marguerite she was conscious of a feeling which was not impersonal, in her heart. The girl had been dependent on her care and affection so long, and the maternal instincts which orphanage brings out in a religious had centered with a peculiar affection on the little American. Besides, Mr. Dalton, the guardian, had given her full authority in regard to his ward's concerns at school, so that after her father's death very few matters excepting bills, were ever referred across the Atlantic for settlement.

Edith looked much more like a young lady than Marguerite, although there was but one year's difference in their ages. She was no taller, but her figure was delicately rounded where Marguerite's barely escaped angles; she still wore her reddish brown hair in a plait, school-girl fashion, down her back, but her fluffy bang and the knot of ribbon at the nape of her neck were managed with a coquetry which the more secluded girl had not acquired. A Harvard student whom she had met at Homburg one summer had told her that her eyes were "deeply, darkly dangerously blue;" and they had a frank, clear expression which physiognomists do not associate with ignorance of the world but fearlessness of it; her skin was soft and fair, her mouth expressive and sensitive, although too large to suit an artist; her hands and feet were perfect, and were the source of a great deal of satisfaction. She had been around at fashionable hotels too much, had mixed with people of too many varying degrees of worldliness not to have learned the value of beauty. She had common sense which really amounted to genius at times in spite of her assumed frivolity, and her practicability, Madame Florac considered a very good foil for the tense ideals of Marguerite.

"Well, my dears, are you enjoying your walk?" said the nun, as the girls turned in their promenade, sixty feet apart as had been prescribed.

Both came running toward her, Marguerite exclaiming, "I thought you would come."

"I am going to stay only five minutes, just long enough to tell you the good news you might have heard this morning but for your disobedience. I did intend to wait until this evening, but I think you have both discovered that the way of the transgressor is hard so I concluded I would not make it any harder. Madame Flaubert sends both of you an invitation to spend the Christmas holidays with Madelene at Chateau Flaubert. She gives the invitation early so that you will have time to write home for permission. Of course this will not be necessary for Marguerite, if she is a good girl I shall let her go, but Edith, you must write to your mamma immediately so that I can accept or decline the invitation for you as soon as possible."

"Oh mamma will say yes, I know. We met Madame Flaubert at Rome during the Carnival; I knew it was Madeleine's mamma as soon as I heard the name. They look alike. When I told her that I was at school with her daughter she kissed me on both cheeks and said she was very glad to know me. She had already said the same to mamma, but not in the same tone; one was the conventional tone, and the other was the George Washington tone of genuine truth."

"Why, does Madelene know about it?" asked Marguerite with unconcealed astonishment that her other chum who stood second only to Edith in her regard, could keep a secret from her, and such a secret too.

"Yes, she knows now, I told her just before the girls went for their walk."

After the invitation had been duly discussed, and the five minutes prolonged to ten, the kind hearted religieuse who believed in tempering punishment with mercy, as well as mercy with justice, said: "Now if you think for the future you can keep from absenting yourselves from the recreation hall without permission, you may put on your things and go with me into the garden to gather geraniums for the chapel."

III.

FOR the first time in her life Madame Flaubert was conscious of a distinct limit to her hospitable impulses which would have excluded two guests her son's thoughtlessness had inflicted on her for the Christmas holidays. Infliction was not the word she used even in her thoughts, for French training would have revolted at any thing so strong as that applied to an invited guest, and at any other time the inconvenience would have been turned into a most decided pleasure. Their welcome lacked inward warmth, which however, bore no outward sign, simply because their coming was inopportune. It meant the possibility if not the probability of a checkmate to her most cherished and carefully laid plans, and human nature, in even the most hospitable breast, could hardly be expected to be proof against such a contingency. Madame Flaubert was a good woman, a good Christian, a good mother, but her goodness had not closed her eyes to material considerations, and it was her very devotion as a mother which protested against the turn affairs had taken. She was not worldly, at least she had never accused herself of being so in the searching examinations of conscience which she made every night, and the good abbé her cousin, who had been staying for a few weeks with her, had not hinted at such an imperfection when she discussed her hopes and ambitions with him.

A mother's first duty was to her children, and what could be a graver consideration than their marriage. In what could their happiness be more vitally concerned : where could a mother show her love for her children more surely than in seeing to their proper settlement in marriage; where could she be more derelict in her holiest duty than by neglecting it; what blessing could she pray for more ardently than for good mates for her children. And now, after many and earnest supplications that a good wife be sent to dear André—a good wife meant one with a very big dot, for Andre was poor; a pretty face,—for Andre was fastidious; of suitable rank, no insanity nor consumption nor other disastrous heritage, docile and pious, French if possible, if not American— —although these things were not expressed in the prayer, they were included in it—when her petition seemed almost on the point of being answered, why should she not feel afraid to fly in the face of Providence by bringing other young men who had mothers of their own to look after their welfare, to interfere with her plans. Why had Madeleine, usually so reserved with strangers and foreigners, become so intimate with two beautiful Americans who were rich beyond all she had dared hope, if nothing was to come of the friendship? It might be that her prayer was to be answered in some other way, but Providence, which often, if not usually, acts in natural channels, ought at least to have a fair chance to fulfil Andre's destiny. He might not care for either of the girls, and she was not one to force her children's inclinations in a matter so serious; and again the misguided Americans might be so insensible to manly worth as not to care for Andre, but prudence required one to make the most of the opportunity. If nothing vital came of the visit she would enjoy the satisfaction of having given a pleasant vacation to two charming girls, and Madame Flaubert's greatest pleasure was in giving pleasure to others. It would have a practical value in laying the foundation for a return of hospitalities, and in paving the way to a greater intimacy with the American colony in Paris of which her sister was always talking. No one could accuse her of selecting her friends on the score of wealth, for her most intimate associates were families like her own, too poor to keep a house in town, and who spent the greater part of the year on their estates, barren of all modern things save a mortgage, and productive of little else than poor crops and vexation of spirit. But rich friends were very agreeable, and very useful to have, and she was not one to think less of an acquaintance because of the possession of money. She always felt that a certain much-quoted passage of Holy Writ had been wrongly translated, and that not money, but the lack of it, was the root of all evil. In the Flaubert family this lack had taken deep root, had grown under several generations of Flauberts, and there was a prospect, humanly speaking, of the estate passing into the hands of a certain Semitic gentleman who held more of the Flaubert paper than was agreeable to contemplate. The outlook was dark, but Madame Flaubert never let her trust in Providence descend so low as to think for a moment, that the catastrophe would really ever happen. Andre would marry suitably, and then all would be well; debts all be paid, and things crooked made as straight as the narrow way itself.

Monsieur and Madame Gaston, her revered brother-in-law and cherished sister, who were coming to spend Christmas with her, had kindly volunteered to bring Madeleine and her companions from the convent, and thus save Madame Flaubert the trouble and expense of the trip. Two days before the great feast of Christmas they arrived at the stately old chateau.

Lord Parkhurst, a young English earl whom her son had met in Paris, and Mr. John Raymond, an American spending the winter on the Mediterranean to ward off a case of nervous prostration, had arrived together the evening before. Lord Parkhurst had been ordered to a more genial clime to save himself from rheumatism, and in spite of all protests that he must go home for Christmas, his physician remained obdurate, forcing him to an exile at the season of all others when an Englishman feels that the whole planetary system ought to wait, if the doing so would facilitate his reaching his own holly-draped fireside for Christmas.

Madame Flaubert received the girls with a motherly graciousness which won their hearts on the spot, and Marguerite declared she was the loveliest chatelaine she ever saw, "just like the noble ladies you read about in the times of the Bourbons."

Edith retorted that her head was turned with

royalist romances, and that she didn't deserve the blessing of having been born under a free flag that waves over the greatest country on earth.

Marguerite and Edith were given adjoining rooms at the suggestion of Madeleine, who had inherited or acquired thoughtfulness for others from her mother; her own room was at the end of the same long corridor; her aunt occupied the state guest room, the room where a royal princess had once slept, and Lord Parkhurst and the American had apartments in the opposite wing near their young host. Madame Flaubert had invited her daughter's friends as convent girls, not as young ladies, and so they brought only simple toilets as became demoiselle who had not yet entered society. The only concession Edith declared her intention to make to the world of fashion was to do her hair up in the prevailing mode, and Marguerite daringly determined to follow her example. Thoroughly tired and out of patience she was still trying to solve the mystery which looked so simple and proved so formidable, of getting her hair rolled in just the right way. Edith came to the rescue, but without success; Marguerite declared that the coil of hair was not in the right place, and that it made her head ache. In despair, for the fear of being late for dinner hung like a sword over her, she plaited her hair as usual, hurried on a ruby colored gown made severely plain, but by one of the great modistes in Paris, and after a finishing touch from Edith, announced herself ready. She followed her friend's more confident footsteps through interminable halls, and down spacious winding stairs, until they reached the drawing-room. The lamps had already been brought in, a wood fire was crackling in the big fire-place, and with the curtains drawn and the easy chairs arranged to the best advantage, the room had a cheery coziness in spite of its size.

Marguerite blushed for no reason, and kept close to Edith as they advanced toward their hostess. She was wondering whether in case they were late for dinner she should explain about her hair. But no one seemed to be conscious of any delay. Madame Flaubert complimented their appearance in an audible aside to her sister who was young and very pretty, and who looked younger and prettier than she really was under the softening glow of lamps shaded to give the most flattering effects to feminine complexions, and perhaps to cast into shadow the threadbare places in the heavy wilton carpet. The young men who happened to be in a group around a beautifully carved, massive mahogany table, were presented with due state. Edith, to whom the dominant sex was no stranger, began to chatter gaily to a tall young man very blonde, and very graceful whom she addressed as Lord Parkhurst.

"I am highly flattered, I am sure Miss Kingman" he said with a profound bow, "and if I did not know detection would swiftly follow I should not undeceive you, I never knew before how musical a title could be, but I haven't the honor—Lord Parkhurst, save me from the temptation of usurping your laurels." He made another bow in the direction of a serious looking, smooth-faced young man, not quite so tall as himself, but with broader shoulders, who carried himself with military erectness in his evening clothes, and who looked, Edith thought, like an Anglican clergyman.

"Oh then you are the American; I have gotten you mixed!" exclaimed the girl in mock dismay, but with no attempt to pretend that she had not heard about the nationality of the guests.

"Only a plain every day American, Miss Kingman, but I throw myself on your mercy."

Madame Flaubert smiled sympathetically, and her smile was one of her greatest charms, but she evidently did not really understand what the banter was all about.

"Well you look like an Englishman, anyhow," went on Edith daringly.

"Do you say that to console me for my lost title, or as a reproach for not wearing the stars and stripes on my sleeve?"

"I am too good an American myself to admit that you need any consolation for a lost title, and in the hearing of Lord Parkhurst I couldn't be so rude as to say it was a reproach to look like an Englishman."

"The Embassy is your place Miss Kingman" said the earl in full rich tones which were marred by a slight drawl. "Such diplomatic talents should never be wasted in private life. It is only a matter of time, if your countrymen are as shrewd as they have the credit of being, when we shall have the pleasure of waiting on you at the Court of St. James, or some other court."

Marguerite said little but her eyes beamed with gratified pride at the way in which her darling Edith was holding her own with these strangers. She sat in a great rocking chair with a tawny tiger skin thrown over it as a background, and Lord Parkhurst, who had a keen eye for æsthetic effects, thought that he had seldom seen a lovelier picture, and many beautiful girls had posed consciously, or unconsciously, for his especial benefit. Marguerite was not posing, he was sure of that, she was evidently thinking of Edith more than she was of herself.

The young Baron Flaubert, who had just attained his majority, and was trying hard to be as dignified as his position demanded, thought the same in regard to Marguerite's beauty, and wondered if it would be just the right thing to quote a couplet about a maiden's eyes and a manly heart, which he had thought poetic enough to remember, to a young lady to whom he had just been presented. He would have incurred any penalty rather than fail in the most punctilious decorum to his mother's guests.

He was small but well formed, with piercing black eyes, and a mustache which would be very black indeed, when it was a year or two older. His manners were simply charming Edith declared afterwards, and his bow the most graceful she had ever seen. She admitted that the American made a very good second though, in that respect. The youthful Frenchman seemed all anxiety about the happiness of everybody, and apparently content to take a subordinate place in the merry persiflage going on around him. In the midst of it dinner was announced by the old butler who had been raised on the estate and had served the family for forty years; first as an errand-boy, then as general factotum, until he received the well-deserved promotion to his present dignity. For years he had stood behind his mistress' chair in the dining-room, which like every other apartment at Chateau Flaubert, was stately and grand. He might have paraphrased the famous lines, had he ever heard of Tennyson; "Guests may come, and guests may go, but I go on forever."

Marguerite went out with Andre, but found herself next to Lord Parkhurst at the table. She was not sure whether she ought to talk to both gentlemen or to confine herself to the Baron, but as Edith talked, not only to those on both sides of her, but to everybody at the table, she decided that there was probably no rule in the matter. She knew that she was hopelessly wanting when it came to social usages, but she did not care to have the fact generally known to the guests at this charming old chateau. After dinner Lord Parkhurst, apparently by chance, took the chair nearest hers, and began asking about her convent life and her studies. Edith was chatting to Andre and to Mr. Raymond on all sorts of subjects.

"I wonder if he thinks I am a perfect baby, and that I don't know anything but the convent" the maiden of seventeen said to herself indignantly. "I know I don't know every thing as Edith does, but I am not quite in pinafores."

Still there was something very agreeable in Lord

Parkhurst's manner toward herself, in spite of its shade of patronage, and he was really very nice, she thought. There was no effort to make himself agreeable, as there was on Andre's part; he did not smile so much as Mr. Raymond, nor talk so much, but there was about him an ease and graciousness, the repose of a dignified civilization, a quiet consciousness of rank of which Marguerite felt the charm, without defining it. He listened with rapt attention to her simple chatter about the convent and Madame Florac and Edith; she told him about her penance on the day Madame Flaubert's invitation was received; about her occasional trips to Paris, and about her father's death, and he listened sympathetically, as was expected of him, without betraying so much as by a look that he was perfectly familiar with her history, and with the fact that she an heiress to five hundred thousand pounds. Presently she shifted the conversation to England to let him see that she knew all about Mr. Gladstone and the Marquis of Salisbury and the Irish question.

"I have never been to England. We sailed directly from New York to Havre when I came over, but I shall stay a long time in Great Britain after I finish school. I am going to spend a year in travel. Edith has already been to nearly every place, and she is only a year older than I." The earl said that he would have supposed there was a greater difference, but seeing that juvenility was not accepted as a compliment, he passed lightly on to speaking of his own travels. Marguerite, accustomed every night of her life to going to bed at half past eight, was not in the least sleepy when a distant clock struck eleven. Madame Flaubert jumped up with an exclamation about not knowing it was so late, and ordered the company off to their rooms at once. "Madame Florac will never forgive me if I send her children back to the convent pale and worn out for the want of sleep."

IV.

ALTHOUGH there was no little bell to jingle at six o'clock the next morning, Marguerite awoke at the usual hour, and for a moment forgot that the one never-remitted penance of her school life was abrogated, and that she could sleep as long as she choose. In the joy of being awake and at liberty to stay in bed it seemed like an abuse of opportunities to go to sleep again, but the dissipation of the evening before, mild as it was, had left its effects on her heavy eyelids, and she was soon lost in the luxury of a morning nap.

After breakfast at which a beefsteak was served in compliment to the Americans Madeleine offered to show her companions the picture gallery, and Mr. Raymond begged to be allowed to go too. Madame Gaston with the exquisite tact which belongs by right of birth to every French woman, immediately put aside her embroidery and rose to accompany them. Lord Parkhurst who had been out for a morning walk and was just returning was asked to go along, and Andre, who had paused as if uncertain what to do, was somehow included in the invitation to view his own gallery. Madame Gaston and Madeleine pointed out the different portraits, narrating quite simply and in a matter-of-course tone, the history of the illustrious originals. One grim-looking ancestor had gone with the sainted King Louis to the Crusades; a dapper little man in periwig and ruff who looked better able to lead a cotillon than a forlorn hope, had commanded a division at Agincourt, and died fighting bravely; a merry looking girl with no waist to speak of, a grandmother, with three or four 'greats' prefixed, had gone to England in the train of Henrietta Maria, but returned to her own land to wed a noble young Flaubert. Mr. Raymond seemed to be battling with suppressed amusement which appeared in a twinkle of his blue eyes. To Edith's query, expressed by a look ending in the plainest kind of an interrogation point, he replied; "I am thinking of my sisters. They consider the Raymonds among the old families because one of them happened to have been a colonel in the revolution; I was wondering how the old gentleman would feel in this gallery along with these august Flauberts, who had returned to highly respectable dust some five or six centuries before he was born."

"Every thing depends on the point of view in this world," replied Edith, "and I wont have you saying anything about your grandfather the colonel, for I am related to the revolution myself. It is quite distinction enough to come in with the birth of one's country."

"As I said before, I was thinking of my sisters" retorted Raymond, and then they both laughed.

In the afternoon Madame Flaubert invited her guests to accompany her to the school-hall where the children of the parish were to have their Christmas tree. Mr. Raymond said that such a chance to study an important phase of French life was too rare to be neglected, and Lord Parkhurst remarked that he seemed to be very fond of study.

"Well, you see it is what all good Americans do

over here. It is a duty we owe to our consciences or to our countrymen who are too busy to get away to study for themselves. We cannot even look at a sunset in peace without feeling that we must whip out our note books and record our impressions. The dimensions of a statue and the proportions of a church must be secured before we can enjoy looking at them, and in an old cathedral the original cost and the time required to build it, so prey upon our minds that we cannot indulge at all in the proper reveries; fortunately the guide books have told us what our thoughts ought to be, and these little drawbacks are but the thorns in the rose of travel."

"You Englishmen do the same over in the States," put in Edith.

"Oh well, with us there is a fraternal feeling of affection which makes us want to understand you thoroughly so as to point out the rocks in your onward course. We study America for the good of the Americans."

"And with an eye to the main chance" Raymond wanted to retort, remembering certain transactions in land in which the English syndicates had gotten the better of their innocent American cousins, but he was afraid it might sound rude: so he only made another bow, which Edith had already discovered was a habit of his.

At the school hall recently built, and which seemed to the strangers to be about the most modern thing in the village of Flaubert, they found the children already assembled; the boys were on one side, the girls on the other, and their parents were beginning to fill the seats reserved for them. Representatives from neighboring Chateaux who had no schools of their own to claim their attention joined Madame Flaubert and her guests, and it transpired from their talk about the tree that they had furnished the greater number of the articles on it. What struck Raymond most as a student of foreign social conditions, was the attitude of the classes toward each other. There was a manner at once affectionate, deferential and confidential with which the villagers and tenants answered the questions Madame Flaubert put to them. She asked about the rheumatism of one, the cough of another, whether one woman's baby had cut all its teeth, and she seemed to know all the children by their names and something of the individuality of each. It appeared to be more like the visit of an old and dear friend in whose wisdom and goodness they had every reason to believe, than like the presence of a Lady Bountiful bestowing her charities. And yet there was the most profound respect on the one side, and the security of acknowledged rank on the other. Raymond thought it was an attitude which if carried out in America might do a great deal toward the mutual benefit of the rich and the poor. He was not very familiar with the different phases of feminine benevolence there, but he did not believe there was anything approaching this footing, at once so admirable and so well defined. In the first place the conditions were against it; the kindest intentions in the world were in danger of being misinterpreted by the poor, ever on the alert to assert their perfect equality with the richest in the land; impertinence and open rudeness he knew had followed his own sister's attempt to aid the denizens of Cedar street. To be sure he had his doubts at the time as to her manner of showing the kindness of her heart, and his doubts, in the light of the charming graciousness of Madame Flaubert and her friends, were amply confirmed.

To Lord Parkhurst there was nothing unusual in the scene, for he was accustomed to hearing at home all about the school, and the village poor, and the needs of the tenants; but what impressed him was the grace and animation of the children. They moved lightly and noiselessly over the floor as their names were called by the curé, and when Andre dressed up as the good Santa Claus, handed them their little presents from the tree, they bowed first to him and then to the audience as gracefully as any children he knew in a Belgravia drawing room. Their eyes fairly danced with animation and pleasure, and he thought he had never seen a prettier group of children. He was a true Briton, with all a Briton's hereditary belief that in England was reached the apotheosis of human well being; but he had the sense of justice of a Briton, and that forced the admission to his mind, whether it was strong enough to force it to his tongue was another question, that the children of his own tenantry were more awkward, more stolid, not nearly so attractive in any way, as these little French urchins, their hereditary foes. He did not believe it was any defect in the English character, but rather a defect in their training, and he

resolved, that when his affairs were straightened
out as he hoped to have them soon—the thought
brought a sigh—he would work reforms in his own
people, that would eclipse these French as the sunlight puts out the light of the moon. In case of war
he felt sure that one of the sturdy Yorkshire lads
could vanquish three of these slender French
striplings, but it seemed base ingratitude to even
think of war in the presence of his affable French
hostess.

Marguerite decided on the spot to buy land close
to New York, build a mansion in the middle of it,
something on the style of Chateau Flaubert, and
settle a colony of poor people on the estate in little
white cottages which she resolved to have bigger
than those she had seen as they passed along; but
white and dazzlingly clean as these appeared to be,
and to have a school and a Christmas tree at which
she would have presents for the parents as well as
for the children. In that thought a more satisfying
outlet for her money was presented than any of
her vague longings and plans had shown her before.
It was grand to be rich after all.

Her thoughts were summarily brought back from
her estate in New York by a ripple of excitement
caused by the drawing for the prizes. Madame Flaubert had given one for plain sewing, a gold piece
hidden in a box of bon bons, and as there were a number who had merited it the contestants were to draw.
The class in Catechism did the same for a beautiful
prayer-book presented by the curé; the boys who
excelled in writing and arithmetic were marshaled
out for another drawing,—for a florin presented by

a noble tlady belonging to the parish. After the
prizes and the presents had all been distributed, the
curé made a little speech in which he wished them all
a merry Christmas, and adroitly mingled a little
sermon with his remarks; he told the old, old story
of the Babe who came into the world poor and
humble to suffer more than any one could ever
understand for the salvation of mankind. At the
end of his remarks he contrived to throw in some
witticisms which Lord Parkhurst thought were
really very good for a Frenchman, and with bows
to everybody, sat down in the easy chair placed by
the little wooden table which had held the lists of
prize winners and the prizes.

Raymond wondered to what class the curé
belonged; had he dared put the question he would
probably have been told by the curé himself that a
clergyman has no rank, but is the father of his
people, the rich and the poor alike. At the close
of the exercises the children sang the Adeste Fidelis
in which Madeleine joined as a matter of course;
after the first verse Marguerite and Edith added
their voices to the chorus, and Madame Flaubert
hummed it under her breath.

When the crowd began to disperse, Marguerite
noticed with an indefinable pang, that the children
all clung to Madeleine with the endearing expressions in which the French tongue is so rich, and
that their parents lingered to say they were glad to
see her, hoped she was very well and that
she would soon be home to stay. She thought it
must be very nice to be so loved by people, and to
have it in one's power to make them happy; she

regretted that her estate had not already been founded so that the children of her prospective tenants could welcome her home to America. She wondered how many girls in New York could come and go from boarding school for years without one soul outside of their families and circle of friends, knowing or caring anything about them.

On their way back to the chateau the talk fell inevitably into the old channels—the relations of the upper classes to the lower.

"But you see in America we have no upper and lower classes" protested Raymond. "The rich may think so, but the poor do not. Toss a beggar a quarter and he says thank you in a surly way, but he does not really mean it; in his heart he thinks you are merely sharing your ill gotten gains."

"Our poor in America don't want charity, they want justice" interrupted Edith, who happened to be in one of her sensible moods as Marguerite would have said.

"We don't consider what we do for our people in the light of charity, at all" said Monsieur Gaston, a man much older than his wife, who seemed to think as a rule that she did talking enough for both.

"Of course the distinction in classes is too well established here, and I was under the impression in your country as well, Monsieur Raymond, to be questioned. We believe, although some of us let our belief remain only a theory, that there are no rights without their corresponding duties. We consider ourselves placed by Almighty God in a position superior to our dependants, and that we cannot shirk our duties to them without at the same time shirking our duties to God. The poor have their obligations to us too; we expect them to be honest, frugal, industrious, and to protect our lives and property if necessary; in return they have a right to all that develops and makes more perfect their intellectual and spiritual life as well as their mere physical existence. Education must be attended to, their children encouraged to make the best of their talents, their social nature has its demands, and we, as their employers, their natural superiors, and benefactors, owe these advantages to them, not as a charity but as their right. The Revolution, terrible as it was, taught us that whatever may be the gulf between the classes there is no gulf at all between man and man, considered as members of the human family. The vocations of our people and their limited means preclude their seeing to these matters themselves, and the leisure classes are naturally expected to assume this duty." "Ah, there is the trouble with us" exclaimed Raymond. "We have no leisure classes, we have only wealthy classes. The men slave all day to make money and the women to spend it."

Madame Gaston here interposed that she had always heard it was the happiest state possible, next to being an angel, to be an American woman, and for her part she would be perfectly willing to give up her days to the spending of money, provided she could have the evenings for rest. She thought it must be far more delightful than to devote one's time to saving it. As for the men, it was strange they did not come over to France to learn the dignity of laziness from people like her husband.

Raymond responded that they never got time until ordered off by their doctors and then it was generally too late. "Why my own father worked himself to death, and half the men I know are doing the same."

"So his father is dead too" thought Edith.

"Money-getting is a sort of an epidemic with us. A man starts out to make a fortune and when it is made he keeps on making it larger from mere force of habit. Our rich men never know where to stop. The average American millionaire works harder, I assure you, than some of his own clerks."

The Frenchman was not certain that the American gentleman who was reported to be a millionaire by inheritance was really in earnest or not.

Lord Parkhurst, who did not understand French as readily as he spoke it, missed too many of the points of the conversation to express any opinions on the one side or the other.

"Besides, we have no landed proprietors as you have in France and England" went on Raymond. "We build cottages by the sea, shooting lodges in the mountains, and occasionally a daring spirit buys a farm in Jersey, but he is an exception. Our country homes are occupied but three or four months in the year, they have a few acres of land around them, often not enough to raise provisions for the owner's horses; we rent cows to make the scene picturesque when we have picnics, and decorate our hay wagons in ribbons and invite pretty girls to gather in our hay. Life in the country in America is only a brief holiday and no one ever regards it seriously. Perhaps at our next centennial we shall have advanced to the stage of the landed proprietor."

"I think the trouble with the most of us, regardless of nationality, is our failure to realize our obligations to those around us" said Lord Parkhurst soberly. Marguerite had explained to him in English the meaning of the phrases he had not quite understood.

"We are all taught that no man lives for himself alone, but I am afraid we do not always keep the truth in mind as vividly, or at least as practically as does Monsieur Gaston."

After a due acknowledgement of the compliment the Frenchman continued; "In America we older and more hampered nations are expecting great things. There you have the conditions for an almost ideal civilization; vast territory, fertile soil, a teeming immigration, mines, manufactures, commerce, unlimited capital, in a word, every thing to make a great and prosperous country. Of course, by birth and tradition I am a Royalist, but I am not sure that I am not a Republican by conviction; not a Republican as we have here in France, nor exactly as you have in America, but a Republican of the ideal Republic."

Monsieur Gaston was enjoying his opportunities to air his views and to show that unlike his wife, he only talked when he had something to say. He was a close student, especially since a tendency towards indigestion had debarred him from the pleasures of the club café, and he was not averse to letting these distinguished foreigners know how well a Frenchman could talk when he was so minded.

"I think every body will admit, excepting a few rabid demagogues, that such a thing as social equality is an impossibility. Some are refined, gifted, cultivated, ladies and gentlemen in a word; others are boorish, ignorant, low; the one class is bound to rise, the other to sink."

Raymond suggested that if position depended only on personal worth there might be a change of places.

"That is very true," continued Gaston, "but there would still be the survival of an aristocracy. What I mean is this; let there be a general leveling of rank in one generation, social destinctions would again appear in the next. And since there must be destinctions we might as well keep those we have, which are quite as good as those we would inevitably come to, if the socialists had their way."

"There's the grand thing about America" cried Edith. "All men are not born equal there any more than they are in any other country, but we give everybody a chance. A ploughboy may become President. Talent wherever found is sure of a reward. With you the children, unless in exceptional cases, are apt to remain in the same condition of life as their fathers. With us our greatest and most successful men are, many of them, the sons of people who were both poor and obscure. Our limitations are personal not social."

"We all admit that, Miss Kingman, and we envy the country where such a state of affairs exists," answered Monsieur Gaston. "That is one of the reasons why we people of Europe are expecting to see America take her place as the banner country of the world."

Madame Gaston looked at her husband, as if she doubted the sincerity of these views for a conservative Frenchman, whom she had heard rail at the government in republican France for hours at a time. She remembered that one of his standing reproaches for a high official was that he was the son of a shoemaker. She did not quite understand the difference boundary lines may make in one's convictions.

"I am afraid that Monsieur Gaston's opinion of us is too flattering" answered Raymond. "We are progressing, and at the same time, to be paradoxical, there is a retrogression. The conditions of success are getting to be harder and harder to control. There are obstacles in the paths of ambitious boys which were not there twenty five years ago. Obstacles, not requiring more talent, but more luck, to surmount. Our best men, Miss Kingman, do not reach the presidential chair I am afraid. In fact I must acknowledge that our best men, as a rule, are developing a lamentable tendency to keep out of politics altogether. Of course this rule has many brilliant exceptions, perhaps too many to permit of the rule at all. Politics are getting to be too corrupt to engage the attention of our best men.

"And you say this without shame, when you have the ballot in your own hands to make your country what you please" answered Monsieur Gaston, not considering that the same assertion could apply to France.

"The ballot is one of the causes of our corruption. In America every man sees in each individual the potential aristocrat, and the grand chance of making him an active one. Life is a mad rush for personal ends; in individual aims we lose sight of the general welfare, and in the ballot a corrupt class recognize their grand chance."

"I am glad I am an American anyhow" said Marguerite softly, and Lord Parkhurst answered fervently that America must be a paradise if all her daughters were like herself, and that one might well overlook a little thing like a corrupt ballot.

"See here, Mr. Raymond, it is hardly fair in you to expose our national weaknesses abroad in this way," said Edith. "We have our faults of course, but our virtues outweigh them a thousand times, and a true patriot would conceal them or deny their existence. Now I should suffer the rack rather than admit that we are not the grandest nation on earth, and everybody supremely happy."

"I have'nt admitted that we are not the greatest country in the world, but only that we might be a little greater."

They had reached the chateau by this time. Monsieur Gaston declared that he must go to his room immediately to put down Monsieur Raymond's remarks in his note book. Raymond replied that that was exactly what he was going to do in regard to Monsieur Gaston's ideas, adding that he would like to cable all these flattering opinions to the Sunday papers at home.

V.

MADAME Flaubert announced at dinner that the first Mass on Christmas morning would be at four o'clock, and that the music would be very fine, but hinted that perhaps the hour was too early for even good music and solemn ceremonies to tempt heretics out of their beds. She said heretics with such an enchanting smile that Lord Parkhurst felt that she had given him an additional title. Every body declared that the Christmas Mass could not be missed even if it necessitated one's sitting up all night. And it really seemed like getting up at midnight when the faithful butler knocked vigorously at each door, and chirped a Christmas greeting. The old fellow chuckled delightedly when Raymond called out "Look here Jacques, you have made a mistake, I have been asleep just fifteen minutes." Edith declared that her eyes were not half opened until she got out into the fresh air.

As they emerged from the chateau gate the stars were shining with all the scintilating brilliancy of a winter's night; the air was crisp and clear, and cold enough to make heavy wraps a luxury. No one spoke a great deal, the majesty of the heavens and the sublime associations of the day, filling each heart and silencing the banter. Only Marguerite murmured so low as to be unheard, she thought: "When Shepherds kept watch in Judea" and the young baron answered in the same tone: "And the star arose in the East."

"Somehow I always imagine myself in Palestine on Christmas," continued the girl shyly, feeling that she had a sympathetic listener.

"Couldn't you fancy our being in Bethlehem and hurrying along the silent streets to find the new born Savior?"

The streets were already lit up, the peasants were trudging along on foot, and from each cottage a light gleamed, showing the Christmas branches in the windows; branches not so precisely arranged as the wreaths of an American florist, but perhaps, as a symbol of the earnest faith and devotion of the hearts that prompted the rude fingers in their fashioning, more beautiful in the sight of the good God. When the Flaubert party arrived the church was already pretty well filled, and the altars were simply a blaze of light and loveliness. The choice plants in the green houses for miles around had been sent to shed their beauty on the Christmas altars; candles by the hundred gleamed in burnished candelabra, and tall palms rising tier like behind the altar formed a background with shadow-like effects. At the side where the Crib was placed, the aisle was almost impassable because of the kneeling throng. To Lord Parkhurst it seemed a primitive, almost childish faith that could require, or even admit of these extraneous aids to worship. The waxen image in the crib, the ox, the manger, the rather gaudy statue of St. Joseph bending over the Infant Savior, seemed to him almost like an abuse of sacred things, but he felt at the same time an admiration for the very evident devotion of the worshipers. "After all, we never knew the point of view of other people" he candidly admitted to himself; "it does make the story of the Divine Birth very real and vivid, and perhaps it is no little thing to keep the story fresh even if the means be crude," he thought, with self-satisfied superiority. There was nothing in his life or training that could have given him the breadth of vision to really understand the feeling of the kneeling throng. But the Mass itself inspired him with awe, and still clinging with all the pride of race to his own national faith, he yet could feel the sublimity of its rites. It was a sacrifice with all the splendor that could be thrown around the act, and whilst he did not admit the necessity of sacrifice in the worship of God, he was not disposed to quarrel with those who did. After all, sincerity is the one great thing in religion, he thought, and if the temperament, the environment, the heritage of these people demanded a faith that to him seemed obsolete, and belonging to dead ages and dead traditions, he yet could respect the spirit which animated its rites. Raymond, fresh from the very modern pursuits of a young business man, felt as if he had been suddenly transported into a bygone age. He closed his eyes, and the throng vanished; the old church was immediately filled with knights in armor and ladies in the costume of the Bourbon courts. Peasants crowded the aisles in picturesque sabots and caps, and princes and courtly youths served at the altar. The bishop's throne at the right was draped anew in richest velvet, and a mighty cardinal in his robes of state, arose with the calm majesty of conscious power to bless the worshiping multitude; from out the shadow of the sanctuary advanced two figures in the garb of friars who knelt at the Episcopal throne for a blessing on themselves and their undertaking—

they were missionaries going to African wilds to win barbarian souls to God. The Crusaders flitted by, their red crosses shining; then came a wedding procession with all the splendor of wealth and rank; a funeral cortege wound its slow way up the aisle, and he opened his eyes at the slight stir made by the hundreds sinking on their knees at the tinkling of a silvery little bell.

After the last gospel had been read there was a profound silence for a moment, and then the old Christmas hymn, the *Adeste Fideles*, soft and clear with only a chord of the organ to bear aloft its sweetness, fell on the air; the birdlike tones of a flute took it up, and another voice joined the first, then a burst of melody rich, full enchanting from the tenors, and the violins, pure, passionate, almost human, vibrated through every nerve; a double quartet, with only the organ again as accompaniment, chanted *venite adoremus*, then a mighty harmony filled the church, organ, flutes, violins, harps, basses, tenors, contraltos, sopranos, rising, falling, beseeching, triumphant; *Venite adoremus Dominum*. Music stirring up all the latent longings for nobler, higher things in careless hearts; banishing the world, hurrying sin, cowed and ashamed, from human souls, vanquishing temptation, glorifying grief, overturning despair.

"I thought I was in heaven," said Marguerite, when they were once more in the open air. The stars were still shining but with a less vivid glow, and a faint streak of dawn was beginning to appear in the East, as a herald of glad tidings to the world.

"No wonder the people are so good; such music in such a church and with such a ceremonial could almost nerve a stone to martyrdom," she continued enthusiastically. She was feeling vaguely that a grand act of self-abnegation, persecution in China, or death in the service of a plague-stricken people might be more heroic than founding a great estate for the poor in America.

Madame Flaubert explained that the music was the result of a munificent bequest for that purpose, of a wealthy nobleman, a former lord of a neighboring chateau, who was passionately fond of music, and who believed that it was that one art, preeminent over the others, intended to elevate the spiritual life. Four times a year, at Christmas, Easter, Pentecost and the Assumption, he desired that the music in his parish church be second to nothing in the way of church music in Paris. "And I think his wishes have been fulfilled" she added with gratified pride.

Immediately Marguerite's thoughts went back to her model estate; not only would she provide fine music for her tenants, but a series of free concerts for the poor in the city, were projected in the field of her dreams.

"I wish you could see Christmas in England" Lord Parkhurst said to her later in the day, and she guessed from his tones more than from his words, that he was homesick.

At dinner there was plum pudding in compliment to Lord Parkhurst, the young Baron said, and the Cranberry sauce he added hesitatingly, "is a tribute to our American guests."

Every body laughed, and Raymond said that cranberries were a more desirable national dish than plum pudding, for the one caused indigestion and the other did not. Edith declared that the roast turkey seemed more national to her than either the sauce or the pudding.

In the evening there was an informal dance in the grand ball room. "It is not a real party" Madame Flaubert explained, "for none of the young ladies have come out, but just a little affair to make you all enjoy yourselves." An orchestra of villagers, a a part of the same that had played so enchantingly at the Christmas Mass, furnished the music. Marguerite danced the first dance with Lord Parkhurst.

As the preluding notes sounded, and he drew her arm in his she felt a thrill that was strange and new and not unpleasant.

"Do you know," she said at the conclusion, "You are the first gentleman I ever danced with in my life."

A curious look, half tender, half determined, came into his eyes, but he answered ardently; "Let me hope that this augurs well for our future—regard, Miss Clayton."

VI.

THIS holiday week was like no other that had ever been to Marguerite. It was not merely a break in the monotony of school life, nor the ending or beginning of any thing, but a period detached from the rest of her life and set apart wholly by itself. So strong was this impression that she was almost surprised that the dull landscape had not changed any since she had viewed it ten days before from the Paris express. The poplars stripped of their foliage, the leafless vineyards on the hills, the chalky stretches of land, a knarled tree by a switch, she remembered all the details because her mind was fresh for all new impressions and received them hungrily, rushed on her with a sense of strangeness, because they were so entirely the same. The complexity of her images formed a background for sensations even more complex.

"Wont we have a lot to tell Madame Florac;" she said ecstatically to Edith as they sat together in the compartement of the train on the way back to the convent.

"And wont we have a lot not to tell Madame Florac;" said Edith nonchalantly drawing her traveling rug about her and extending her slender boot until it touched the hot water pipe.

"Why you know I tell her everything" replied Marguerite reproachfully. She was prevented from pursuing the subject any further by the presence of the Gastons and Madeleine.

And when it came to talking over the week's pleasure the girl was quite honest in believing that she told Madame Florac everything. She certainly told her about Lord Parkhurst, and Mr. Raymond and Andre; about the Christmas tree and the Christmas Mass, the music, the party, even the battle with the hair pins and old Jacques' rheumatism, and what more was there to tell?

The girls resumed their studies and days settled back into the same placid and pleasant routine.

Mrs. Kingman came over in June for a few weeks at the German baths, and announced that her daughter was too much of a young lady to be kept at school any longer, and that this departure was final. Edith had gone and returned so often that Marguerite was accustomed to short separations, and regarded them as the inevitable bitter she had theoretically been brought up to expect with all the sweet; so she was unable at first to comprehend the enormity of the blow this decision entailed on herself. Even the pleasure of going with Edith and her mother, for a little outing in Germany, could not banish the awful thought of the lonely year before her at the convent without Edith. Older people are apt to forget the passionate depths of a school girl affection between natures capable of feeling a strong attachment, and to underrate the poignant sorrow of parting. When Marguerite returned to school in September it was with the determination to study so hard that there would be no time left for unavailing regrets, and so firm was this resolution that she even demurred when Madame Florac insisted upon her resting the first day, and commanded her not to think of her books. Constant work proved almost the panacea she had hoped to find it; still there were times, especially on holidays and Sundays, when her loss rose with all its keen misery, but she fought against it valiantly. Again there were hours when she was in danger of becoming almost as fond of Madeleine as she had been of Edith, and from this she recoiled as from the basest kind of disloyalty. As a graduate-elect she was allowed to have a private room, and in the old quarters formerly occupied by Edith, she loved to picture her friend, in the moments of day-dreaming she allowed herself, reclining in unblushing idleness on the little sofa, and herself on an ottoman at her feet.

"You don't know how lonely I am without you, dearest," she wrote to Edith on Washington's birthday. There is no one to help me celebrate the day, for all the other Americans are juniors. The flag flies from the top of my bed but it flaps mournfully as if conscious that the day lacks its wonted pleasure in your dear room."

From the first year of her school life Marguerite had refused to study on Washington's birthday; the other Americans followed her example, then an English girl wanted a holiday on the birthday of the Queen, and a German lassie put in a plea for one on that of the Emperor. In dire perplexity Mother Salette promised a half holiday on the national festivals of all the foreigners, provided that they afterwards made up their lessons thus missed. This charming old French gentle-woman did not mind in the least the American holiday, for she had an undeniable fondness herself for Washington, and besides, had he not been the friend of Lafayette;

but it went sorely against the grain to celebrate for England and Germany.

Marguerite, who had been scarcely anywhere, and whose life for years had been bounded by the precincts of a French convent, was intensely patriotic, and American to the finger tips: Edith who had been over half the globe, was thoroughly cosmopolitan; she loved her own country after a fashion, but agreed that there were others just as good, and an exile from her native land would not have caused her a tithe of the pangs it would have entailed on Marguerite. The younger girl regarded America much as the Israelites of old must have regarded the Land of Cana. If the thought of leaving the convent made her sad, the thought that she was going home to America brought consolation.

Hard study this last year was not altogether a matter of choice; there was much to be done before the honors which were to crown her labors on commencement day could be secured. The final examinations loomed in her pathway, examinations before the curé and a score of clergymen and all the nuns. There was to be the final rounding off of the branches she had studied or skimmed through in following the course of study, rather broader than it once was, in deference to the American expansion of the feminine sphere and the feminine mind. There was no doubt that she was a very accomplished girl; she spoke French beautifully as was to be expected; she knew Italian almost as well, which was not a matter of course by any means; she spoke German fairly well and had taken a course of German literature; under one of the finest masters from Paris she had learned to play the piano in a way to give pleasure to cultivated ears ; she could play the harp and the guitar and the mandolin, and her voice, never very strong but sweet and sympathetic, had been cultivated to the utmost; she could draw and paint fairly well as amateur work goes; she had experimented in the laboratory only lately added, knew something about acids and gases and chemical laws, could analyze flowers and classify rocks, and had a speaking acquaintance with the philologists of her own tongue. She wrote a graceful semi-Anglican, wholly foreign hand, could dance like a nymph, and with steps that would have been a puzzle to the nymphs.

And underlying all, the foundation-stone of her education, the prevading essence of it was the religious training which Madame Florac had made a personal concern. She wanted to guard her charge against the frivolities and worldliness of a mere woman of fashion on the one hand, and the aberrations of fanaticism on the other into which, without the ballast of a reasoning faith, a young and ardent soul might be led. She wanted her spiritual nature to be developed to its utmost, but developed evenly, rounded off to a symetrical whole, and not emphasized in one direction only to be dwarfed in another, She had tried to teach her to see the poetic and the beautiful, as well as the unchangeable and the true. She wanted her heart to feel the grand significance of the spiritual life and her head to know the why of it all. She was sometimes troubled by the thought that she had not altogether succeeded. Marguerite was charming and lovable and spasmodically pious, but her character seemed to Madame Florac to lack stability. The girl was capable, she felt of the grandest heights of spiritual heroism in some moods, and of the most reckless yielding to temptations in others. She had trained her not as a nun, not as her teacher merely, but as a true and tried friend, a foster mother having her best interests here and hereafter at heart. She knew that after twenty one Marguerite would have unlimited control, no one to say her nay, of a large fortune, and she had tried to make her realize both the power and the responsibility money would bring. She wanted her to go into the world equipped in thought, feeling and impulses for the struggle of the world. A struggle which she knew would be none the less real because it would lack all the elements of a struggle for fortune and position. She would have felt more secure about the future of her charge had Marguerite been less impulsive, even if the being so had meant a less affectionate temperament. Sensitive hearts bleed so easily.

Above all she dreaded the influence of an insidiously lowering environment. She had encouraged, although it was not the rule of the community to encourage particular friendships among the girls, her regard for Edith Kingman; for whilst Edith had some traits she did not like, and had been too much of a young lady in experience when she should have been a school girl, yet, on the whole, her principles were good, and she was thoroughly attached to Marguerite. Her practical nature would detect a sham more quickly than Marguerite, whether in people or opinions, and her honesty and independence of character would prevent compromise with shams of any kind. She was not very deep, but she was true as far as she went. And she was deeper, Madame Florac knew, than she was generally credited with being.

She thought too, that Edith by being with Marguerite constantly, and occupying the place, after a fashion, of a mentor and elder sister, might prevent, should there be any danger of it, a disastrous marriage. She was not sanguine on this point however; even her own limited experience of the world had taught her something of the wilfulness of maidens in matters matrimonial. A girl with no parents to look after her was certainly in great danger of making a shipwreck of her happiness when it came to marriage, and Americans even those with parents, were constantly marrying whether in haste or otherwise, to drag out a long and most miserable repentance.

Edith made her debut brilliantly at the beginning of the season, and wrote to Marguerite that she was having a most enchanting time. She added in a postscript that Mr. John Raymond had sent her a bouquet as big as a half-bushel for her coming-out party.

In June she sacrificed her very natural desire to continue her social triumphs at some of the American watering places, in order to be present at the graduation of Marguerite.

Although the exercises were always strictly private, not even the parents being allowed to attend, Edith with Yankee ingenuity managed matters to suit herself. It was the custom of the nuns to welcome back any of their old pupils who wished to seek the seclusion of the cloister for a retreat, or even for a visit, at any time.

Edith wrote to Madame Florac that she thought she would like "to make a retreat" during commencement week. Her audacity brought ripples of merriment to the calm faces of all her old teachers, for a retreat and Edith Kingman were such antagonistic elements, especially in the month of June, that even the gravest of them accepted it as a huge joke. Madame Florac, who understood perfectly as Edith intended she should, replied that they would be only too happy to receive her. That a cell would be fitted up for her accommodation, and that Mother Salette and the Curé would be delighted to look after her soul. She regretted that during commencement week the place might not be as quiet as could be wished, but she would try to prevent unnecessary distractions. On the afternoon of the graduating exercises, since Mother Salette and the Curé would both have to be present, she might recite the penitential psalms by herself.

Mrs. Kingman who made a sea voyage every year for the benefit of her health, finally consented to spend the summer in European travel.

"I should think you had seen enough of Europe by this time and would want to settle down for the summer at some cool place where you could have a nice time," she said to Edith.

"But Marguerite has seen nothing at all of Europe," retorted Edith. This argument was unanswerable and conclusive Mrs. Kingmann acknowledged if she once admitted her obligations to her daughter's friend.

She murmured plaintively, when they were three days out from New York, and she was beginning to feel a certain physical uneasiness, that it did seem hard for a woman of her years to be deprived of needed rest during the hot season. Edith, who was never seasick, laughed merrily at the allusion to age, for her mother was barely turned forty, and did not look thirty five. Mrs. Kingman had declared more than once, when she was feeling perfectly well, that Edith was the one unreconcilable element in her existence.

"I tried to keep her a child as long as I could; insisted on her wearing short frocks until everybody was shocked, and always spoke of her as my little daughter, but she most ungratefully sprang up into young ladyhood at the earliest possible opportunity. Now there is Marguerite Clayton, only a year younger, but a perfect child. I could go on being a young woman indefinitely with her for my daughter, but Edith betrays me unmistakably. I did think seriously of being her stepmother, but she foiled me again, for she takes after the Carter side of the house; so all expedients failed, and I am reduced to the barefaced truth."

The exhibition was like thousands that had taken place before and like thousands which will take place after it.

There were rows of girls of gradated sizes in simple white frocks, on a stage decorated with growing plants and bunting. There were some creditable recitations, much admirable music, a dialogue in English for the French girls, and a dialogue in French for the Americans. Marguerite very pale, did beautifully all that she was required to do by the programme, and as a graduate and so old a pupil she was not spared. At the end she bade a tearful farewell to her teachers and the dear old convent home, in what was declared to be the best valedictory of the school for many years.

But the real farewell came an hour later. She had already made a sad little pilgrimage to all the old haunts endeared by years of childish association; to the summer house where she had loved to read during the long vocations; the garden with its wealth of flowers, the barn where the cows and the gentle old horse and the chickens and the ducks had ever given her a friendly welcome. "Good-bye Nanon" she said to the horse; "I hope you will be as gentle with the other girls as you have been with me." "Good-bye, Capitaine old fellow, you wont forget me will you," and she put her arms around a great shaggy New Foundland and gave vent to a burst of tears. Capitaine seemed to understand, and wagged his tail and fawned on her cheeks in a way which said plainer than words: "I am sorry you are going away."

Her little cell, which Madeleine had occupied during the last year, seemed suddenly to be the dearest spot in the world, and the room which she still called Edith's room, a haven of peace. The class rooms, recreation hall, the spacious court, even the gloomy state drawing-room received her tears of farewell. When she saw her trunk going out to the express wagon it seemed like a coffin with her heart in it. She had pictures and locks of hair as cherished keepsakes, packed tenderly away in her writing portfolio.

At the very last she stole up to the beautiful old chapel, the chapel where she had made her First Communion, received Confirmation at the hands of the great Archbishop of Paris, where she had gone to Mass every morning of her convent life, and sought again in the evening for night prayer, and the examination of her girlish conscience.

Moved by an impulse she went up to a life sized statue of the Blessed Virgin and hung her bright new medal around the sculptured throat. Flinging herself on her knees she buried her face in her hands and sobbed: "My dearest Mother, I am going home, home to America, but I have no mother there, no one to care for me, I know that I am not worthy to be your child but take care of me and be my Mother—for the sake of thy own dear Son who died for sinners." She knelt again for a moment before the altar, just as some one was calling "Marguerite" as if to beg for a blessing on her strange new life opening before her, and then she hurried down to the parlor.

Edith and her mother who were waiting to take her away with them to Paris, considerately turned aside when the last words came to be spoken to Madame Florac; and with warm kisses on lips and brow, she entered the carriage that was to take her away, and bring her back never again a school girl. Her eyes dwelt hungrily on the familiar scene as the carriage whirled down the broad graveled drive; on the stately old pile of buildings which had been added to for centuries, with turrets and steeples and towers, quaint gables and carved balconies and imposing columns; on the vistas of clover fields where she had hunted butterflies and wild flowers, the court where she had played so many happy hours, on the velvety terraces leading to the visitors, gate, the grand old trees whose music had lulled her into sweetest day dreams, even the porter's lodge was not without a pathetic interest. They were well on their way to Paris when the Angelus rang from the monastery, and Marguerite, turning her head in the endeavor to catch a fleeting glimpse through a break in the trees; cried; "There is the Angelus, Edith—the very last of the convent."

At the end of a tour prolonged until the close of November Marguerite gave up her idea of a year's travel, and decided to return to New York with Mrs. Kingman and Edith. During their stay in Paris they had dined informally with Madame Gaston, her nephew being one of the guests. The baron saw Marguerite on one or two other occasions, but he evidently did not think that he had received encouragement enough to put his fate to the test. His mother was in favor of making overtures to Mr. Dalton as the young lady's guardian, but Andre objected. He said that in wooing an American it was just as well to do it in the American way. A legacy from his godfather had relieved him from immediate embarassment, and so he could afford to wait. A tour of the States had long been a dream of his life, and he argued that probably Miss Clayton in her own home might be induced to look more kindly on his suit. If not, well there were other Americans in New York. He confessed that he did not fancy Miss Kingman in that particular way, although protesting that she was a most charming girl. His aunt assured him with a quizzical smile that she thought the feeling was mutual.

"I fancy Miss Kingman will marry an American" she said.

Mrs. Kingman would have liked as well as anything else to spend the winter abroad; she had done so for so long that the habit seemed almost like second nature. There was something very agreeable to her in the easy careless life of the foreign resorts, more so than in the many cares and demands on her time at home. In Europe she posed as an invalid, being assisted to that state of mind by all the surroundings and associations, where it was taken for granted that no American, not on the invalid list, would elect to spend the winters at the resorts when Paris was at one's command. She was really unwell enough to sooth her conscience as to a waste of time, and not ill enough to interfere with her enjoyment or her digestion. But Edith, to whom America had developed irresistible attractions overruled all objections, and in the storms of November, during which Marguerite was very, very sick, and Mrs. Kingman enough so to be out of humor, they crossed the Atlantic.

Marguerite landed on her native soil just eight years after she had left it, a self willed, spoiled, warm hearted little girl.

She was returning—not denationalized, but very much foreignized.

In all her summer's travels she had seen no country so foreign to her as New York.

VII.

IF a fair minded person, knowing only Marguerite's views of her father's marriage, had wondered that a sensible man with the ordinary feelings of paternity, had come so under the sway of a woman, as to practically neglect his child for years, he would have wondered no longer after meeting Mrs. Clayton.

Even in her second widowhood, with two daughters well launched in society, and her age no longer possible to reckon under the forties, she was still a remarkably attractive woman. And the charm about her was not so much in her beauty, which she admitted to herself in moments of candor, was decidedly going off, as in an indefinable personality, and a subtle flattery of manner that have ever proved invincible to men as old and as sensible as the late Mr. Clayton. Why it was that her step daughter did not like her, and those in the confidence of both could have testified that the indifference was not all on one side, could be answered only on the grounds of a psychological antipathy which has ever been the puzzle of the mental scientists. That a spoilt child should resent the coming of another person into her father's affection was natural enough, but after the father was dead and the child grown up into a presumably sensible woman, that the feeling should be kept up was a little surprising; especially when even with the most unjust division of the estate, Marguerite's fortune was still large enough to give her a high place in the Plutocracy she was to enter with all the eclat befitting her rank and aspirations. Mrs. Clayton was not a learned woman, a deep woman, an accomplished one even; she was simply a fascinating one. Some women are born with that elusive quality, and others with every advantage of temperament and environment never attain it. She welcomed Marguerite with affectionate cordiality, gave her a choice of rooms, even offering to banish one of her own daughters to an upper floor should Marguerite's requirements or inclinations in the matter of apartments render it necessary. Their dispositions and widely differing points of view of life, as well as their different trainings, added to a varied and multitudinous experience on the one hand, and the total absence of experience on the other, were sufficient to explain the absence of congeniality or deep attachment, but they did not explain their wholly negative attitude. Had Mrs. Clayton come into the world under auspices more favorable she might have been superficially different, although perhaps not radically so; but life with her had been a struggle; a struggle from the very dawning of her girlhood, when the easy conquests of the youths who came within the range of her attractions, opened to her ambitious eyes the possibilities of a future, of which, it made her dizzy even to dream. The daughter of an obscure corner grocer, born and raised in an unfashionable house, in an unfashionable locality, given over, even in her childhood, to the wandering hordes, known as boarders and the renters of cheap rooms, and sinking steadily in the social scale in each succeeding year, her first rise had been when she married the brainless son of a wealthy restaurant keeper who had come to New York to spend the paternal dollars made in the West. With the assistance of a young and pretty wife it did not take long to spend them, and when, after a few years of the splendors of hotels and watering places, the scion of the Western caterer was killed in a drunken orgie, she was left with two children and a very limited income. A less persevering woman might have been daunted, and relinquished all dreams of a social career in the calmer enjoyment of maternal and domestic concerns; but not Mrs. Wall; she looked into her mirror, smiled into her limpid blue eyes, and took heart; she also took a flat about the same time; it was a tiny affair in a fashionable apartment house, nine flights up, but where, she was assured by the agent, only the best people were received. The flattering implication that she belonged where she had so long dreamed of belonging, decided her for the apartment, but it meant the most pinching economy. She sent her children to a fashionable day school, dressed well and joined an exclusive church where only souls in well attired bodies were wanted, and showed such an unobtrusive piety that the minister was glad to avail himself of her talents for works of charity. As he had a kind heart and genuinely pitied her lonely widowhood, he sent his wife to call on her. This genial shepherdess was so fascinated with the recent addition to their flock that she introduced her to other members, and thus was laid the foundation for a sort of social life superior to anything the widow had hitherto known. She kept one domestic, a raw German recruit in the household service, who consented to accept poor wages in view of the exceedingly poor quality of her work; she had meat but once a day, alleging that her physician forbade a heavy diet, and that it ruined children's complexions and made them gross. She had a sewing machine in her tiny bedroom concealed by a Japanese screen, that was made to whirl when other women were asleep or dawdling about the shops, pricing things they could not afford to buy. When summer came she packed her trunks with the daintiest and coolest of frocks, turned the key on her private room, sublet her apartment and hied away to one of the big hotels, ready with a genuine welcome for her and her trunks.

It was at one of these she met Mr. Clayton. Promenades on dim lit verandahs, sails by moonlight, and long drives in the cool delicious mornings lead to an invitation to the ninth story flat. The finale was inevitable to any one who knew Mrs. Wall, and the engagement was speedily announced. She did not cry out in ecstasy at her good fortune, but she pinched her arms and tried other expedients of her foolish girlhood to assure herself that her good fortune was not merely a dream. Poor Number One who had seemed such a prize when she won him, now paled into the rest of her past, over which she wished to draw a curtain; the vistas opening before her far reaching ambition seemed limitless. Mr. Clayton had only recently moved to New York from the other extreme of the continent, the wondrous city of the Golden Gate, but reports of his great wealth had preceded his coming. She quietly withdrew from the church in which she had gained her first round, alleging a change of religious convictions which made it desirable to transfer her new name to the membership book of a temple to which her new circle belonged. The circle did not become hers as soon as the name, but she had patience and consummate tact, and she knew it would in time.

The different steps in her upward career were as readily discernible as the battlefields on which a general wins his peerage. But there were still summits which she had not attained. It was a part of her genius to turn everthing, every incident, accident, or contingency however trifling to her own advantage, and her step-daughter's home coming was not to prove an exception to the rule if well laid plans could augur success.

She regarded with secret complacency the intimacy between Marguerite and Edith Kingman. It would eventually bring some good fortune to herself, she was perfectly certain, although she could not say in what particular form the advantage would come. Mrs. Kingman's place was among the exclusive few by right of birth and inherited wealth; she had always lived in New York, and had always been connected with the prominent people of the place. As a woman born to the Patriarchs, Mrs. Clayton, who had attained them only after a long struggle, paid her the deference she considered her due. Although her fortune, added to that of her daughters, which she had in the zenith of her power won from her doting husband, made her far more important in a commercial way than Mrs. Kingman, she had sense and perception enough to know that there were a few distinctions, even in a country given over more and more to the reign of a Plutocracy, which money could not buy. She was contented to let the other enjoy her riper honors—for the time. Mrs. Kingman would have been surprised could she have known the amount of thought that was bestowed on her private concerns by a woman whom she hardly knew. Like all people accustomed all their lives to be the leaders, and not the led, she regulated her existence according to her own convenience and fancy, without a care as to what others were doing, or going to do. The rigid adherence of Mrs. Clayton to what she conceived to be the course of action of women socially superior to herself, would have struck Mrs. Kingman as the height of the ludicrous. In the same way that men mark out a career for themselves and set about steadily to attain it, Mrs. Clayton had decided on her pinnacle of success, and spared no efforts in reaching her end. In the meantime she regulated her life according to the most approved standards. Although she was a pious woman by every outward indication, going to church with as much regularity as a very convenient headache and the state of the weather permitted, yet if it had been definitely determined that it was the mode for the socially elect to set up a statue of Buddha and burn incense before it, she would have done so cheerfully and have been among the most enthusiastic in protest that Christianity was crude and unsatisfactory for a civilization nearing the Twentieth Century.

Social position was her standard, and everything was measured by that figurative yardstick. Not only her body but her soul as well came under this rule. If the condition of the working girls appeared on the list of charitable fads she was the loudest and most earnest, in her efforts in their behalf; when it passed she could hector seamstresses, toss dry goods about for the long suffering clerks to put in order with the supercilous insolence of any upstart in town; if hospital work loomed on the social horizon, she could be counted upon for money and visits, although the next week she would be perfectly capable of turning a sick servant into the streets.

She could be congealingly polite to a person one season, and on meeting her the next at a house of unquestioned rank, most graciously cordial. A struggling woman seeking a footing in the arena of art with the daintiest sketches in the world, would have been received in the reception hall standing; that same artist, under the protection, and enjoying the friendship of a charming and fashionable woman would have been voted 'such a dear girl and so bright'. A picture that cost twenty five thousand dollars she could spend hours admiring; its coloring was delicious, its perspective wonderful, its vividness startling, its masterly technique the mark of genius; a picture hanging in an obscure corner, which future buyers will seize upon as a bargain at a hundred thousand, she would pass by as commonplace. A poet dining at Mrs. Van Horn's was so interesting, with a cooing sibilation on the so; a poet whom she chanced to meet on some of her summer outings, was merely a being to contribute to the amusement or welfare of the class to which she belonged, just as did the maid or the footman, the florist or the caterer. She liked the books it was the fashion to like, raved over the operas and the plays which captured the fickle fancy of fashion; she left no efforts untried to be a fashionable woman. No hermit of St. Benedict ever followed his rule of life more strictly than she did her's. And yet the place she wished had not been secured; but she aimed high. The summits that temptingly lured her on were crowned by a coronet, not for herself, but for her daughters; when she could see one of them a countess she felt that she could rest on her laurels or die happy. One of her daughters was older, one younger than Marguerite, but both had come out the winter before, and were having fairly successful careers as belles. To be sure there were some people with a disgusting fondness for social chronology who refused Mrs. Wall-Clayton's invitations and failed to send her any in return, and a certain journal, which she had read with avidity as Mrs. Wall, and hated fiercely as Mrs. Clayton, devoted a two column article to the season's debutantes; pictures of the Misses Wall appeared at the top, with a complete history of their grandfather the caterer, and their grandfather the corner grocer; a paragraph was also devoted to the beautiful mother who had fascinated the boys of her humble neighborhood, when she stood behind her father's counter to sell them apples and taffy. She gritted her teeth in most unfashionable rage at this article in the privacy of her boudoir; to her friends she simply ignored it. Although there was no reason now for her to save, she did so partly from habit, and partly with a view to increasing the fortune which was to bait the titled fish. Accordingly as a thing was costly or cheap she valued it. She could no more help mentally pricing everything she saw than she could help seeing it. Even whilst greeting a caller with all the graciousness of which she was mistress, she had her silently appraised. "Yes, such a lovely day"—it must have cost thirty dollars at least, it's a Virot bonnet and he does charge so frightfully. "So glad to hear it, so sweet of you to tell me"— What a dowdy gown ; I should think she would have decent clothes, she can well afford it. She could listen with rapt attention to a most soulful parlor reading from Browning, and take an inventory of the room, the carpet, curtains, pictures and bric a brac before the climax was half reached. '

In mid winter when strawberries were five cents a piece she thought them delicious ; in June when they could be had at five cents a pint she would not allow them on her table.

People whose tea she was glad to drink as Mrs. Wall were not even on the calling list of Mrs. Clayton. The old minister, who gave the first lift to her ship when it was high and dry on the sands of obscurity, could be kept waiting until she came down bonneted for a drive, to make the most perfunctory inquiries for his good wife.

In a word, Mrs. Clayton was a most finished snob; she was the consummate flower of a type met every day, not only in New York but in every town and hamlet throughout the length and breadth of the land.

But whilst snobs are common enough, snobs of Mrs. Clayton's perfection are rare. She could have carried off at any College of Snobbery in the world the degree of Master of Arts without any effort at all. There was all the difference between her and the great body of snobs that there is between the skilled artisan and the bungling apprentice. Barnes Newcome and Thackeray's other creations could have gone to school to her for the full term of a university course.

But it was a part of her general cleverness that her most characteristic trait was hardly suspected by any but her dearest friends. The woman she greeted with the warmest caress could not know that the iciest of finger tips were given to a former friend; the debutante heiress who found her such an agreeable hostess, could not dream that a girl, poor and obscure, in her place would simply have been stared into social limbo.

There were some women who did not like her; women of birth and breeding to whom generations of wealth and leisure had given every opportunity to develope all that was lovely and lovable in womanhood, and who selected their friends from the same class as themselves. These women might introduce a poor relation into society, take up a struggling artist, or dine in a rented house from kindness of heart or disinterested affection, in the uruffled security of an unassailable position; but for Mrs. Wall-Clayton, as well suggest the plague at once.

There were even a few men who shared this adverse feminine opinion, but as a rule her reign in the masculine kingdom was complete. For who could be more gracious, more sympathetic, more subtly flattering, more interested in one's pet schemes!

She was not at all diffident in gauging her own powers. A woman who had gained so much — why not gain all, she thought. When she could say "my son" to a peer, there was no available chance to say "my husband" unless death would translate some peeress near her own age to a better world, her happiness would be complete. Then those who had not liked her, and had shown their dislike or their indifference, would be figuratively at her feet. In her dreams by the fire which she had in her bed room because it was so English, her triumph over those who had not yielded to her fascinations, was complete. She even pictured them interceding with her for cards to a court drawing-room.

Marguerite came home with the full determination to set up an establishment of her own, and it took the combined expostulations of Mrs. Kingman and Edith, the softest most persuasive arguments on the part of her stepmother, added to the positive disapprobation of Mr. Dalton, to make her relinquish the plan. Even then she did not altogether give it up, but merely consented to let it remain in abeyance. She soon discovered however, that the hatchet was buried in a deep grave so far as Mrs. Clayton was concerned, and that it rested with herself to let it remain so. She was honestly sorry that she could not be fond of her stepmother; and the girls were nice, well mannered pretty girls who would certainly not revive the feuds of their childhood. They were cordial, almost affectionate to her, and certainly could not know how horribly they grated on her nerves when they spoke of "dear papa." Marguerite had shared her father's money, but she could not patiently share her relationship. She would simply have been roused to fury had she known that the Misses Wall had deliberated very seriously on taking the name of Clayton. They argued that if they were to have children's parts of the estate why not be children in name; but Mrs. Clayton, as much as she would have liked it, did not quite see her way to this post-mortem adoption. They never forgot themselves so far as to speak of their own father.

Marguerite, who understood her stepmother from intuition more than from judgment, wondered a little what object she had in view in being so affable to herself.

VIII.

DESPITE intermittent hours of homesickness for the convent, Marguerite was very happy. There were no old threads for her to pick up, but it did not take long to find entirely new ones. Her costumes had all been prepared in Paris under the supervision of Mrs. Kingman, and her mind being relieved on that weighty consideration, she was ready for all the sight seeing and informal gatherings which Edith constantly devised for her amusement. At a delightful little luncheon, to which Edith had given verbal invitations to a quartet of her intimates to come take pot luck with her and meet the dearest girl in the world, Marguerite made her first step toward social success. The maidens in question were representative of the best and most desirable element, and they formed an immediate liking for the semi-French girl whose simplicity of manner, and general sweetness they pronounced the perfection of good form. They reconsidered their determination to decline Mrs. Clayton's cards to Marguerite's coming-out party.

On the first of December this important event took place. Mrs. Clayton had issued the invitations in honor of her daughter Marguerite, but it was Marguerite herself who paid the piper and the other supers of a great social function. However, it was to Mrs. Clayton belonged all the credit for its entire success. She had a natural gift for entertaining, and she was always glad to do it, provided she could get the right kind of people to entertain. "Put no limit on the champagne and have a *chef* who is an artist in his way, and your daughters will never lack for partners," was one of her proverbs upon which she uniformly acted. In this instance not only had the *chef* and the butler been given carte blanche, but the florist and the decorators and the musical director as well. There were two bands in attendance, both unexcelled, and during the evening the seductive strains never ceased, which could send thrills to the very toes of an octogenarian, and make him sigh that his dancing days were over.

There were alluring bowers of palms, the faint odor of cut flowers massed everywhere, the soft trickle of a fountain, the flash of lights, the glass-like floor of one of the finest private ball-rooms in town, rows of velvet divans for the chaperons, the deftest of maids in the dressing rooms, the most obsequious of footmen to relieve gentlemen of their overcoats. There were wines specially imported for the occasion, canvas-backs, and terrapin, boned turkey and truffles, salads and ices and candied violets, solid gold plate and rare china, and sparkling cut glass, and spoons emblazoned with the Clayton crest. Mrs. Clayton, like many another matron, had purchased the crest at a heraldic establishment in London, where she had been given a choice of crests of a half dozen different families of Claytons.

Mrs. Clayton received her guests with all the grace and graciousness of the daughter of a hundred earls; indeed, it was a question whether the earl's daughter could have held her own with the republican matron. A middle aged bachelor who knew her history, said to himself, as he watched her and her train of wealth and beauty through the vista of splendid rooms, that in view of the American woman there was simply no limit to the possibilities of the American race.

Marguerite's gown was of white silky stuff, with puffed sleeves and a girdle, and old lace, of the kind permitted to young girls, at the throat, a gown which the papers spoke of as a French confection.

She took a few turns over the waxed floor by herself, as a preliminary venture, before the guests began to arrive, buoyant with that ecstatic thrill of joyous expectancy which belongs naturally to the desirable concerns of youth.

But in the middle of the party the ecstasy had gone; she could not tell why, she hardly knew when, nor could she say what had replaced it. Not disappointment, for everything had gone off splendidly, and everybody was having a good time, or simulated the aspect of a good time. Every detail, Edith had whispered, was simply perfect, there was no lack of partners for herself, nor for any one else; and yet, and yet the effervescence of happiness had gone, leaving only a sluggish draught of the commonplace which might change to weariness at any moment. The glare of the lights made her headache, she was tired of dancing, and there was something insipid after all, about young men. Why could not she feel all the bliss Edith had experienced at her coming-out party; why was there a formless longing in her heart, when every beat should have been charged with present happiness. Still she danced and talked and smiled and sent arch glances from under curling black lashes, until Edith, who had been watching her, wondered if Marguerite was a belle by intuition, since she had certainly been given no opportunities to learn the art, and a nine years seclusion in a convent was not conducive to a knowledge of even the theories of belleship.

It was the last dance on the program before the supper march, and Marguerite was talking perfunctorily to a Mr. Henry Wilson who had been presented by her stepmother in the early part of the evening. In the absence of any information in regard to his personality, likes and dislikes, she felt that her remarks were rather colorless and uninteresting, and she was just on the point of asking him to take her to Mrs. Clayton when—she gave a little cry, whether of surprise or pleasure or both, Wilson could not tell, which left his question as to her opinion of the States unanswered;—by some primal law of telepathy she had looked towards the door just as a tall, courtly appearing personage was entering it. In a minute Marguerite was shaking hands with Lord Parkhurst.

"I am rather late, I know, but that is the fault of the unfeeling ship; it was due here in the afternoon, but the fogs and a perverse fate delayed us so that I was beginning to think I should have to swim ashore to get here in time for even one dance with you, but fortunately, I was saved from that extremity by the press boat. Newspapers have their advantages after all."

Marguerite was American enough to enjoy the triumph of having an earl go to the trouble of dressing on shipboard, and coming direct from the docks in a shackling old hack, just to attend her party, and she was woman enough to be glad of the devotion which had prompted his efforts. She hardly knew what she said to welcome her cavalier, but he was evidently very well pleased.

"I thought the colored factotum at the door was not going to let me in, for I had forgotten my invitation, and I did not even have a visiting card about me, but I was not going to be balked at the very threshold, after coming all the way from England to dance with you; so I asked him to be good enough to tell Miss Clayton that Lord Parkhurst wished to see her, and took up my stand in the vestibule with all the determination of the Sphinx; then he relented and ushered me in with such a bland smile that I wanted to turn back and give him a sovereign on the spot."

The triumph was tempered by the acknowledgement, which came out presently, that he had run over to see about some speculations in Mexico, and that he had made the trip a month earlier than he would otherwise have done in order to attend her coming-out party. Even a month sacrificed to do her honor was something from an earl, commonly reported to be indifferent to the attractions of women; and if he had come purposely to see her, it would have been too marked, and she did not want that, she told herself; there was no reason at all why his attentions should be so pronounced. He was merely an agreeable acquaintance who had made a week, passed at a French country house, a very pleasant one.

"But come, we must find Edith" said Marguerite, as if she had been derelict in a duty and had suddenly discovered the omission. Lord Parkhurst refrained from saying that he thought he could survive even if he did not see Miss Kingman during the whole evening; but remembering that with Marguerite it was a case of 'Love me, Love my friend' he only said that he should be delighted, but modestly suggested that he would also like to pay his respects to Mrs. Clayton.

"O yes, Mamma, will be so glad to see you."

It was a triumph of grace over nature when Marguerite schooled herself to say mamma to her father's wife. As a child she refused point blank to do so.

"Mamma, I will not say, mother, I cannot. Mrs. Clayton, I may not", she herself had said to Edith, and during her school life she had compromised on Mere Clayton. To please Madame Florac, who feared rather a stormy time in Marguerite's domestic life, she had consented to say mamma.

"Mamma, here is Lord Parkhurst, just arrived from England."

"Lord Parkhurst, dear heaven" exclaimed the voice of the matron's inner consciousness, but the silvery tongue of her corporeal presence voiced the smoothest of welcomes. In that moment she could have embraced her step-daughter with deepest affection.

"We want to find Edith" Marguerite continued after the necessary greetings had been exchanged between hostess and guest.

Lord Parkhurst, since he could not very well monopolize the debutante for the rest of the evening, thought that Miss Kingman would make a very charming substitute. He remembered her as an agreeable girl, of the type which passes current in Europe as the American. For his own part he had long since come to the conclusion that there was no such thing as the American type; the sole national characteristic that he had observed was the tendency of every American to be different from every other American; and if the only common ground was the ground of individual differentialization he did not see how any question, or any calculations could rest on the type.

Edith's first feeling on seeing Lord Parkhurst was a resentment she could not show, but which she vented to herself in the thought; "Oh I don't want Marguerite to marry an Englishman, and go to live in England;" but when she found that the earl was merely on his way to Mexico she recovered from her displeasure, which she acknowledged, since the danger was passed for the time, had been decidedly premature. She talked to him with the animation natural to her, and with the interest his own personality inspired; for she really liked the young man, although she did not like some things about him; and he on his part found genuine enjoyment in her society; but she did not give him a great deal of it. "I shall make myself cherished for life," she thought, with a humorous smile, as she introduced the earl right and left. The most popular girls were wild because their dances were nearly all taken.

"Miss Wall, my sister, Miss Stella Wall — my second sister," she said very sweetly.

Marguerite had taken pains to present the earl to her step-sisters soon after his arrival, from a desire born of happiness and natural goodness, to practice the golden rule.

All things considered, Lord Parkhurst found that the dances which Marguerite gave to her own countrymen could be made most enjoyable by her countrywomen. He had always been fond of Americans, although he had never for a moment conceded to them an equality with English maidens until he met Marguerite; and she, he reflected, was not representative of America.

And Marguerite discovered that her spirit of pleasure was merely resting, and had not vanished for the evening. It was something to make her party memorable, that a peer of the realm had braved all the discomforts of a November voyage to be present. He had laughingly told her at the little dance at Chateau Flaubert on Christmas night that he would cross the world to attend, if he got an invitation, but she had accepted it merely as a joke. Still the invitation had been sent to his London address, and he must have sailed on the next steamer. He certainly was a very agreeable partner; and she could talk to him with more ease, and with a greater wealth of ideas than to any other man she had ever met; of course she had met only a very few.

Those who had thought her lacking in animation at the beginning of the evening, confessed that their judgment had been hastily formed.

"There is nothing like one's first party after all",

the girl whispered gaily to Edith; and Edith could not keep from replying that there was certainly nothing like it, especially when a handsome man with a hereditary right to a seat in Parliament, was numbered among one's partners.

IX.

MRS. Kingman's invitations had already been out for the regulation fortnight to a dinner in honor of Marguerite, when Lord Parkhurst appeared on the social horizon. Edith, who was disposed to afford him all the pleasure possible in view of his speedy absence in Mexico, as well as anxious to make Marguerite's first taste of society as agreeable as she could, was equal to the emergency. Or at least she was able to meet it through the assistance of a good natured second cousin, a young girl, not rich, but very pretty and moderately popular, who consented to act as a Convenience for the occasion. Since it was to be a Convenience for a Lord, she declared that she considered it as having greater distinction than an invitation in the first place. So a card from Mrs. Kingman bidding him to dinner, was not the least prized of the social trophies which began to gather thick and fast about the visiting earl.

Although the presence of Lord Parkhurst put a sort of embargo for the time, on a little dream of Edith's, who had the match-making instinct which belongs to some natures, her friendliness towards him left no room for suspicion of any disappointment.

"Carroll is such a perfectly charming fellow, that he can wait for his chance," she thought; but there was marked cordiality in her tone when she said; "Marguerite, I want to present a dear old friend and playmate of my innocent youth, Mr. Kirwin."

And Marguerite delighted her by showing all the graciousness she felt toward a friend of her friend.

The young man immediately conceded that the reports of Marguerite's beauty, which always grow in ratio to a new belle's fortune, had not been exaggerated.

Marguerite found him a good talker; he appeared taller than she had at first thought him, and his eyes, which looked black, proved to be dark blue, and to have a humorous twinkle where she had imagined an expression of melancholy. "But perhaps they are changeable, some people's eyes are", she thought. His tones were deep and sympathetic, with that indescribable prolongation of the s, which even her limited experience recognized as Southern. She knew something of his history from the Kingmans. He was a lawyer, and lived in bachelor quarters, in a house on a side street near the Park, which he had bought simply to oblige a friend; so the story ran, although Mrs. Kingman, with her prosaic way of looking at money transactions, the outcome of her years and long experience in personal management of property, had said; "I suppose it was a pretty good investment, anyhow." Marguerite went in with Lord Parkhurst, but found herself with Mr. Kirwin on her left. The question of precedence had been deliberated long and seriously.

Edith was for carrying out her original plan and assigning the honor to Kirwin, of going out with Marguerite, but she at length decided on doing as she would be done by, although not for one's own best good.

"We manage things differently in Maryland," Kirwin was saying to the lady at his right.

"I knew it, I knew he was not a New Yorker" Marguerite thought exultantly to herself, with the pleasure one feels in making a discovery unassisted.

"Lord Parkhurst has come over to point out a few of the rocks on which our ship of state is liable to split," began John Raymond in jocose allusion to their last conversation on the subject of America and the Americans.

"Ah, that is hardly fair," said the earl; "when I spoke for the glory of England, I had to take a different tone from what I should have done had it been a personal question. In the light of what I have seen I am tempted to add there are no rocks, but only the most buoyant of tides, but even Mr. Raymond's patriotic feelings will not demand quite such a concession."

"The most flattering of the compliments Europeans pay us" said Wilson, "all the more flattering because it is done unintentionally, is the fact that in speaking of America and the Americans, the United States are always meant; now when we remember South America and Mexico and Canada, to say nothing of the rest of the Bristish possessions, that habit of speech certainly does speak well for our national preeminence."

Lord Parkhurst ventured the suggestion that this might be the result of the limitations of the language which had no other name for the habitants of the country which owns the stars and strips for its flag.

"One can say Canadian, Mexican, Brazilian, Chilian, without any particular twist to his tongue, but when it comes to United Statesian one's vocal chords rebel."

After this question had been satisfactorily disposed of, the talk naturally drifted to other phases of the United States, as conversation usually does when a foreigner is present.

"You ought to get Kirwin here to explain reform," said Raymond: "he got the fever some time ago, and still has it pretty bad; if you get him started right he can give you more information in an hour than you could dig out of a two volume quarto of statistics in a week."

"So he is a reformer" thought Marguerite. "I wonder what particular thing he is reforming." His modest disclaimer of being a reformer at all did not enlighten her any.

Marguerite was to spend the night with Edith. As a matter of fact she stayed two thirds of her time with her friend, and had a room to call her own in the Kingman mansion, which Edith had decorated for her especial benefit. After the guests had gone the two girls went up stairs, ostensibly to go to bed, but in reality to spend a good portion of the night in an exchange of confidences.

"Did you notice poor Mr. Wilson" asked Edith as she sat Turkish fashion on a rug before the open fire, "when Lord Parkhurst and Carroll Kirwin were talking about reforms: and Lord Parkhurst said we had better reform our marriage service or else do away with it altogether, so as to save the divorce courts their overwhelming work; Why, you know his father and mother are divorced; they separated when he was a child; there were only two children of them, and the father took the boy, the mother the girl. Poor fellow, he has never seen his mother since. Do you know there is something fascinating about the man, although mamma does not like him."

"He is very good looking," said Marguerite, non-committally. "I never before, saw black eyes that were so very black and his mustache and hair match his eyes. He is quite distinguished looking too, almost as if he might be the king of the bandits."

"There is something sad about him, to me"; continued Edith, "I always feel sorry for him, although for no especial reason; he seems to be doing very well and to be quite able to take care of himself."

"Did you know his parents," asked Marguerite, with a feeling of interest in any one who was an orphan like herself, only more so.

"Oh no: nobody ever knew his parents; I really believe they were quite unknowable. We met him at Nice; he was there with Carroll Kirwin; he and Carroll went to school together as boys, and are still very good friends. Henry Wilson went to Heidelberg for a year or two and came back a complete infidel; I don't believe in sending boys to some of those Universities, and I should think one could learn all he chose at our own schools." Marguerite did not remind her that that sounded somewhat inconsistent from a girl who had herself been educated abroad.

"As a boy he had lived around with his father in one boarding house and another without home training of any kind. Then his father died, and he went abroad; I heard that his mother was dead too, or married again, I am not sure which. When he came back to New York he was practically a stranger, as his father had formed no social ties and of course could not give his son what he did not possess himself. No one knows just how he got to be so popular. He began life as a clerk in a bank, but was promoted rapidly so that now he is the assistant cashier. I suppose he is really very bright, and a bright man can always get along in the world.

"There was a rumor that the daughter of the president of the bank had taken a fancy to him that was more than passing; but nothing came of it, and last spring she married a charming man from Chicago.

"Everybody considers him a very promising young man, excepting mamma; she says, she prefers promises fulfilled. He is a great student and talks well, don't you think so?"

Marguerite replied that her opportunities to judge of either point had been limited.

"He is very aesthetic in his tastes; is fond of music and pictures and old china. They say his apartment at the Hannibal is sumptuously furnished; I suppose he puts his salary in those things, and trusts to his eyes and his mustache and his tongue to win him a fortune along with a wife. There is no accounting for tastes. Now there is Carroll Kirwin with an income of forty thousand at least from his estate and his practice —he is with Roberts & Roberts, the railroad lawyers, you know, and he lives like a clerk. He has two old servants who used to belong to the Kirwin plantation in Maryland; his house is ordinarily furnished, the only extravagances he owns up to are rare books in fine bindings, and fast horses. He belongs to the clubs but seldom goes to them, and he accepts just about one third of his invitations. He only came to-night because the chance to see a new belle and a live lord was too good for even him to miss. It was you Marguerite, who formed the attraction. I was jesting about the earl, for he he does not care in the least for titles, he is a thorough-going, old colonial American."

"Since when did you take to calling gentlemen by their first names, Edith?"

"Oh, Carroll, why I have known him all my life, and mamma knew him before I was born. Besides he is a sort of relation; his cousin married a cousin of mama's that is."

"Mr. Raymond told Lord Parkhurst that he, I mean Mr. Kirwin of the attenuated cousinship, was a reformer," said Marguerite. "What particular thing is he reforming, inebriates, convicts, election laws".—"None of those; his great scheme consists in building sanitary tenement houses and putting them on a paying basis. Considering the kind of hovels our poor live in and the kind of men who own them for the most part, one might say that he is trying to reform the rich, the landlords," answered Edith.

"Oh, how lovely; and does he put his fortune in tenement houses?"

"None that he does not expect to get out again. It is philanthropy, and philanthropy of the best kind, but it is on a basis of four per cent. The nicest thing about Carroll is that he is not a bit of a crank. And he does not make people feel uncomfortable by being oppressively good. One is apt to imagine a man with a scheme of that kind going around with long hair and a shiny coat and looking spiritualized. But you would never suspect Carroll of being so good. The one thing that he needs, and needs badly, is a wife who could appreciate him. I'd marry him myself, only I never could live up to his ideals, I am too frivolous he thinks; besides he never indicated in any way that he wanted me to," concluded Edith.

"It must be grand to do all those noble things with one's money. I want to use all my income, I mean over my expenses, for the poor. Do you remember the model estate I was going to found when we were at Madame Flaubert's that Christmas? well I have not forgotten it, only there have been so many things to think of since I got home, and besides you know, I do not get control of my property until I am twenty one, and that will not be for nearly two years. I wonder though, if Mr. Dalton would not let me put some money in those tenement houses; I should think he would, since there is no loss. Would Mr. Kirwin think it strange if I were to ask him to invest some money for me?"

"Why no, indeed, it would be just the thing; he would be delighted," cried Edith. "Now if they would only get mutually interested in that scheme it might lead to something," she was thinking to herself, delighted that Marguerite was lending herself unconsciously to her matchmaking idea. She had decided on the union of Carroll and Marguerite long before the girl came home from school.

"If ever two people were created for each other those two are, Carroll, and Marguerite. Now *I* see it if *they* do not, the perspective of a third person being naturally broader than those immediately concerned. Both have aspirations and aesthetic tastes, and an Arcadian disregard of the flesh pots of Egypt: And he has practical sense to counterbalance Marguerite's inexperience and angelic innocence."

Marguerite, all unknowing that her friend was getting her married and her life work mapped out for her, as they sat toasting their toes before the wood fire, continued; "I have not forgotten all that Madame Florac said about great wealth carrying with it great responsibilities. I wish sometimes that I did not have so much: I used to be glad, and I intended to do so much good with it, but I don't seem to be doing anything."

Edith suggested that as she had been home just five weeks, and her property still in the hands of her guardian, that she was reproaching herself too soon.

"I envy you and other girls who have fathers or mothers to take all the trouble and worry about money; you have the pleasure and benefits of it without any of the responsibility. I have always wanted, since I have been old enough to think about it, to make my money an instrument of good for others; not simply to be given in charity—anybody can give who has anything to give, and there is no particular merit in bestowing what one does not need or want, but what I would like would be to make my money an instrument in my hands; I to be the dominant power, my money simply the machine," said Marguerite earnestly.

Edith told her there was no hurry, as the poor would probably not become extinct in New York, at least for a few months anyhow.

"But I don't seem to have time for anything now but enjoying myself; and I have just come out; I can't help wondering how I shall even find time to say my prayers if the invitations continue to pour in as they have begun; I promised Madame Florac that I would lead a regular life, give a certain time to reading, and study, and music, and physical exercise, and works of charity, and all that; I had a most beautiful rule of life laid out, and I do not observe one single regulation."

"After you have been in society for a few years you will get everything reduced to your system. If you don't get married, that is, but not much danger of your failing to do that Rita?"

"But I want some sort of order in my life now" cried the younger girl smiling. "The morning is gone before I get up, and when I sleep late the day seems to be all out of gear. — And here we are chatting away at two o'clock in the morning and both of us will be in bed until noon tomorrow."

"And just fancy, not two years ago we were getting up at six o'clock in the morning." Answered Edith. "Ugh, that bell, I hope I shall never hear a rising bell again while I live."

"You always were lazy, Edith. So am I, only I know better. Theories are so easy, and practices are so hard."

"My dear, that is really such an original saying; I am sure nobody ever heard it before," said Edith with good natured sarcasm.

The maidens were beginning to feel a certain heaviness about the eyes, so they scrambled to their feet, gave a yawn, allowable in the privacy of one's own room, which is usually described as pulling oneself together, and prepared to go to bed;—just about the time the milkman was starting on his daily morning rounds.

X.

MARGUERITE'S success as a belle was all that the most insatiable vanity, or the fondest pride could wish. The most desirable men in New York vied with one another in sending her flowers, and begging the favor of being her partner for the numerous cotillons it was the fashion that season to give. And she was equally popular with the girls of her own age. Perhaps, if she had shown by so much as a lift of her straight dark brows, any elation at her popularity or consciousness of it, there might have been barbed shafts of envy aimed behind her back; but her manner of receiving the homage so freely offered was adorable, and those who knew her were firm in the conviction that her manner simply expressed her heart. Her way of sharing Lord Parkhurst, as much as anything else, contributed to the high favor she obtained with her own sex. Although the girl herself insisted on the story that he was going on to Mexico on important business, it was generally understood that the earl had come to America to see Marguerite. People made it a point to ask them to dinner together, and when at receptions and parties they rested on palm-embowered stairways, everybody said it was such a pretty romance. So marked had been the attentions of the earl to Marguerite from the start, that no one thought of entertaining any matrimonial designs on him, and all were well content to wine and dine the young peer, and dream, possibly, of the bliss of an invitation in the autumn to his country seat, when Marguerite would be the countess of Parkhurst. In the gossip of afternoon teas and women's receptions, the two were already married, before, in reality, they had seen each other a half dozen times. The story of the Christmas holidays spent together at Chateau Flaubert was woven into a very pretty little idyl, and further embellished by the assertion that his Lordship had hired a special cutter to bring him ashore, to be in time for Marguerite's party.

When mildly chaffed by his intimates at the clubs, at which he had been introduced by Carroll Kirwin and Raymond, on his budding romance all Parkhurst would say was, that any man might be proud to win a smile from Miss Clayton.

An affair of this sort, when it has the misfortune to enlist the interests of the community, always moves at the rate of the fast express to its vision, when in reality it is progressing at the stage coach pace.

Lord Parkhurst and Marguerite had talked about books and pictures, Europe and America, life in France and life in England, the condition of the poor every where, the inhabitants of Mars, the responsibility of the human will, and a hundred other subjects, besides the stock phrases of the weather and society; but they had not talked of love. The earl seemed very well contented with his life in New York; and with reason, for if society had welcomed Marguerite it gave a regular ovation to the peer. He might have dined three times every day, and still have been compelled to decline some of his invitations. Then some ingenious woman, knowing she could not secure him for a dinner asked him to breakfast, and another one followed it up with a luncheon, so that, after the first few days, he was allowed to sleep a few hours out of the twenty four at his hotel, but nothing more.

He soon got into the habit of dropping in informally at the Clayton abode, where Mrs. Clayton made him not only very welcome, but thoroughly comfortable. He soon developed a genuine regard for the agreeable woman who seemed to know just what he liked. If he asked Marguerite to go walking with him and the girl demurred, she urged her to go with gentle insistance that she had been cooped up all day and needed fresh air; if he was tired of talking and in a mood bordering on the sentimental, Marguerite was coaxed to play for him, or to sing the songs he liked. There was usually a box of cigars of his favorite brand on the library table, and receiving the assurance that Mr. Clayton had always smoked in the luxurious room, and that smoke was considered very good for the books, he not infrequently stopped there to enjoy a cigar.

No mother, with designs on a coronet for a child of her own, could have paved the way for the course of love more ingeniously than did Mrs. Clayton for Marguerite's affair. In the light of so much kindness the girl was growing almost fond of her.

People who were not dazzled by the title were pleased with Lord Parkhurst on his own account. He was gentlemanly and courteous, dignified and considerate, entertaining and companionable; and when it was remembered how many young men with no title to compensate for stupidity, lack these attractions, the popularity of the earl ceased to be a wonder.

Lord Parkhurst had been brought up with a great respect for his mother and his mother's opinions; and among the opinions insisted upon most strenuously by the dowager Lady Parkhurst were those which concerned the marriage question. She had no patience with the absurd romanticists who profess to believe that marriage concerns only the two persons, who in the language of the Court circular, are the high contracting parties. They sometimes had the least to do in the matter, she contended. It concerned the families, society, religion, the whole political and social universe. It was desirable of course, that the couple be congenial to each other, but love she maintained, had very little to do, either with the happiness, or the good results of a marriage. There were so many people who had married for love who would have liked to be unmarried for something else; and so many who had entered into a matrimonial contract from a high sense of duty to the family, its past traditions and its future hopes, whose union proved most fortunate, that her skepticism in regard to the purely romantic aspect of marriage had taken deep root. She was not at all the stern parent of the melodramatic stage, who would have forced a child against any well defined disinclination to an alliance; but neither would she have listened to any rhapsodies about love as an excuse for an unequal marriage. If the two were suitable to each other in every way—in station, fortune, education, refinement, love would come after marriage as a matter of course. In regard to the prevailing custom which had attained such growth in late years of American heiresses capturing impecunious peers, she had nothing to say provided the fortune were great enough to really be a fortune, allowing for shrinkage in values after the connubial knot was indissolubly tied.

No well-bred Englishman would marry an American, of course, when an English girl equally rich and desirable could be had, but as wealthy English girls recognized by Burke and Debret were not as numerous as anxious mothers could desire, the Americans might be a great convenience. A gentleman could not so far declass himself as to marry the daughter of trade, however beautiful and rich when it was a question of British trade; but in America where there are no Plebeians, and where any one may be a Patrician who has money enough, and no questions asked as to ancestors—in a country where the children of men who began life as butchers or bakers or candlestick makers, hucksters or errand boys, may enter, by grace of their own charming personality and their fathers' money bags, any circle in the land, and be eligible for any honors, it was quite a different affair. Americans were received every where, even kings liked to talk to them, and queens did not disdain to give their royal finger tips to the rosy lips of American commerce—in the person of its daughters.

The question of her son's marriage had given Lady Parkhurst a good deal of concern. She did not approve of early marriages, neither did she approve of late ones. By thirty a man ought to be married and settled down into his proper sphere in the world, and assume the duties which his rank imposed. Just what these duties were in her son's case she did not stop to define, and no one would have had the assurance to ask for an explanation. It was now past thirty with the earl, and Herbert, his dashing younger brother, Herbert who would have been the maternal favorite could he have taken the talismanic place of the first born, was nearing that age; and it was eminently desirable that he settle down to sober married life and the diplomatic service, in which it was her dream to see him. This could not be accomplished until the Earl married the expected fortune and made the promised settlements. With these anxieties before her she hailed with no little delight the announcement of the young peer that he was going to America; he had always wanted to see the States, America really was a most extraordinary country, and the people delightful; besides he thought he saw his way to making some investments in Mexico. Of course she knew all about Miss Clayton and Miss Kingman; it was quite natural, considering that she had seen neither of them, to prefer Miss Clayton, the undisputed heiress to two millions, over Miss Kingman who interposed a youthful mother between herself and a scant one million.

On the night when Lord Parkhurst was dancing with Marguerite at her coming-out party, his mother was courting insomnia on an ancestral bed, beneath ancestral walls, and tucked in cozily between sheets old enough to be ancestral, planning the changes which must be made. Financial difficulties would be untangled, the crooked path of debts made the straight way of cash payments, and every thing vivified in the general prosperity, when the earl would bring home his American wife to those same ancestral halls,—draughty and out-of-repair halls as they were.

To do Lord Parkhurst justice he went about his wooing in a business like way, which ought to have delighted the shades of his maternal grandfather, a manufacturer who had made a fortune in Birmingham, and mounted on stacks of cotton prints to the daughter of a baronet. Although the earl took a pride in his family seat—Parkhurst, it had come to his grandfather by purchase, and he himself was but the third Lord Parkhurst, the title having been revived for his grandfather, through some remote claim of his wife. The claim was backed, it was whispered, by money lavishly placed where it would do the most good.

The third earl took his title very seriously however, and if it had gone straight back to William the Conquerer he could not have been more alive to the dignity of a hereditary legislator of the Realm. He would not have relished the suggestion that his business talent came to him by the right of inheritance from his grandfather, although he was glad to avail himself of business methods in his career.

He had been a good student of human nature as well as of human affairs, and he realized instinctively that in winning a girl like Marguerite Clayton he would have to do it on his merits as a man, and not on the title of an earl.

Besides, he was noble enough, warm hearted

enough, poetic enough in spite of his mother, to feel that there would be something very sweet and beautiful in a marriage for love. Marguerite liked him, he was sure of that, but he had not, as yet, the least reason in the world to believe that her liking had a warmer tinge than mere friendship. She was even more uniformly charming to Carroll Kirwin than she was to himself.

But then there were so many agreeable girls in New York, surely a man ought to find one who would both love him devotedly and pay his debts.

XI.

THE play was just over, and as the stream of fashionable and well dressed humanity surged from the vestibule of Palmer's theatre into the flashing radiance of the electric lighted streets, a box party of eight paused just outside the entrance, as carriage after carriage came swiftly up, received the impatient occupants, and whirled away. It was during the Christmas Holidays, and the party was given by John Raymond in honor of Edith Kingman. It fell to Carroll Kirwin's lot to be Marguerite's escort on the occasion, and he seemed to be duly grateful for his opportunities. Lord Parkhurst had been invited, but as the affair was almost impromptu, having been decided upon at the last minute so to speak, after Edith had expressed a desire to see an unknown actress in a well known role, he was of course engaged.

"I believe in encouraging obscure merit" said Edith, "and besides I am tired to desperation of dancing. I feel like the bad boy who was punished for stealing jam by being put on a diet of jam for a week."

They were chatting all the gay nothings which a public performance of any kind seems to bring to the slowest of tongues. Marguerite appeared the very embodiment of beautiful and joyous girlhood, Carroll was thinking as he deftly drew her opera cloak more closely around her shoulders, remarking that the Northern winds were no respecter of persons. She had caught his interest at first as the representative of a type, and she retained it by the magnetism of her own personality; but his attentions had not been persistent enough to please Edith, altogether, who would have liked for him to make a proposal of marriage at first sight, since she in her wisdom, had decided that theirs would be an ideal union. She was in hopes that the earl would soon take himself and his opposing fascinations away to Mexico—or Japan, now that the holidays were about over.

Mrs. Kingman, whose appreciation of posttheatrical badinage, especially when taking place in a snow covered street at eleven o'clock at night, was not keen, was beginning to feel a little impatience which she vented in a dry cough, when Raymond called out cheerily; "here are our carriages." The party immediately separated into quartets. Marguerite was declaring that she had had a lovely time, and her heightened color and sparkling eyes gave the force of truth to the conventional assertion.

"Marguerite takes to society as naturally as the proverbial duck takes to the proverbial water," Edith answered gaily; and Marguerite retorted; "If you have any more proverbs, bring them out, I am good natured, and willing to be a living illustration to your little remarks. Illustrations are the fashion of the day from articles on Siberia to sermons."

The first carriage, containing Edith, her cousins, Mr. and Mrs. Farr and Raymond had rolled away, and the second was trying, amidst the rush of countless other vehicles to get to the curbing; the crowd was still pouring out of the doors, for the hordes who seek their holiday amusement in the theatres had been out in full force and "Standing Room Only" had been the welcome legend which gladdened the manager's eyes. The remaining quartet had succeeded in reaching their carriage, and Marguerite was just entering, when their attention was attracted by a commotion a few feet away, and a woman in the firm grasp of a policeman, came into view. She was clawing, screaming, shrieking, cursing—her Christmas had evidently been celebrated in such strong and steady draughts that reason and womanhood had fled together, leaving only the ribald degradation which a vicious life had engendered.

"Thief, thief" she was shrieking between a string of oaths. "The daughter of a thief in spite of all your fine clothes and your carriage, and the ground too hard for yer to walk on. A fine bird she is, too good for the likes of me to tech, in her stolen feathers and her grand airs; and her old daddie what took the bread out o' honest folk's mouth, a restin', under his fine moniment; mighty lot o' good it's a doin' him now. Hurrah for old Dick Clayton's daughter! Hurrah! Hurrah!"

Marguerite, paling, gave a startled look, as if she could not realize that it was her father's name that the old blear-eyed, drunken hag was shouting. Then every vestige of color left her face, as more horrible words and laughter fell on her ears like blows. It was only a moment until the creature, still fighting and screaming, and laughing the most demoniac laughter the girl had ever heard, was borne away.

"Shocking! I am afraid you are quite overcome."

"How in the world did the poor wretch ever get hold of your name. Probably some one to whom your father refused money for drink years ago. One never knows what absurd fancy these people may take into their heads; there is a socialistic element which resents as a personal grievance any evidences of prosperity, and the sight of the rich provokes them into a fury. They would like to put a bank president at breaking stones;—they consider every man who has three regular meals a day a thief."

"Here, are you better, please don't think of that miserable creature." Carroll Kirwin was eagerly holding a vinaigrette to Marguerite's nostrils, although she protested that she was not going to faint.

"I can't understand why the police allow such wretches to be lurking around a respectable place; surely we pay taxes enough to be spared from insult on a public street," Mrs. Kingman added petulantly, to a series of more disjointed exclamations.

"Well, she will have time to sober up and repent of her tirade in the work-house at her leisure," answered Kirwin indignantly.

Marguerite was deposited at her own door, with a chorus of protestations that she must not let a little thing like a drunken woman steal from her a single wink of sleep.

Once in her own room, however, she stood before

the fire, without even taking off her wraps, locking and unlocking her hands, a gesture she had when excited, trying vainly to hit upon some clue to the night's insult. She knew so little of her father, and nothing at all of her father's business, but surely he could have had no dealings with a creature like that. Where had the woman even heard of him. Mr. Kirwin was right; she was probably some vagrant beggar to whom he had refused money. And were there really such people she thought; people with human lineaments, although distorted and deformed by drink and infamy, people with immortal souls. The last consideration made her shudder. Here in the glad holiday time, with its rounds of parties and receptions and home gatherings, this pleasure-seeking and present-giving time, the time of peace on earth; here in the very shadow of steeple and dome, of charitable institutions and private palaces and happy homes, were there really such beings. She kept thinking, thinking, going back over the past, the past that seemed so like a dream. Her father had lived only a year in New York when she went to France to school, but in San Francisco she remembered him a jolly, easy going man, generous, kind hearted according to her childish recollections. Certainly not one to injure a living being. Of course it was absurd, and she would think no more about it. Any one is liable to insult in a big city, and a drunken woman is really not responsible. And she shuddered anew at the image of a drunken woman. A drunken man was bad enough, but a drunken woman—God in heaven! what sort of a world was it in which people could be happy and careless and free and yet such terrible infamy brush against one, not in a purlieu given over to poverty and vice; but in a broad, splendid thoroughfare!

She went to bed, but sleep refused to come. She tossed and turned restlessly, with the words ringing in her ears; "Thief, thief, the daughter of a thief. Dick Clayton a thief." Then visions of the old creature lying in her prison cell and going to the island to serve her term, came before her. She had scarcely even read of such things, for native refinement recoiled at the details of police news, but her fancy pictured the scene in lurid horrors. And perhaps she had little children at home in a garret wondering why their mother did not return to them. Then she thought of the Christmas merriment that was not innocent; of men drinking, drinking until their very souls were in the clutches of the demon drink. She had heard of men, not only in the haunts given up to liquor, but in clubs and beautiful homes, making beasts of themselves over their cups, and worse than beasts, for beasts are at least, temperate and having their fall shielded from the world by discreet valets, or sorrowing wives. There might be some excuse for the half-starved vagabonds of the streets, tempted beyond resistance by the bad whiskey and the gilded brightness of the drinking hells; there was none for the other class, and something of pity at the unjust proportion of punishment meted out to the outcasts filled her heart. Her indignation at the drunken old crone was dying out, and she was half sorry that the policeman had not let her escape. Of course it was all a mistake of her drunken fancy, and how terribly it would be punished. Perhaps her children might die whilst she was in the workhouse; or go to the bad more completely than their mother.

Marguerite fell asleep at last, but only to dream most frightful dreams. The drunken hag was breaking rocks, handcuffed to an ogre, some one was hissing "thief! thief!" and three little children belonging to the woman, were being buried in one grave.

XII.

NOTWITHSTANDING her harrowing vigil and troubled night, Marguerite awoke with a start early next morning, feverish and nervous, and strangely depressed. Although not a soul was stirring in the house she got up, opened the blind and stood looking absently down at a newsboy on the deserted street.

"I wonder what time the trial will come off; I suppose they will have to have a trial, and then sentence her to that dreadful Island," thought the girl, her mind still on the adventure of the evening before. She would not have minded so much had it not been the Christmas time. That was a season for everybody to be happy, and she did not want to be the cause, however remotely, of unhappiness to any one.

"It is dreadful to be insulted in a crowd that way. But she was not responsible for what she was saying, and I am almost sorry she was arrested. And maybe she is crazy; I am sure she is; I wonder if they will send her to the work-house if they find she is crazy. Oh I wish, I wish I had not been the one she took to vent her insane fancies upon; I don't want a human being, and even a drunken woman is human, to suffer on my account."

And then like a flash, came the thought of going to the Police Station and paying the fine. She knew that this could be done, although how she knew she could not have told. This act of forgiving beneficence appealed to her generous impulses, her enthusiastic desire to be of some service to the unfortunate; at the same time it would lift her out of the commonplace life of a mere butterfly of fashion, as her strong minded sisters, who wrote articles for the heavy reviews, called girls of her class. It was a deed which she thought her good angel might like to record. It would certainly be forgiving one's enemies.

With Marguerite to conceive a scheme was to carry it out, if it could be done before the heat of the impulse cooled. She rang the bell which, after an interval, was answered by a sleepy maid, and ordered a cup of chocolate and her brougham to be got ready. She had a "turn-out" of her own in which she and Edith spent half their days.

She hastily donned her shabbiest gown which was shabby only by comparison, nibbled at a roll, and in half an hour was entering her brougham. She was not without misgivings as to her very unconventional course, but she was not going to back out after starting. Then the puzzle arose as to how and where she was to find the object of her benevolence. She knew nothing about police stations, nor in what particular one the woman might be incarcerated; and she did not know where to find out. But a blind trust in luck, she called it luck although in her heart she meant Providence, for Providence surely ought to guide one in a matter of charity, buoyed her spirits. She thought of asking her coachman, but there was something so like propriety both personified and petrified about Hilton, who had once driven for the Honorable Miss Aldgate, that she prudently decided to keep her own counsel. She thought of

Edith from force of habit, only to remember that in the first place the young lady was still taking her beauty sleep, and in the next, that Mrs. Kingman would probably ask questions it would be puzzling to answer, for it was hardly in that worthy matron's nature to approve, exactly, of two girls going to a police station.

"Ah, I can look at the directory" she said to herself with a flash of inspiration, and the conviction of the provincial, that in the directory lies the safety of the stranger and the source of all municipal wisdom. She saw a whole array of police stations, but how to locate the particular district wanted was not so easy; so she called for a glass of soda water from the youth in sole charge of the drug store, and then timidly ventured to inquire if he could tell her at what station a prisoner would be found, arrested the evening before on Broadway near thirtieth street; she did not want to be too explicit. "I wonder if he thinks it is a brother or some friend I am going to see about," she thought to herself with a faint blush. But the youth had lived in New York all his life, and considered it beneath the cosmopolitan importance of the great city to wonder about anything which took place in its limits. He gave the desired information as imperturbably as if she had asked her way to the Fifth Avenue Cathedral.

Hilton, for the first time in his career as Miss Clayton's coachman, had to ask to have the directions repeated; Marguerite gave her orders again without in the least betraying the trepidation she felt, and was whirled away. She was thinking that she would like to know what Hilton was thinking.

Arriving at the prison, she was told that the prisoners had all been taken up to the police court. The policeman in charge, to whom she explained her errand, said, with a patronizing air which policemen, old in the service effect towards the young, especially if the young be well dressed and with an air of affluence, about them; "now, if I was in your place, I don't think I'd bother about her; she's probably a bad lot altogether, and it 'ud do no good to bail her out; like as not she'd be up agin before mornin' ". But Marguerite was determined, now that she had come so far, and asking the nearest way to the police court she gave Hilton the second order which he appeared to have some difficulty in understanding. She alighted before a very modern and very imposing building, which looked not unworthy to be a temple of justice in the abstract, and far too dignified for the harrowing details of the concrete forms daily enacted within its portals. She explained to a blue coated guard whom she found in the lobby, her mission, but in the absence of any clue by which to identify the woman he could only conduct her to the court-room, and let her wait for the case in question to be called. She felt her courage oozing out at her finger tips, which were beginning to get cold, and benevolence, which had seemed such a beautiful and heroic thing, was beginning to wear a very doubtful aspect. If she only had the moral support of Edith's presence she would feel different; she might even enjoy it; no, she could not let that word stand, if only in thought, for anything so dreadful, but be interested in what was going on around her. Alone, the situation was formidable. The cases were called and disposed of with a celerity that made her dizzy. 'Found drunk on the streets;' 'disorderly conduct' were the usual charges; 'three months;' 'six months;' 'two months'—the verdicts were becoming almost monotonous. "Let off on probation," was a youth who pleaded extenuating circumstances for a first offence. "Discharged" came once in a while, followed by a subdued buzz, meant she supposed, for congratulations. There was a hum of voices going on all the while from the crowd which seemed to have no particular interest in any one, and to have been drawn there by unhealthy curiosity, and morbid love of excitement in its most degraded channels. There were women too, she noticed with the same shudder she had experienced the evening before. Blear-eyed, coarse, degraded, with frizzly bangs or unkept locks, covered by battered old hats, with a faint caricature of adornment in their dirty plumes, and faded flowers; thin shawls were thrown over threadbare calico frocks, soiled and torn, with half the buttons missing, and exhaling that peculiar tenement house odor, which contact with the very poor has made familiar to sensitive nostrils. A general air of shabbiness and dirt, of disease and degradation seemed to characterize the throng, and caused the young beauty to instinctively recoil from even a momentary contact with them, as one and another scrambled forward to see and hear all that was going on, as if it were the first night of some great tragedy. Tragedy it was; the saddest most hopeless tragedy, with real men and women, real life, real sin and suffering, to make the action darkly, terribly real, with a real part of the great world for a theatre. It was horribly repulsive. Poverty is pathetic, but brutalized, crime-stained poverty, is revolting, and the unkept, besotted appearance of the prisoners was hardly more pronounced than that of the spectators. Marguerite was wondering how she would ever have the courage to speak to any one when her case was called, and tried to peer into the prisoner's dock to see if she could distinguish the old creature, when the official, to whom she had spoken in the lobby, touched her respectfully on the shoulder; "I thought maybe you mightn't like to go up to the bar, and I can speak for ye when yer man's called."

"Man, it's a woman," explained Marguerite, blushing for no cause.

"Oh, them's the hardest kind o' cases; when a woman is mean she can beat a man all holler; but they aint gen'rlly mean."

"Look! there is the one, standing up now," cried the guard. A mask of a woman arose, ashen-hued, trembling, her grey hair falling in disheveled strands on her shoulder, bent and thin, mud-bespattered and woe begone, more so even than those who had preceded her in the prisoner's stand.

"Martha, Grigsby, drunk and disturbing the peace." All her ferocity of the night before had disappeared, and she looked up pitifully at the judge, but the look changed to apathy in the thought that no future could be worse than the past. The details were soon over, and sentence was about to be pronounced, when the policeman stepped up and signaled his desire to pay the fine. An expression of bewilderment spread over the old creature's countenance, and she looked as if she hardly understood the judge's parting injunctions to mend her ways or she might not be so fortunate the next time. The policeman piloted her over to where Marguerite was standing, with the look of bewilderment still on her face.

"I am the one whom you insulted last evening" said Marguerite not unkindly, but with the calmness belonging to her superior plane. "But, as I did not want any one to suffer, even justly, on my account during the Christmas time I came down to pay your fine. I should like you to tell me in what way you think my father ever injured you."

At this the dull eyes wakened into something very like a flash, and the expressions of gratitude suddenly froze on the bloodless lips.

"'Taint no thinkin' ma'am; it's him what brung me to what I am; But it wa'nt no fault o' your'n, and I'm sorry I spoke to ye, Miss."

The policeman, with the instinct of a true gentleman, seeing that the interview was becoming private, repressed whatever curiosity he might have had to hear the details of this most unusual case, and turned away as if deeply engrossed in the proceedings of the bench.

"You are certainly laboring under some extraordinary delusion" answered Marguerite repressing her indignation, and maintaining her dignity; "But tell me all about it."

"Well, you see Miss, me an' my ole man was a

livin' down in Konnettiket, Hilsborough, Konnettiket, an' Jim, that's my ole man, or was, Miss he's dead now, was a workin' for Mr. Bienvenue, haulin' freight, and doin' odd jobs, when he didn't git no teamin' to do; we had our own home and gyarden; I sold aigs and chickins, and sich: them was happy times; I didn't know what trouble was; we was gittin' along fine, gittin rich, I'd tell Jim, when Mr. Bienvenue, Jim sot a heap o' store by Mr. Bienvenue and he was a fine man, he got the minin' fever, eve'y body was gone plum daft on the subjec' o' mines; buyin' stock, they called it stock ma'am, but there warn't no stock about it Miss, jest bits uv paper; then long comes big posters, the Golcondy Silver Mines, sorry day fur Hilsborough that was, and me too, and Jim, and all uv us. Mr. Bienvenue, he brung em from New York, whar he got in with a fellar what called hisself the agent for the Golcondy Mines; and come home crazy on mines, crazier a heap, that is, than what he was before that; he said he had the inside track, and was a goin' to make us all rich. He sold his store and broke up his law bus'ness, and sold his farm, he had a good farm too, and put ev'ry blessed cent in them mines. Nothin' ud do Jim but he must go into mines too." They had stepped out into the lobby by this time where the tones of the woman, getting louder and louder, would not be so apt to attract notice, and over to a window where no one was liable to disturb them. Marguerite listened with scarcely an interruption, but with growing impatience at the lenghty explanation which was explaining nothing. As soon as the mines were mentioned she thought she understood the whole matter. Her father had been connected with mines and mining as far back as she could remember, and this old creature was no doubt some one who had taken stock in a mine which had not turned out well. She knew something of the indignation of ignorant stock holders, who thought that every dollar put in a mining company ought to yield twenty, regardless of the worth or worthlessness of the mine. She smiled at so simple an explanation, when she had half expected to hear something of a tragedy. But she heroically allowed the old woman to air her imaginary wrongs. She thought at the same time, she would ask Mr. Dalton if he knew anything of the Golconda Mining Company.

"Jim, he sold our house in spite uv all I could do and say, puts the money into them thar' mines, and set down to wait fur the silver an' gold to begin pourin' in his lap. Mr. Bienvenue he moved to New York, whar he said he could git more law bizness, and his minin stock would support him in style. Nuthin would do Jim but he ups and moves too, and me a pledin' and a beggin' with all my might and main, and the two children, one uf em was a baby, same age as Mrs. Bienvenue's Kit. So we ups, and we goes. We stayed with Mr. Bienvenue fur a while; then we went to housekeepin in two little rooms in a big buildin', Miss, whar, yu couldn't git no breath of fresh air, but good Lord, I didn't know nothin bout trouble even then. I guess I'd a gone stark mad ef I'd a knowed what wuz comin' to me; Fur three months it was all right; Jim got work; Mr. Bienvenue he give him a recommend; and them papers brung in money every month, and we thought the land o' promise had come sure, and I wuz a scoldin myself that I'd been sich a fool as not to want Jim to put his money in the mines. Mr. Bienvenue, he was so tickled that he put every solitary red cent, and said he wuz a goin t' be a rich man right off; then sudden like the mines busted. The papers warn't no good; a man what Mr. Bienvenue saw, sed they never wuz no count; stock not wuth makin' kinlin' wood uf. It was jest the bigges kind o uf a swindle, the mines was salted, I dont jest know what that was, but it wuz a big piece of devilment all the same; Mr. Bienvenue he was fur goin to law, and puttin the raskels in the penn, but a losin' his money broke him up somehow, and he jest died; Then Jim he died: then the chiluns wan't used to havin' no place to play, and no sun, an nothin, and they took the diphthery and died; then I jest seemed to go from bad to wors'; start a dog down hill an' it don't take long for him to git to the bottom. An' the man that swindled us out uf our money, as honest men worked fur, salted them mines, and made believe he was a gittin silver whar' thar warnt no silver to git, put up the whole infernal job, was your father, Miss. He was President of the Company. I don't want to hurt your feelins' Miss, you war'nt to blame, I reckon; you was jest a little girl then, bout like Miss Delphine, but you see its agin human natur' to stan' all that; and when I seed your name in the Gazette and read all about yer bein' one of the best ketches uf the season an' all that, it riled me; sez

I, 'I reckon she is, her old daddie a makin a billion out uf us poor folks': But I didn't know ye then Miss, and I'm plum sorry I spoke to ye."

Marguerite smiled at the thought of her father getting a billion dollars out of one single mining venture. A million would have been out of the ordinary but a billion was quite startling.

She tried to explain to the old crone that mines were all a risk, and that her father, because he happened to be president of a mining company which did not pay, was not responsible for her losses. He risked his money as did everybody else who went into mines. But she soon saw that all explanations were hopeless. The crone only reiterated with dogged persistency; "Mr. Bienvenue he said it wuz a swindle, and he wuz a lawyer, he wuz."

Marguerite took the woman's address, the rear room in a court tenement, the location of which she had not the remotest idea; she drew out her purse meaning to empty its contents into the hands of the miserable creature, for the thought of the two children who had died for the want of country air, and the terrible suffering of their poor mother since, touched her heart, and she could forgive the unjust resentment against her father: but remembering the woman's condition the evening before, in time to check her misplaced liberality, she said; "Now if you will promise me to go straight home, and not touch a drop of liquor all day, and get yourself something to eat, I will see about obtainng you some means of support." She was on the point of saying "Not to touch liqour ever again," but reflected that if she imposed conditions which she was morally certain would be broken, she would be conniving at another person's falsehood.

The old creature began to cry, and Marguerite forgetting all about the liquor, pressed a bill into her wrinkled, grimy hand. Amidst a volley of brokenly uttered thanks and protests of penitence for past misdeeds, the girl escaped to her carriage.

XIII.

MARGUERITE took Edith off the next day, quite unmindful of her protests that they were both due at a committee meeting for the Charity Ball, to see her protege. Edith pronounced the whole affair absurd, at the same time confessing to a wee bit of curiosity to study her friend's first plunge into radical philanthropy.

They took a cab, Marguerite declaring that Hilton would undoubtedly give warning if his livery were any further disgraced by being seen near police courts and tenement districts. They alighted at the entrance to a dismal court, for the very good reason that it was too narrow for the vehicle to pass, and made their way, over broken cobble stones and washed out gullies, in which little pools of water from the melting snow, were still standing, until they found, at last, the number Martha Grigsby had given to her young patroness. "There is not much danger of a tall man's falling here because he would not have the room," said Edith. An odor that seemed to be a mixture of decaying vegetables and escaping sewer gas, filled the air, although the thermometer was low and rapidly falling. They groped their way up the first pair of stairs, down a passage in which the odor was more pronounced, up another flight and into a hall wrapped in total darkness, except for one flickering blaze, obscured by a dirty chimney; then more steps in the middle of which Edith stopped to take breath, smiling wickedly at Marguerite's very evident fatigue.

"Higher, higher, remember Longfellow's boy and Excelsior" she called. Another flight presented itself, at the foot of which Marguerite declared that she could go no further, and leaned against the wall with a determined air of remaining, unmindful of the tragic whisper: "There is worse than dirt on that wall."

With a supreme effort they reached the top floor.

"Cold, damp, dark, dirty; how is that for alliteration?" said Edith as they started down the long hall.

"I am afraid we have gotten our directions all turned around," murmured Marguerite plaintively, "You know they were not very explicit."

"I am thinking they have gotten us turned around" answered Edith, bravely taking the lead, and stopping at last before a door bearing the right number, which a gleam of light, from a broken transom opposite, enabled her to read.

"Come in," said a thick voice, at the same time the door swung back with a sharp creak of its rusty hinges, and the two girls found themselves in a tenement room. The old creature looked ill, but she was sober at least, and Marguerite felt that that was a point gained.

Edith expected to see the withered cheeks suffused with blushes, or she so declared afterwards, at the sight of Marguerite, but there was nothing of the kind; only an apologetic show of hospitality as she invited the visitors to be seated. Obviously this invitation could not be accepted by both as there was but one chair in the room. Martha hurried into the next room, and after a parley with the occupants, there seemed to be more than one, judging from the shuffling feet and the sound of voices, she returned, bringing another dilapidated chair, the match to the one on which Marguerite had selfishly dropped, leaving Edith to await the result of the borrowing expedition. The old woman seated herself on the poor little bed, with its torn and patched covering, and its one dingy pillow. The floor was perfectly bare, excepting for a strip of faded carpet at the bed; there were a rusty little stove holding about a quart of coal — Edith said a pint; a rough pine table, a shelf covered with a fly specked newspaper cut in scallops; a tin-type of two boys, almost babies, framed in cardboard, which at once invested the place with the pathetic interest the hard, sad story had awakened in the breast of Marguerite. An old hat and a shawl that the girl remembered, hung on a nail against the door, and some other articles of apparel kept them company. There was no book, not even a Bible, to be seen; a wooden chest stood by the bed, and pushed well under the table were a tin basin and a battered water pitcher. One narrow, dirty window, which looked northward into a small court, gave the only light and ventilation to the room. Great ugly blotches in the plastering overhead told of a leaking roof, and suggested a chapter of horrors in the way of malaria and rheumatism, coughs and colds. And every where was that stifling odor, added to the mouldy smell natural to a room into which the sun never comes for even one bright moment.

The little stove seemed to be burning as well as it could, but it gave out scarcely any heat, and the girls, wrapped in sealskins and glowing from the exertion of climbing four flights of stairs, were not too warm.

"Oh you can't, you mustn't stay here any longer," cried Marguerite impulsively, a great wave of engulfing pity sweeping through her heart which familiarity had not made callous to human misery.

"Have you been here long ?" interrupted Edith.

"Two years Miss; I used to have two rooms, down on number three, but I couldn't git no work, and so me and Mis. Johnson and Mis. Smith her sister, we took these here two rooms between us."

It did not require much encouragement to draw from her the details of her miserable, poverty stricken, sin-stained life during the twelve years of her widowhood. Marguerite wanted to cry, she felt as if she were choking. She opened her purse realizing that its contents afforded the quickest, surest relief to sufferings such as these; but Edith more practical and better versed in the force of the temptation to drink, said: "Wouldn't you like to stay for a few days in the Home for Friendless Women; I am on the committee of finance and I could send you there immediately if you wish. It is growing very cold and you seem far from well." Even Edith's experience did not extend to a knowledge of the terrible ravages the thirst for liquor ungratified makes in the personal appearance.

"And I will pay for you, you can stay there as long as you like, all your life," cried Marguerite.

"That is certainly very kind in Miss Clayton,"

answered Edith, and since she has so generously offered to pay for you, we could easily arrange to have you live there permanently; or in some one of the other homes. They are comfortable and warm, and since you have no children to look after you, or to be taken care of, that would be the best thing for you."

"And you must have warm clothes and medicines," continued Marguerite, making a move toward opening her purse.

"It would be better to wait until you get to the home to see about your clothes, and I will have the doctor prescribe for you," interrupted Edith who saw at once the danger of letting such a creature get hold of ready money; and that Marguerite, in the glow of her pity, was liable to do a very generous and very ill-advised, and because ill-advised, almost a wicked act, from the purest motives that ever filled a girlish heart. Edith wrote a note on a scrap of paper torn from her note book, to the directress of the home, compelled Marguerite, by a look, to put away her purse, urged Martha to go at once, and said that they would call in a few days to make arrangements for her permanent residence.

When they were again on the outside, breathing the fresh air, the air in the foul court seemed fresh by contrast with the fouler air inside, Marguerite exclaimed, overcome by the horror of the place: "Is it possible Edith, that human beings can own such dens and actually make money out of them? Why, that is worse than the Pagans ever did."

"Certainly they do; sixteen per cent," answered Edith sententiously.

"You must ask Carroll Kirwin about tenements; they are his hobby, you know. All New York has been agitated on the subject of tenement houses, but the agitation is going out of fashion now, and we are begining to take up profit sharing instead. Don't think that you have discovered any thing new, or that you can advance any fresh ideas on the subject, they have all been exhausted; tenement house theories are all below par, a drug in the market, but if you want to invest in them on a basis of four per cent with a gradual rise to six, there is plenty of room in the field. In fact, only Carroll Kirwin and a few others have invaded it at all. You see it is too expensive to follow up one's theories of reform by really reforming."

"I should think that people who have comfortable roofs over their heads would never let such a subject rest until those old rookeries were torn down and comfortable apartment houses or tenements if you prefer, built in their places," Marguerite answered passionately. "It is an outrage to civilization, and more than an outrage to Christianity."

"Christianity and money-getting are not always on good terms," returned Edith dryly.

"Tell me about Mr. Kirwin's plans," said Marguerite after a pause.

"Carroll Kirwin is one of the very few who believe in the combination. He got started on the subject of tenement house reform by being on a charity committee for visiting the poor. He maintained that tenements could be made comfortable and sanitary and homelike, and put on a paying foundation at the same time. He showed his belief in his own theories by testing them. He hired an architect, and together they planned a building which houses eighteen families, or about a hundred persons, which is well lighted and well ventilated. It is built with a court in the middle, but instead of having it paved with brick it is laid out in flower beds and grass plots with a fountain in the centre, actually a fountain, my dear, and broad gravel walks for the children to play in. The most scrupulous neatness and cleanliness are exacted, and whilst he has an agent, he sees to the place himself. I feel that I am talking quite like a reformer myself, but I have heard all about the plan so often I know the details by rote. Drunkenness or disorderly conduct is the signal for dismissal, eviction if necessary. He furnished two of the apartments as models, and offered to furnish any of the others for his tenants on the monthly installment plan. I forgot to say that whilst the floors are not hard wood, they are smooth and stained, so that there is no reason for the wretched excuses called carpets; some of those tenement floor coverings are regular vermin nests, he says; he wants his people to have bright new rugs so that sanitation and aesthetic effects are accomplished at the same time. It really is a revelation to go through that house. You must let him show it to you. He declares that the kernel of the hobby is, that it pays; five per cent, clear of taxes and insurance, and he only counted on four. Some of the apartments have three rooms, and some four; he says that no family with children can get along with less than three rooms. And the rents are scarcely any higher than in the old rookeries we have just left. I do hope we are not bringing any souvenirs away with us; Marguerite you must take a bath as soon as you get home, and hang your clothes out to air. Carroll's latest venture, still on the tapis, is a home for working gentlewomen and art students from the country, not as a charity, but as a paying investment. Perhaps if you are very good he will take you into partnership in the enterprise."

XIV.

MARGUERITE changed her mind about going home, being persuaded by Edith into some project for the afternoon, and dismissed her brougham at Mrs. Kingman's steps. Edith opened the door with a pass key which she carried under a faint protest from her mother, who regarded it as pandering to her daughter's boyish inclinations. The sound of voices from the drawing-room made them pause at the foot of the broad stairway; "Marguerite, Edith, did you get back alive," called Mrs. Kingman, and the two girls, interpreting an invitation to enter, in the inquiry, walked in to find Lord Parkhurst seated in friendly tête-à-téte with the entertaining matron.

The earl shook hands with an air of effusive amiability with the returning philanthropists, and Edith thought she detected the ghost of a twinkle in his eyes when he asked about the success of their mission, and whether Miss Clayton found her protege wearing a blue ribbon or lost to mundane concerns in the oblivion of malt potations. "Mamma has been telling tales, that is not fair!" cried Edith in mock anger, but she went on to give a serio-comic account of the morning, even to Marguerite's selfish pre-emption of the one chair.

"Marguerite is for selling her stocks and bonds and building tenement houses by the block," she continued, "but a flinty-hearted guardian, with a full amount of common sense, has to be consulted about all expenditures until she has attained the age required by a wise government for its voters;

and by that time it is to be hoped that she will have learned the value of a good balance at one's banker's sufficiently to prevent her making ducks and drakes of her fortune."

"And spending it for 'chips and whetstones', why don't you add," retorted Marguerite. "One phrase is just as sensible and as comprehensive as the other."

"No my dear it is not; I appeal to Lord Parkhurst if 'making ducks and drakes' is not an old Saxon expression which comes down from the market days in England, when to buy ducks and drakes was a bad investment because the market was liable to be overstocked ; 'chips and whetstones' is a modern American hybrid which has no origin beyond a possible small boy, so far as philologists have discovered."

The discusion was kept up until luncheon was announced.

"Mrs. Kingman has been good enough to ask me to stay for luncheon," said Lord Parkhurst. "We were afraid that the demands of charity would make you forget that there is such an institution as a mid-day meal."

"Marguerite might have forgotten it; she always had a genius for those spiritualized ways of existence," piped Edith, "but as for me, I confess to a genuine appetite three times a day, with candy and plenty of soforths between meals; and just now I really think I could do justice to a broiled chicken. Mamma dear, please say that you have ordered broiled chicken."

Marguerite, who could talk brilliantly at times,

had a way of lapsing into silence, not of inattention but of most flattering interest, subsided into the latter mood after one or two flashes of wit and repartee, and Edith, who knew her so thoroughly, guessed that she was not feeling quite well after her morning's work.

"Marguerite wants a cup of tea and some Angel's food," said Edith.

"Leave Marguerite to me; she is going to take some broiled chops and a glass of claret. I won't have any nonsense at my table from a girl who ought to weigh at least ten pounds more than she does," retorted Mrs. Kingman. Lord Parkhurst made a mental note of the fact that the girl in whom he was especially interested, seemed very much more at home here than she did at the splendid Clayton mansion, and that Mrs. Kingman was evidently more of a mother to her than was the charming matron who, by courtesy, enjoyed that honor.

Almost immediately after luncheon he made a move to go, expressing the hope, with an interrogative inflection, that he would see the three ladies that evening at Mrs. Van Demian's reception.

"Yes we intend to go," answered Marguerite, "if we can find a Chinese-English Dictionary in town. I want to be able to say a few words to the guest of the evening in his native language. I am mortally afraid however, that I shall lose all my new found knowledge when the time comes to use it, and that I shall say 'washee, washee', instead. Do you think if I did he would regard it as an international insult and require our government to send an envoy over to his government to apologize?"

Lord Parkhurst thought there was no great danger, and Marguerite continued: "Well, I don't see why we are all going there to meet that Chinaman, any way. Isn't it strange what weathercocks we make of our ideas! Now here is a man who has left a dozen wives at home and a private temple in which he worships all sorts of idols, come over here to be feted and made much of, simply because he is the son of his father, and the father is only above other men because his father was such a monster as to murder a whole town of unprotected women and children, in the interests of the Emperor, and get promoted. We claim to be a Christian nation, and here we are, every one of us, going to pay honor to the veriest Pagan in the country; if he were a learned Pagan, a heroic one, there might be some excuse, but this one is half-civilized, except in his capacity for Washington punch, he is said to be wholly so there. Now, why we are going to 'salaam' to him, and eat ices in his honor, and put on our prettiest gowns, is more than I can understand. If he were in a museum, and we paid ten cents to go in and see how a Chinaman of the upper class dresses and looks, and if he would wear his court costume and hang his other toggery up on pegs around him, or spread it out in glass cases, I could enjoy that, for I like curious things, and am reasonably fond of study, but to go to meet him socially, and smile and seem pleased and wonder what he thinks of us, and if he thinks in the gibberish he talks, I confess that is a puzzle."

Lord Parkhurst admitted that he had not analyzed the motives which actuated the civilities of the Occidental hostess to the benighted Oriental, but promised to study the question if she would allow him to call and compare notes the day after the reception.

"Marguerite always could advance more problems in five minutes than a philosopher could answer in a life time," interposed Edith.

"Last year we were really quite intellectual in our entertainments, and now we are having the reaction; the Chinaman comes in on the neap tide of our passion for novelties in visiting celebrities." Mrs. Kingman looked as if she wanted Edith to remember that Lord Parkhurst himself might come under the head of visiting novelities.

"All last winter we were screwed up to a most transcendental pitch," continued the girl. "Mrs. Van Demian gave a large reception to a poetess of the Unknowable; who appeared in a cotton velvet gown, trimmed with imitation jet, and bobbed up and down, and could only smile, and look supremly idiotic. I say poetess, because that is how she herself would pronounce it, but I should say a scribbler of rhymes who admired 'poetesses,' and 'writeresses', and 'studentesses' of her own particuliar cult. Then we paid our respects to a bishop from Australia with a fat little wife who kept tugging at her gloves all the evening, and was worsted in a battle with the Subjunctive Mode; next came a scientist, who couldn't speak English at all; then a Buddhist who lectured on ancient Buddhism, and spoke English like a cockney — each was made much of in our desire to show a republican appreciation of learning; this winter we are going in simply for social nonentities who can be agreeable and entertain us in return."

"Edith!" came warningly from her mother, who sometimes regretted that her own exuberance as a young lady had reappeared so strikingly in her daughter. "Never mind Mamma, I am not going to tell Lord Parkhurst that he is a social nonentity, and that we expect him to invite us all over to England in return for a cup of tea."

The earl protested that all Parkhurst was at their disposal at any time they would honor him with a visit, and that Miss Clayton might inspect the family portraits, and the accumulated curiosities without paying her ten cents.

And in a continued volley of banterings the young man took his departure.

XV.

AMONG the puzzles which American social life presented to the earl, was how the men could work all day and dance two thirds of the night. He broached the question at a little bachelor dinner which Carroll Kirwin gave in his honor on an evening when one of the largest receptions of the season was to take place; the lack of feminine society at dinner could thus be atoned for latter by the bevy of lovely maidens and fascinating matrons assembled in Mrs. Gillette's gorgeous new mansion.

"Kirwin is the last person in New York to answer that question," cried John Raymond. "He believes in short hours for making money, and long ones for enjoying it. He is not typical at all. Ask me, or any other down-trodden business man, and he would tell you that, in the first place, it is owing to our native vigor both of mind and body, preeminent over that of other nations." At this the company glanced from Lord Parkhurst's broad shoulders to Raymond's narrow ones, and laughed with keen appreciation of the irony. "And secondly, because we simply must," Raymond went on composedly. "Necessity knows no law, physiological or any other kind, and the man who doesn't hustle is going to get left. You, as a student of American life and language will forgive the term I am sure; 'hustle' is in the new Dictionaries, or it ought to be, although you probably have not observed it. Thirdly, I am really not going beyond the thirdly, although I could reach the teens; the Ten Commandments and the Municipal law secure one day of rest out of every seven, and a man can do a lot of recuperating in one day when he has no more."

"And why is Mr. Kirwin not typical" asked the earl after the question had been discussed under the heads presented by Raymond. "I thought he was one of the shining lights of the New York bar."

"Oh so he is," admitted Raymond, but he only gives to the law from nine in the morning until four in the afternoon, and not even the President of the road that retains him could make him stay in his office after those hours."

"You see I am trying to convince an ungrateful city that if business hours were cut down one third or even a half, that just as much business would be transacted in that time as is done now in a whole day, and I endeavor to act on my own theories," answered Kirwin. "We have a few men who do nothing at all, and a great majority who do too much, and I am an advocate of the golden mean."

Parkhurst would have liked to hear Carroll elucidate his ideas more fully, but as host he naturally shrank from making himself a subject of conversation. The Englishman was beginning to feel a genuine regard for the young Marylander, and was interested in him in many, ways not as a type, but as an individual. He seemed different from the generality of young men whom he met; these were, for the most part, either absorbed in business, taking even their pleasures in a restless, nervous way that seemed to be making large draughts on their vitality, or else they were very young men given over to amusements and idleness altogether, spending in a reckless extravagance the fortunes which doting fathers had slaved, or schemed, or cheated to amass. Here was a wealthy, scholarly, cultivated man, rising steadily in his profession, fulfilling all social obligations, indulging in none of the vices allowed by a lax code, going his way quietly, ignoring all the outcry of the professional reformer, and yet doing in his own fashion a monumental work. Edith had told him a great deal about the tenement house investments, and in her shrewd, humorous practical way, something of the theories underlying them. In some respects the lawyer was typical of a new generation of gentlemen in England, who accept their positions with a grave sense of the responsibility attached, and with a desire to fulfill their duties to their dependents and to society at large. These were not in sympathy with what a witty and caustic duchess characterized as the 'rowdy element of the peerage'. Whether the Earl of Parkhurst would have been capable of serious self sacrifice in support of his own convictions, opportunity had so far left undecided. He looked around with more curiosity than Kirwin's modest domicile, really merited, anxious to learn the taste of his host as manifested in his domestic surroundings. The drawing-room was furnished in the conventional drawing-room style, evidently fitted up by a professional decorator, whose taste whilst good, could manifestly give nothing of the personality of the owner. There were some very good paintings on the wall, and by the piano stood a large music rack, overloaded with music. He would have liked to examine the pile to see what style of music the American preferred; a collection of Beethoven's sonatas, on top, and 'Little Annie Rooney' he accepted as an index to versatility at least. In the dining room the walls were lined with family portraits, and the dinner was served on dainty china and sterling silver, much of it old fashioned and massive. A cut glass bowl of roses in the center afforded the only decoration. The viands were unexceptional, and the wines of rarest vintage. Kirwin did not entertain a great deal, but when he did, he believed in giving his friends the best at his disposal, without descending into Épicureanism. Two colored people, an old woman raised on the Maryland Plantation, and her husband, who had served Carroll's father as valet, comprised the staff of his servants. The old woman was not the equal of a French *chef* exactly, although in her day she had enjoyed a reputation in the culinary art second to none in the country, but cooking had progressed like every thing else American and modern, and she had remained stationary; still it required all the diplomacy of which Carroll was master to get Sherry's men into the kitchen when he wanted to give a dinner. Cooking that had been good enough for the Pickenses, and the Randolphs, and the Jenkinses, and old General Carroll Kirwin, was good enough for any of young Carroll's friends, she thought; and only when he convinced her that she was too aged for so much extra work was he successful.

Ordinarily, he hardly knew what was placed before him, especially if he were hungry, or engrossed in some study, but when guests had assembled around his board he was disposed to be critical. After the coffee the quartet adjourned to the library for their post-prandial cigars. "Here," thought the earl, "personal taste begins to manifest itself." The luxurious stamped leather chairs, the heavy carpet dull and rich, the engravings crowded thick wherever a bit of wall space permitted, the busts of Shakespeare and Dante and some classic statuary copied from the Greek, the low book cases filled, and overflowing on to the table and even the floor, were all very modern, and very sumptuous, and very individual.

"Ah, you have hit my pet weakness!" exclaimed Kirwin in reply to some complimentary remark of the Englishman's on the collection of books, proceeding to show some rare editions, a parchment manuscript, Greek vellums and an illumined Testament, with all the pleasure of a born collector. "We see finer things every day of course, in the museums and the public libraries, but the pride of possession, of knowing a thing is really one's own, appeals to a fellow's vanity I suppose."

"I see you do not despise fiction" said the earl pausing before a case given up entirely to novels, American, English, French, Spanish, German, and translations from the Russian and Norwegian.

"No indeed, and I imagine there are very few who really do. I could never understand the outcry against fiction. I admit that novels are not the roast beef of our intellectual life, but they certainly make a most palatable dessert. When I was a boy I used to get many a penance for stealing off with a story book under my arm. And now, in my maturity, I am willing to draw the line at fiction for children."

"Happy children," murmured Raymond.

"We find life in all its phases in a novel," continued Kirwin; "we can sit down for an evening's quiet in our libraries and enjoy all sorts and conditions of men, and women too; wits, bores, oddities; home life, social life, foreign life, life sad, grave, gay, life as it is, as we would like to have it, or as it never was on earth or Mars, can all be found in the pages of fiction. A bit of philosophy, here a condensed sermon, there an epigram, on one page, a crystallized poem on the next."

"In view of the power of a popular novelist and his tremendous responsibilities I am in favor of requiring a certificate and a license from all aspirants," interposed Raymond. Kirwin agreed that the idea was not bad. Lord Parkhurst asked if the certificate and the license would not be a curtailment of the right of every American to do as he pleased, and this being settled, Carroll went on: "A novel that is false in logic, false in teaching, false in perspective, false even in art is an excrescence on the body of literature, and should be weeded out of existence; but if it be a picture of the true in whatever field it invades it is worthy of a place. A bad picture is a blot in a gallery, and a bad novel is a greater blot in our libraries." Raymond declared that if the rule of the true were acted upon, novels would all vanish in a day, for no two people could agree upon all the points of logic and theology and perspective, to say nothing of the sciences, art and society, law and the moral code which find place in the novels of the day. The Earl said interrogatively: "Then you only ask of a novel to be true to life, to photograph the phase selected, and give a free lance in the choice of subject?"

"No; most emphatically I do not. There are certain scenes no respectable artist would depict on his canvas, so there are certain phases of life that have no place in books. Vice, for instance, is a deformity of nature, and a deformity, as a deformity can have no place in a novel of the true. As an illustration, as means to an end, a novelist may bring in crime, but as a gratification of a morbid curiosity, or as mere food for the imagination, never."

"But my dear fellow," replied Raymond, "crime does not always serve as a desirable illustration, not by a long way, in these days, if it ever did. The old Sunday school books, with their sinners coming to grief, and the suffering and virtuous hero mounting to victory, are in direct opposition to your canon of the true. Crime if it illustrates any thing, illustrates success, honor, happiness. The gnawings of a guilty conscience, philosophers and students of human nature, have decided to be very much overdrawn, for much conscience and great crime are incompatible terms."

Kirwin declared this to be merely a superficial aspect. Wilson thought that both crime and conscience depended on the point of view.

Lord Parkhurst admitted that he had no theory on the subject of fiction in its ethical bearings. "I never cared a great deal for novels, any way, at least since my Oxford days. I used to like them there as a relief from Greek verbs and Latin odes. I prefer life that is true in fact as well as true in perspective, so instead of a novel I take biography or history. In a novel you must accept whatever the writer chooses to give you; as Mr. Kirwin says, philosophy, sermons, or what not, are put before you, and I prefer to choose my own sermons and my own philosopher and to take both in my own time. It requires the intellectual agility of an American to read a good novel, and appreciate all its points."

"I am afraid the average American does not read a great deal of any thing excepting the newspapers and the magazines, and he gets a variety of subjects in both," said Raymond. "We haven't the time," put in Wilson, who had been rather silent all evening. He was given to conversation by spells, all wit and gaiety one evening, and all taciturnity the next; besides, he was subject to nervous headaches that were liable to come on at any time, and physical pain generally successfully concealed, made Kirwin forgive in him much that in another we would not have pardoned.

"That is the great trouble with us in every way," answered Kirwin, "we have no time; and therein lies the reason of my strike against nine hours at my office. A man that is engrossed in business all day cannot help but neglect his intellectual and spiritual life; and yet all philosophy, all religion emphasize the theory that a man's intellect is superior to his body. If we ever get a leisure class like you Britons we will show the world what a very gifted nation we really are."

"I am afraid we do not appreciate our privileges in that respect," answered the earl. "Englishmen are too athletic, too fond of sport, too much given up to the details of their estates and too lazy, with shame I confess it, to be very scholarly; excepting our men who are professional scientists and scholars; we expect them to leaven our general and particular ignorance." He was still examining the books, with a cursory but genuine interest, when he exclaimed with a flash of enthusiasm: "Ah, here is the man —Newman,— Newman was a great Englishman, as well as a great scholar. — I mean that his mind was an English mind, distinct from a French or a Roman mind, and that is why we English admire him so greatly as a man and a thinker, althought we do not accept his conclusions. His book 'The Idea of a University' did more for me than any one book I ever knew. He gives one an intellectual hold of things; shows the arts and sciences in their true relation to one another; he saved me from being even more superficial than I am. No author I ever came upon, presents so clearly as Newman the reason for knowing a thing thoroughly well; he elucidates the well worn text, 'A little learning is a dangerous thing'. I had always cherished a vague notion that it refers to quantity; Newman taught me that it is quality that is meant. The power to see both sides of a question, to see it in its relation to other questions, to seize the weak points of an argument as well as the strong ones, is a great power, and this Newman possessed. If his one lecture on 'Accuracy of Thought' could be studied and absorbed by our students it would spare the world a lot of senseless argument."

"What book is that? I must get it at once," said Raymond. "One of the troubles of my life is the intellectual short sightedness of other people. Brown sees one side of a square and pronounces the whole square green; Jones sees another side and calls it red; Robison sees still another side and calls it yellow; Johnson comes along and from his superior point of view, or breadth of vision proves it to be parti-colored, with green, red and yellow sides and a side of no particular color."

"Isn't that a free translation of the story of the shield," said Kirwin quizzically.

"No, it is a kindred illustration."

"To return to Newman, all his greatness of mind and accuracy of thought did not prevent his being a bigot," chimed in Wilson with more animation than he had hitherto shown.

"All enthusiasts are more or less bigots" answered Raymond. "And yet because a man is an enthusiast, a bigot if you like, it does not follow that he has not seen both sides of the question. His decision may be the result of a most critical act of judgment; he may have weighed both sides, examined the pros and cons, pondered over the possible results and deliberately embraced one side. Of course after committing himself to a defined line of action or thought, it is no longer possible to keep

ORCHIDS.

up with both sides. He is then busy with his
All the great deeds of the world, all the
revolutions in thought, have been achieved by
of iron determinations who had cast their ene[rgies]
on a particular side, resolved on attaining a ce[rtain]
end, and letting no obstacles stand in the way.
"Wilson said that might be true of great men [and]
great deeds, but that in ordinary life preju[dices]
were more common than convictions; that accid[en]-
not choice determined a man's actions and
allegiance.

"The trouble with you Wilson, is that you [are]
not enough of a bigot on any question. You [are]
too coldly critical without ever formulatin[g a]
judgment," replied Kirwin. "Even you agnostic[ism]
is a very negative sort of agnosticism."

"My bigotry lies in not being a bigot," reto[rted]
Wilson. My vocation in life deals with matt[ers]
financial not intellectual. The force of my will m[ust]
of necessity be directed to material ends."

"Oh, no one ever doubted your will powe[r,"]
interrupted Raymond.

"I have had no time to form my judgment[s,"]
continued Wilson. I am merely a looker-on [in]
the intellectual forum, and as a looker-on, I ha[ve]
seen certain phases of thought rise, flourish th[eir]
brief day and disappear; each may, or may n[ot]
have left its fruits behind to enrich another epoc[h.]
As students of history we all know the phases [of]
religious belief which the world has gone throug[h]
and it was on the religious phase that Newm[an]
left his mark."

"We can admire Newman without admirin[g]

Newman's beliefs," said the earl quickly, who was an ardent supporter of the Establishment.

Wilson continued: "Superstitions, idolatries, the childish beliefs of a childish age, flourish and then pass away. Even in Christianity there is nothing stable but the name.

"New beliefs, new doctrines, new rites, new codes of right and wrong have all come up since the beginning of the Christian era. We are all given to taking too narrow a view, and in our narrowness we lack toleration. Now, in America not to hold some vestige of the Christian belief is to mark one as an oddity; in Asia and Africa not to be a Mohammedan or a Buddhist or a worshiper of idols would mark one as equally strange. We do not think as our forefathers thought, and our successors in this vale of tears, as some poet calls it, will doubtless look upon us as childish and crude."

"But you lose sight of the fact Wilson, that the true is somewhere—must be; and as a member of the human family, a student of human affairs, it rests with you to distinguish the true from the false," said Kirwin.

"That is what no man can do, because the false and the true are inextricably mixed. There is always some truth in every system which holds men's minds. You believe it exists in Christianity alone; I believe it is to be found in every creed, and in none."

"We are getting into rather deep waters," answered Kirwin, "but what I want to say is this; we judge a tree by its fruit, and I ask that the same rule be applied to Christianity: it teaches men to live nobly, to die bravely; all the ideals of mankind, even of the Pagans, have ever been founded on Christian standards. Lastly, the line of progression, of nations as well as of individuals, has ever been the line of progression of Christianity. There is not a spot in all the globe desirable as a place of residence, that has not been made so by Christianity. Our laws, our customs, our habits of thought are the result of Christianity. There is no argument possible on the question, because the facts bear witness."

Wilson was looking away into space, seeing his Pagan heroes, and a line of kings and reformers and diplomats who were Christians but not heroes, and a fire of indignant protest was in his eyes. No one had ever brought to his comprehension the justice of reversing the operation; of seeing the kings and statesmen who were Pagans but not heroes, and the line of kings and scholars who were both heroes and Christians.

"Oh, Christianity has done its work," he answered, "sometimes well, sometimes ill, but a real work I grant. It has benefited the race, because all selfishness benefits either the race or the individual; and Christianity in its present stage, is but organized selfishness, a purely business arrangement; only unlike ordinary business the reward, or the gain is always sure. The only difference between the militant Christian and the man who does a day's work for a day's pay, is that the Christian expects the reward to be so very far out of all proportion to the work. The compound interest for waiting I suppose."

"I cannot let that pass," said Kirwin. "The reward is the lowest motive of a Christian. True Christianity means the complete negation of self. The love of God, the desire to do His will, to follow His example, form the pole star of a Christian's life."

"Leaving aside theory," answered Wilson, Christianity as we see it, is merely a mass of conventionalities, of forms, of cut and dried thought. In the matter of sins, for instance, some are treated as 'unpardonable, although a God is theoretically supposed to pardon every thing, and a man draws the lines very closely around certain crimes he commits himself, although they may be more offensive to the Supreme Being, according to his own standards, than others he condemns pitilessly. A fellow overreaches another in a business transaction and he is merely a shrewd financier : a poor wretch takes an overcoat to protect himself from freezing to death and he is branded as a thief. The Ten Commandments are supposed, in our time, to have been given to women, not to men. The world is a mad struggle at best, for all but the very few. A rushing, eager, selfish mass appear on the scene, then the little drama is over, and another set take the vacant places."

"Wilson's theories are abominable, but his practices are all right," said Kirwin with good natured toleration ; "especially if he is not feeling well, or has been out too late the night before, or something of the sort, but at heart he is one of the best fellows going."

Wilson smiled, and admitted that Kirwin generally got the better of him in one way or another, in an argument.

"But we have been wasting time and talk," he continued.

"You are all Christians because you inherited the Christian belief; I am not, because I was left without even the traditional penny when it comes to a faith of any kind. If I were to judge Christianity by some Christians I know," he looked at Kirwin at this, "I should consider it divine, judged by the many it seems simply a huge farce. The Brotherhood of Man for instance — there is no situation in comedy to equal it; the majority of the 'brothers' starving in hovels, the few feasting in Richardson mansions."

"Surely Mr. Wilson," exclaimed the earl, who thought that he was being initiated into American ways with a completeness beyond his most sanguine hopes, "surely you are not a communist or a socialist."

"Oh no; logically I do not have to be. — I am not a Christian."

"Come Wilson, that is hardly fair to spring a question of socialism on top of Christianity; such deep problems after so good a dinner are bad for digestion," put in Raymond.

"It is a part of our general selfishness to believe in private ownership as soon as we have any thing to own," concluded Wilson.

"Life is a struggle, and the world, the prize for which we contend, and take our chances on, in the grand lottery of existence."

"Don't mind him," cried Kirwin. "Wilson works for honest dollars, and regularly draws dividends on his stocks or demands the reason why, just like the rest of us."

"Oh, I don't pretend to be better than my neighbors," said Wilson.

"And he is too sensible to be either a socialist or a communist," replied Kirwin. "The carriage is waiting to take us away to Mrs. Gillett's gilded salons. That is merely an exigency of speech; they are not gilded at all, but most artistically subdued."

"I second the motion to adjourn our symposium," said Raymond. "It was clever but exhausting. I feel as if I had been listening to essays from the North American Review and the Forum."

XVI.

FOR Henry Wilson the drive to Mrs. Gillette's was something in the nature of a triumphal procession. It was the first time that autocratic matron had condescended to recognize his existence, although she had entertained constantly for seasons immemorial. The young man had been duly presented to her the first winter after his return from Heidelberg, but on their next meeting, when he was prepared to make his most deferential obeisance, she calmly looked over his shoulder. He was a proud man and the cut had rankled deeply.

Those who think that only women scheme and strive and struggle perpetually up the social ladder, in herculean efforts to know other women who have, by accident or intention, failed to know them, may not receive with unqualified belief the assertion that Henry Wilson had registered a vow to meet Mrs. Gillette on her own grounds. He had given no sign of his mortification during the several years his vow remained unfulfilled, but he waited; and all things come to him who waits, was conviction of his, as far as he had any convictions.

But Mrs. Gillette's omission of the young man on her invitation lists had not been by accident. Soon after that unfortunate meeting at which an inconsiderate acquaintance had introduced the young man to her, she gave, what a slangy maiden called a 'ram-jam reception', for all the world. A niece, who assisted her in sending out the invitations, suggested Henry Wilson as a young man who ought to be invited.

"No, my dear, I don't think he ought," said the matron energetically. "Why should he be? Nobody knows any thing about him, he has no family, he is not distinguished, and he is as poor as a church mouse, or as a mouse would be if we permitted mice in our churches. I think this fashion of indiscriminate invitations to young men is most deplorable if not positively wicked. We would not have so many unhappy marriages if hostesses were more careful in this regard."

"We might not have so many marriages of any kind," the niece suggested.

A year later Mrs. Kingman happened to mention Wilson's name in connection with a cotillon, to Mrs. Gillette.

"Now Clara Kingman, I did think you were a woman of better sense; Henry Wilson is far too good looking, and too utterly impossible to have around among our girls; Some of them are such simpletons anyway when it comes to getting married."

"No body was thinking about marriage," retorted Mrs. Kingman.

"Oh no! nobody ever does, until the mischief is done, and it is too late to think. I believe in doing as I would be done by; I should not thank a woman to invite fascinating no-bodies to meet my daughters, if I had any, and I am not going to throw temptation in the way of other people's daughters."

No one knew just what made her change her course; it might have been the alarming disproportion of dancing maidens to dancing men, and it might have been the conviction that the average girl, excepting the debutantes who are figuratively tied to their mother's apron strings, is quite capable of taking care of herself.

Mrs. Kingman had once suggested that the young men of the City be divided into two classes, the Socially Eligible, and the Matrimonially Eligible, and that the former class be required to sign a pledge at the beginning of each season, that they would not abuse their privileges, if invited to parties and receptions, by making love seriously to the young ladies with whom it would be their privilege to dance or to talk.

The fact that Wilson had been seen of late at all the great houses in town, may have had something to do with the clemency of Mrs. Gilette, although he had not signed Mrs. Kingman's suggested pledge, when she was sending out her invitations to the reception which she had determined to make a Social Event.

Just how this was to be done was a problem which had occupied her waking thoughts and even her dreams for months before the given date.

The ordinary affairs of the social whirl had palled on Mrs. Gillette, had palled especially on her taste as a hostess. The ambition, which ten years before was satisfied if she could give savory viands in rooms modestly decorated with palms and ferns rented from the florist, relieved by a few cut flowers banked on the mantlepiece, and get the socially desirable people to enjoy them, was now eagerly clamoring for other and strange fields to conquer. Each mounted round in the fairy ladder of entertainment only revealed to her the possibility of other rounds, and what had seemed sufficient once was the veriest insipidity now. Yet she was considered to have entertained lavishly during the five years she had lived in her new house, the pile which had risen as a monument to American ability, expanded and developed by American opportunity, and pushed forward by American shrewdness, in ways which might not have born a strictly Scriptural interpretation. She had exhausted the gamut of Pink Teas, Yellow Teas, Japanese dinners, Cotillons with Parisian favors, Receptions with professional talent to amuse the guests; she had seen, more than once, her best efforts eclipsed by some one else in the same line; her dinner to a baronet had been followed by a rival's dinner to a peer; her lion from China forgotten for a bigger lion from Africa; her reception to a returning explorer outdone by a reception for an outgoing ambassador. The ambition which may be typified by dinners and diamonds, is quite as insatiable as the ambition of battle fields and diplomacy; Mrs. Gillette was proud of her reputation, and her supreme desire was to evolve an entertainment from her inner consciousness, or the inner consciousness of somebody else whom her money could command, that would be different and superior to any thing New York had ever seen. She studied the chronicles of Court Balls given at the Tuileries and at Versailles; fetes held at English country houses; entertainments in Washington and New York to visiting foreigners, as a practical illustration of American simplicity;

happy conceits in teas and favors, ready to cribbage any bright idea found, and disguise it with details of her own; the poetic possibilities in a flower ball; the novelty of a tete poudre fete; the unlimited scope of a ball masque—but could hit upon nothing at once new and delightful. "Women are getting so clever nowadays, she sighed; "they have tried every thing, every thing."

She stepped into her florist's one day to substitute an order for chrysanthemums instead of roses, as a compliment to the Japanese Minister who had come over from Washington, and was to be her guest at dinner. The proprietor himself, with the subtle flattery practiced so successfully by those who make their living by the humors, rather than the necessities of society, begged she would do him the honor to inspect some rare orchids just obtained at great cost and trouble. The moment her eyes lighted on the mysterious, gorgeous, wonderful flowers, their costly beauty appealing to the love of the unattainable implanted in the feminine breast since Eve, the idea, which had been in mental solution so long, was suddenly precipitated. "I have it, I have it," she thought exultantly. "I must give an Orchid Reception." She plied the deferential florist, with the lackey soul and the Yankee eye to the main chance, with questions about orchids in every conceivable form. The difficulty of obtaining them in large quantities was just what she wanted, provided the difficulty could be overcome. She waited until the season was at its zenith, so as, the more effectively, to focus the attention of Society on its crowning, most glorious event. And then she began her preparations. With orchids as the key note to the decorations, there was absolutely no limit to the daring effects of startling gorgeousness she might attempt. Opalescent crepes, Persian rugs rifled from Eastern shrines, cloth of gold hangings, a miniature Hindoo temple, marble fountains supported by Pagan gods, were all included. The house was thrown open literally, from top to bottom to the fortunate guests; a flood of light from electric globules, cunningly arranged by an artist in color effects, although he came from the Electric Light Company and modestly called himself an electrician, linked the Occident of material prosperity and practical comfort with the Orient of limitless splendor. So spacious was the interior, so deftly were the vistas of apartments arranged, so charmingly placed were the little retreats intended for a half hour's delicious rest, or a lovers' tete-a-tete, so alluring were the broad stairways, transformed into flowery ascents, so enchanting was the effect of the whole, that one priviledged to enter from the harsh winds and the cold of the streets, with their distinct modernity, their leveling democracy, had at once the impression of having been instantaneously transported into Fairy Land. The caterers had been given carte blanche, wines had been specially imported, servants in full livery stood elbow to elbow around the horse-shoe table. Two perfectly trained orchestras discoursed the sweetest of music. The guests had done the part expected of them, and appeared in charming toilets. All these details were given with the greatest elaboration in the daily papers of the city. A score of reporters, admitted on the presentation of a card bearing certain cabalistic signs, treated the entertainment with the dignity and respect belonging to a great national event. Glowing adjectives, flattery laid on with a trowel, a riotous profusion in description, attractive headlines, comparisons with every thing on the earth or under the sun, thickly dotted the columns. Paragraphs were sent out by the associated press. — In a word, Mrs. Gillette had been supremely successful.

Carroll Kirwin and his friends were among the late arrivals, and the rooms would have seemed crowded had they not been so spacious. The moving figures of charming women exquisitely gowned, and men, some distinguished and all passable looking, in sober black, with a background startling in its beauty, appeared a most enchanting picture to the quartet, as they stood a moment, lost in genuine admiration. Mrs. Gillette was simply radiant, and with the light of a gratified ambition beaming from her eyes; even her husband had caught a reflex of her spirit, and showed himself the genial, companionable fellow he might have been, had the duty of amassing a fortune left him any time during the period of character formation. The new comers advanced in a small phalanx to salute their hostess. And what psychologist could have analyzed the subtle gradations in her welcome ? The well-bred greeting to Wilson, the easy friendliness to Carroll, the familiar bon camradeship with Raymond, the self-respecting deference to the peer ! Or tell how she invited leniency of judgment with the tongue, for the crudeness that must be manifest to one used to the hereditary perfection of London entertainments, and daringly challenged comparison with her eyes!

As they moved away Wilson's face did not share the smile of good humor and satisfaction of his companions.

"You see here the apotheosis of American ambition," he said to the earl, not without a trace of bitterness. "Money speaks at every turn, money unlimited practically, and that is what every body must have over here if he wishes to be any body, or meet with any consideration. A fellow who lacks the ability to make a fortune had better hang himself in the start, and save himself a lot of useless bother of living. There is a tradition that a circle exists where refinement and culture, and all that sort of thing, are the ends, but no one ever saw it. An amusing comedy in real life swept over our country a few years ago, and people took sides as to whether the sun-flower or the golden-rod was our national flower — flowers that a milkmaid may have; just as if everybody does not know as well as Mrs. Gillette, that the orchid is our national emblem; it symbolizes our highest ambition."

Lord Parkhurst was saved the trouble of a serious reply, by Mrs. Kingman, who, happening along at the moment, exclaimed that four men together was nothing short of a crying shame. It was only the work of another minute for each of the four to be paired with a not unwilling maiden. Edith Kingman herself took John Raymond in hand.

Henry Wilson was soon chatting agreeably with a little blonde fairy who would some day be the sole inheritor of the paternal millions. Every body in the house was related to millions excepting himself, he thought bitterly, but his conventional smile showed nothing of this spirit. He could not have told what tantalizing influence called up the image of a tall, dark eyed beauty in a simple white muslin frock, with a mass of yellow flowers at her belt, or why, above the strains of the orchestra he should hear a clear, sweet voice caroling tender old ballads.

There was nothing in the little blonde who chirped away as pleasantly as a sparrow, to make him picture that other girl moving in regal grace through the splendid vistas, he felt she would adorn so much more fittingly than some who were there. Why did fortune play such cruel jests? why was he not rich, rich? With money, plenty of money, he could be radiantly, blissfully happy with — but what a fool he was, he was not rich and the speediest road to a fortune was to marry one. It was done every day by less attractive men than he; the life of a poor devil with his way to win in the world, had no place for sentimental dreamings. But if he were only rich, even moderately well off. — He pitied himself, for the lack of money which cramped and hampered his genius; he did not define in just what form the genius existed, and which shut away from him the bliss which comes to more fortunate men. In his thorough selfishness he forgot to pity — The Girl.

During the course of the evening Carroll Kirwin found himself with Marguerite Clayton.

"This is certainly a beautiful scene," he said, "a scene to be remembered; Mrs. Gillette has placed us all under obligations for an artistic treat, as well as for a most charming evening. But don't you think, Miss Clayton, that so much enchanting magnificence has a tendency to make us lose our sense of the relative values in social intercourse? to make us, in a word, accept the case for the jewel? After all, the real pleasure of this evening is supposed to be the enjoyment of the society of our friends under agreeable conditions. With so much to tempt us, we might be misled into thinking it only an occasion for feasting and drinking, and gratifying our delight in the beautiful. Yet to yield to this temptation, and to acknowledge one's fall, would be to offer an indignity to our charming hostess and her guests."

"Marguerite laughed a little, and said that she did not think Mrs. Gillette would question the motives of her guests very closely, so that they enjoyed themselves, and did not make a scene by imbibing too freely of the wines so lavishly provided.

Carroll reverted to his original theme.

"But don't you think that our ancestors enjoyed themselves quite as much as we are doing, although they certainly never dreamed of such a scene as this? I remember my grandmother telling me, when I was a litte fellow, about the inaugural festivities for General Washington, but I am sure they would have appeared very tame compared with this. I am certainly very far from quarreling with those who are able and generous enough to give us such an artistic feast as we have here, but we are in danger of learning to estimate the success of our entertainments by what they cost; then some of our most charming hostesses will cease to entertain at all, and that would be a serious loss to society at large. Our grandmothers in their sprigged muslins, or their stiff brocades, were conscious of no lack to their pleasure as they danced the minuet on floors waxed with candles, or sat down to a banquet of three courses. And we too could enjoy ourselves without — well, say a background of orchids. Here in New York we are in danger of losing both the understanding and the spirit of a cultivated simplicity."

"What is that we are losing?" cried Edith coming up at that moment on the arm of Lord Parkhurst.

"Nothing that the presence of Miss Kingman could not atone for," answered Kirwin with a mock obeisance.

" Now Carroll, I didn't think you would say any thing so perfectly absurd as that, and to me too, a mere cousin."

And then another change was effected, and the Earl was well pleased to be again with Marguerite.

XVII.

LORD PARKHURST'S business in Mexico was apparently not very pressing, for he announced that it had been settled satisfactorily by mail. The afternoon following Mrs. Gillette's reception he called on Mr. Dalton.

He came to the point at once, and asked the consent of that gentleman as Miss Clayton's guardian, to pay his addresses to his ward.

Mr. Dalton was not a little surprised. "Why my dear fellow," he said "I manage her property and take the greatest interest in the world, in her happiness and welfare, but in a question of her marriage I do not feel at liberty to interfere in any way; it is a matter which concerns herself alone, and even her own father, would have little to say beyond a warning or approval, if she decides in your favor. Of course, I know over in your country the parents and guardians cut a big figure in this matter, but in America the young people themselves generally attend to the business. If Marguerite likes you, I shall have no objections; and you will have to find that out, young man, for yourself. She does not come into her property until she is twenty one, but there is nothing to prevent her getting married to-morrow if she chooses to do so. And I wish you joy, I wish you joy. — And good luck to you," the old gentleman continued warmly, with genuine liking for the young man, so respectful and deferential to himself, and so manly in every way. He had the hereditary dislike of his native Island to an Englishman, and the patriotism of an American citizen to oppose to all class distinctions; but in Lord Parkhurst he thought he saw an unusually fine Englishman, as well as an exceptionably sensible peer.

"If Marguerite likes you, all right; I think she might have found a husband among the clever men of our own, but if they are not spry enough to keep Englishmen from poaching on their preserves it is their own lookout, not mine."

Lord Parkhurst went directly from Mr. Dalton to Marguerite. It was a charming, clear cold day despite the calendar, which marked the last of January, and logically called for snow and a falling thermometer. He strode buoyantly along the Avenue, the exhilarating atmosphere in keeping with the exhilaration of his hopes. He was apparently not apprehensive of his answer, and he had no reason to be. Although she had not intended it, did not know, would have suffered agonies of shame had she found it out, Marguerite had shown, by the glad light in her eyes, if in no other way, her liking for the young earl. Maiden reserve, and American pride had kept the liking from crystallizing into love, but the potentiality of love was in her heart, and a word was all that was needed to effect the transformation.

It was the hour for five o'clock tea when Lord Parkhurst reached the Clayton abode, but there was no one in the drawing-room, and the footman did not know whether Miss Clayton was at home or not. To any one else she would probably have been out, but Watkins knew the earl, and had already guessed rather shrewdly at his business in New York, so he said diplomatically that he would see. Watkins also knew the earl's preference for the library to the drawing-room, and so showed him into that delightful apartment to await Miss Clayton's appearance.

The interview was not very long. The shades of evening were approaching when the suitor came, and the darkness of night had not yet fallen when he went away. But it was an hour measured by the pendulum of happy heart-beats, and time lost its normal value.

Marguerite had entered the room bringing all the charm of a pure, sweet, joyous girlhood. The subtle depths of womanhood were limned in her soul when her lover left her with his kiss of betrothal on her lips.

For every pair of lovers, it is said, the world is created anew, and to Marguerite, not only the world, but every phase of life had been revivified and restored to some beautiful, enchanted, glorious planet.

It was decided to defer the wedding until after Marguerite's majority when she would come into control of her property. It was Marguerite herself who suggested this, for the earl had been perfectly honest with her in regard to his debts and financial embarrassments, and she understood without the telling, that her entrance into the English nobility would be attended with more dignity after her money had put the ancestral home in readiness for her reception. The earl had acquiesced, frankly admitting that to wait would perhaps be best; but he accompanied the admission with such a wealth of endearing protest that the necessity of waiting existed, and that he would be cheated out of a year's bliss which under happier circumstances would be his, that Marguerite's loving heart was more than satisfied. In view of its long term, the engagement was not to be announced publicly. Of course it was told in semi-confidence to Edith and her mother, Mrs. Clayton, Mr. Dalton, and a few others. Edith confided it to her cousin Mrs. Farr, and she, like a dutiful wife, repeated it to her husband, after enjoining an iron-bound secrecy which he straightway forgot, on seeing the earl, and congratulated him right heartily. When taken to task by his spouse, Farr argued with masculine obtuseness that if the engagement were really a secret Marguerite would have kept it to herself.

"Little you know about it," retorted his wife. "The more important it is, the more she would be bound to tell it to somebody."

Marguerite wrote a glowing rhapsody to Madame Florac, telling her that the noblest, best of men was to be her husband and that she was very, very happy.

However, in spite of all the caution observed, the Sunday Comet announced that it was currently reported that a visiting peer had succeeded in winning a beautiful American heiress, recently returned from a prolonged sojourn abroad. The Comet was a big newspaper, with a big circulation which it strove to increase by every means known and unknown to legitimate journalism. — A paper of nondescript character, it was just on the borderland between the solid, respectable dailies, and the vulgar sensational sheets, sometimes veering in one direction, sometimes in another. This same paper had previously dilated quite freely on the attentions of an impecunious peer to a wealthy and charming young lady, expressing the greatest concern for the latter's happiness, and ending with the hope that the peer would have to return to his ancestral halls alone. Although no names were given, they might as well have been blazoned forth in capitals so far as instant recognition was concerned, for Parkhurst happened to be the only nobleman in New York. Another paper, not usually received in good society, but which had come to Marguerite through the post, with a vivid blue pencil mark on its margin, indulged in a little biography of her fiance, with an account of his grandfather, the Birmingham manufacturer, and his marriage to the passé daughter of a bankrupt peer, with a history of the revival of the title now borne by the third Earl of Parkhurst. Marguerite read it with a growing sense of the impertinence of the press, and a shiver of loving admiration for her noble, handsome lover, but missing the point of its sting altogether — the attempt to belittle the title and to show that the patrician blue blood was most freely diluted with the plebeian red. Tears of indignation filled her eyes when the article went on to comment upon the reported engagement of the peer to the young heiress, and his business discernment in selecting a girl with no parents to interfere with his control of the fortune of which he had come to America in pursuit.

"Heiress, heiress, have they no other word to describe a girl who is not a beggar!" she cried indignantly.

But not the shadow of a doubt disturbed her trust in the earl. She knew, of course, that in England marriages were sometimes made for family or pecuniary reasons, but Lord Parkhurst had told her that he loved her, that she had stolen his heart during that enchanted week at Flaubert, that she had been the idol of his fondest dreaming ever since, and she believed him with the unshaken trust of a heart that had never been deceived. Why should he have selected her when there were so many others, if it were not for the one reason, — he loved her and did not love another? And the insinuation that she might have loved less, or perchance not loved at all, had a title not dazzled her eyes, seemed to her innocent soul little short of sacrilege. Although reared in France where marriage is more a matter of business than of sentiment, to be arranged by the worldly-wise heads of the respective families, she had really lived in an atmosphere where matrimony, either as a subject of conversation, or as food for girlish imagination, had very little place; the girls were sent to the convent to be fitted for their future sphere as wives and mothers, but not to plan in advance their lives as such. It would have been considered bad form, if not positively indelicate for a young girl to express a preference for a particular type of manhood, or to have owned to any theories about managing a husband and the rights and prerogatives of a wife. Of course the maidens expected to be married: an American would express it as getting married, and the unthinking auditor might not recognize the difference, although the difference is vital with the force of a national differentiation. To get married, would imply a certain active co-operation on the part of the girl; to be married placed the matter wholly in the hands of the parents and guardians.

Marguerite without being French, had nevertheless imbibed necessarily much of the French character. In her freedom from control after her return to America, joined to the exaggerated reports, which floated to her ears, of the emancipation and advanced ideas of American girls, she began to weave her own little dreams, and to build castles dimly outlined in a roseate haze. She ventured timidly at first on the subject of love, the veriest shadow of a dream, then something a little more definite; as a child, who in learning to swim, puts first one foot into the water and then the other, afraid yet fascinated; then both dimpled feet go in, then one step, then another, so advancing farther and farther, until a wave comes along with unexpected force, and the safe footing is lost. Once, before Lord Parkhurst made his appearance on the horizon of her New York existence, Edith had taken Marguerite to a meeting of a club composed of young maids and youthful matrons, and the subject of discussion was love. It made her cheeks burn to hear girls no older than herself, give their views: — one read passages and scenes from certain famous novels dealing with the tender passion; it was discussed from the point of view of temperament, congeniality, its phases before and after marriage; it was analyzed, dissected, postulated. Platonic friendship versus Love, also came in for another prolonged argument. Marguerite could almost imagine herself in a laboratory, or a museum, where some strange, new force in nature was being analyzed and classified. After Lord Parkhurst had transformed the world for her she indulged in speculations, on her own account, wove beautiful ideals into the warp and woof of a maiden's fancies, but she would have shrunk, as from a profanation of something holy, from unfolding her heart to any living creature. Not even to Edith did she tell all these musings and vague fancies.

She seemed to understand as she had never understood before, the Divine Beneficence in the plan of Creation. All life seemed beautiful because her own life was happy. How good God is, what a tender father to his children! ran her thoughts. And how unworthy she had been of so much happiness; ah! but she would try to be better in the future; she would live a life superior to the ignoble motives and fretting, harrowing cares around her; she would be so grateful to the good God, and show by her life that she was worthy of the blessings given her by being true to the duties they imposed. And her money — she was glad that she was rich; — she would make a source of benediction to every creature who came within her reach; the poor, the sorrowful, the sinful even, should share in the wealth which God, in His goodness, had entrusted to her keeping.

It was not hers, absolutely, but only as a trust. —

She was God's almoner for the suffering and the poor. And who could be so blind as to say that God had willed the unhappiness of the world; there was wretchedness, yes, but the wretchedness did not come from God; He willed that all His children should be happy; it was only by sin, by the fall of our First Parents, and by the personal falls of succeeding generations, that sin and unhappiness had come into the world. God was good, so good; He had created human hearts with that strongest, most ineffaceable law of love; and love was beautiful, noble, divine, because God in His wisdom had made it so. The deep, delicious undertone ever sounding in her heart, in her dreams, in her waking hours, sounding above the most trivial act of daily life, sounding when listening to music or looking at any thing beautiful and inspiring — was the strange new melody of love. Her heart had not been frittered away in unworthy flirtations, nor the freshness of its emotions wasted on passing attachments. It was the precious treasure of a girl's first love she had yielded up so gladly, so generously in the moment of betrothal. And Lord Parkhurst, with all his worldly wisdom, his experience, not always what he would have cared to make known, was stirred in every fibre when he realized instinctively all that he had won. With a rush of tenderness he had cried: "I am not worthy of you Marguerite, but I shall devote my life to making you happy."

Under the spell of her new happiness, she said to Edith: "You know I used to be puzzled over the inequalities among people; why some are rich, others poor; some high, others obscure, at the hard lot in life of some, and all that, but now I understand things that were a mystery before. There is not so much difference among people after all, I mean those in normal circumstances, not the degraded and the vicious, the squalid and the crushed, but ordinary people. The great centre of happiness, is the home, the talisman of a happy, rounded life is love, and these blessings, ordinarily, may come to all. Wealth and station are merely the accidents, not the essentials of a happy life. Love, home, the air and the sunshine, the stars at night, the joy of living,—belong to the poor as much as to the rich. These things know no monopoly. I sometimes think that it is we who are rich who ought to be envious of the poor. I do not mean the very poor, but the people in moderate circumstances, the people whom your Mr. Raymond calls the salt of the country." Edith was not sure, but she thought that she would try to bear the load of being rich with becoming resignation. She told Marguerite that if the burden of wealth became too great she would have no difficulty in ridding herself of it, by selling her possessions and dividing the proceeds among the denizens of the Eastside, who might, for the sake of a change, consent to being rich. There was also a certain club she had read about, with decided anarchist tendencies, where one might be relieved of his troublesome millions.

"Oh, I don't want to be poor, Edith, but I should like to have the money without having the responsibility of it. You are wrong, for once; I cannot be relieved even if I wished, by giving my inheritance away. It has come to me and I am responsible. Besides, I am not a free agent any more." Edith understood that this last was an allusion to the unfilled coffers of the House of Parkhurst.

But the sense of her responsibilities could not ruffle the girl's enchantment. "I never knew Marguerite Clayton was so beautiful," was the refrain of more than one of her friends. Happiness is the best cosmetic, and in these early days of her engagement her eyes shone with a new light, her cheeks were suffused from the quickened pulses, her voice was musical with laughter, her step as light as Titania's tread on a bank of roses. When the weather became fine and the first buds of a belated spring put forth their petals, Lord Parkhurst and Marguerite could be seen sauntering up the Fifth Avenue, or on new and unexplored thoroughfares; in the afternoons they went driving, under proper espionage, in the Park; they lunched together almost daily, either at Mrs. Kingman's or at Marguerite's home, or sometimes with a party at Delmonico's. They appeared together in public with well-bred indifference to each other's proximity, and exchanged vows in the fleeting moments they chanced to be alone. It was the springtime of a girl's life, — a spring with naught to mar its rare perfection.

XVIII.

ALTHOUGH the round of pleasures crowded into the last weeks of the season, left little time for the more serious affairs which Marguerite had promised her conscience to attend to, she did not quite forget them. There was always an uneasy feeling as of something undone, which could only be soothed into a comfortable state of mind by a mental renewal of the promise to see to them very soon.

"It is so easy to plan, so hard to fulfill," she confessed to Edith in a mood of penitence, with the spirit of good resolutions strong within her, on their way up town from a Saturday Matinee.

"'We love the good and do the evil,' as Madame Duval, your particular aversion used to say, and you are bound to admit, in spite of your prejudices, that she was very nearly right," answered Edith.

"It takes a great deal of time, this being engaged," concluded the younger girl with a sagacious intonation that Edith always found amusing.

As a prelude to the series of good works she proposed to herself for Lent, Marguerite went the next day to see her protege, Martha Grigsby, in the Old Women's Home.

She was let in by the cheery faced portress, who had carried into the convent some of the superabundant good nature and sunniness of soul which had characterized her in the world, and after a word, flitted up the broad stairway to the third floor, where Martha had her cozy little room.

Marguerite preferred this to playing the Lady Bountiful in the parlor, usually crowded on Sundays with visitors to the inmates, their friends of better days. They all claimed better days; these were as much a part of their lives as the obvious fact that they had been born into the world. The poor creatures would have lost their self respect immediately had it not been for these mythical better days which wrapped them like a mantle from all the humiliating aspects of a home, partially charitable. Old Martha, who had reformed after a serious illness and a wild attempt to get liquor, was now living out her life in uneventful contentment, in the most homelike home she had enjoyed for many a long day. She claimed, and was granted a sort of distinction which came from having her own income and paying for herself. As she looked upon her income as her right, and considered Marguerite as merely having returned what rightfully belonged to her, the girl thought, with a smile half of amusement in spite of her annoyance, that since she was deprived of all earthly credit, the reward might be the greater in another world. She paid the money every month out of her own allowance, and no one but Edith knew any thing about it. She was far from thinking however, that the poor creature had any claims on her, beyond the claims of common humanity; to admit that she had would be an insult to her father's memory, and Marguerite, however hurt she might have been with her father living, had only the tenderest feelings for him dead.

She opened the door at Martha's invitation to

'come in,' but her usual greeting: "And how is our rheumatism to day," was cut short by the sight of a visitor. Martha appeared slightly perturbed at the entrance of Marguerite, but her instincts of hospitable politeness came to the rescue of her evident embarrassment.

"Miss Marguerite Clayton, I'll make you acquainted with Miss Delphine Bienvenue," she said with stately formality. Marguerite was instantly trying to think where she had heard that name. "A pretty name," she thought. The first comer, a girl like herself, perhaps scarcely so old, bowed stiffly and arose, as if to take her departure.

"Pray don't go Miss Bienvenue, I have just looked in on Martha a minute on my way to a committee meeting; I am on two committees and it seems to me that we are continually meeting. We don't usually meet on Sunday however; to-day is an exception."

She was wondering to herself who the girl might be, and why she was calling on Martha Grigsby. The girl had an interesting face, and an interesting personality altogether, Marguerite decided. She was quick, and generally very good at reading character. Marguerite noticed that Miss Bienvenue was tall, and that she carried herself with an erectness supposed to be regal, but which royalty seldom attains. She was dressed all in black, and the frock was something the worse for wear and constant brushings, but a gold ring on the ungloved, slender hand, and a fancy pin at the throat, dispelled the suggestion of mourning. Her eyes were large and dark and sad, veiled by straight black lashes, and surmounted by a pair of straight, well defined brows. Her nose was a prettily shaped, straight nose, and the whole face had the general effect of being made up of straight lines, which a rosy mouth dimpled at the corners, did not destroy. The oval profile was accentuated by the way she wore her bangs, a fluffy little tuft of hair coming down into a point on her forehead.

Miss Bienvenue did not linger, but saying a few kindly words to Martha, adding a promise to come soon again, and with a nod, almost curt, to Marguerite, she was gone.

Martha Grigsby felt called upon to frame some sort of an apology, for whilst not openly expressing any gratitude to Marguerite, she secretly felt a great deal, and she did not want her patroness to suffer any annoyance, least of all, in her room.

"You mustn't mind Miss Delphine bein' sort o' huffy like," began the old woman. "Of course you wasn't to blame, and maybe nobody was to blame," she went on regardless of her previous assertions, in her desire to pour oil on what appeared to be troubled waters. "But it's only natch'ral that she feels that way."

"Feels what way?" answered Marguerite completely bewildered. She was not even conscious of being offended, or of having been treated with coolness.

"Oh I thought you might kinder noticed she wa'n't quite friendly like."

"Why Martha, what do you mean? why should she be? I never saw her before in my life, that I know of."

Martha's embarrassment increased, and she seemed not to know what to do with her hands.

"I thought I told you about her—it was her pa, that got my man to put his money in them bonds, the Golcondy, you know."

Like a flash the whole story came back to Marguerite. So this was the daughter of the man who had claimed that her father ruined him. The attitude of the girl to Martha Grigsby was thus understood.

"It is very stupid in the young lady to look upon a business transaction in that way," Marguerite answered. "I daresay my poor father lost many a dollar in speculations; indeed, I know he lost a great deal in mines. Her father took the chances just as mine did, only mine was successful in other channels and did not go to the wall after one failure, and hers unfortunately, was not. I fail to see why she should cherish any ill feeling towards me or my dear father."

Marguerite spoke hotly; it was bad enough to have old Martha acting as if she were a thief making restitution, without having this girl, presumably an educated, sensible being, doing likewise.

"Well, well! I guess Miss Delphine aint as much to blame as her ma. Miz Bienvenue always was a master hand at complainin'. I ric'lect when we was both down to Hillsborough she was always low spereted 'bout somethin' o' tuther. Some people's made that way you know and nothin' on earth aint goin' to change em; it seems to be a plum pleasure to em to have somethin' to happen jest to prove that they was right." Martha chuckled to herself as if impressed by the humor of her own discovery of the vagaries of human nature.

"Have they nothing to live on, are they very poor?" asked Marguerite, interested in spite of her pique.

"They've got Miss Delphine's wages; she's cashier at Skinner's on Sixth Avenue and gits twelve dollars a week; and her ma does fine needle work when she can git any to do, and her back aint a troublin her, and she aint got the neuralgy."

"And is that all their income, is there a large family, where do they live?" Marguerite asked her questions hurriedly, without pausing between them for an answer.

"They lives on Martin Place — I don't jest rick'lect the number; I got it on a piece o' paper in the mug on the washstand there. No, there aint a big fam'ly of em, the Lord be praised, or I declare to goodness I don't know what they would do; I jest don't. There's Miss Delphine and her ma, and her little sister. — She aint so little nuther, most fourteen." Then after a pause to make her conclusion more impressive — dramatic effects come naturally to women, she added:

"The little un's a cripple; white swellin' in her leg, limb I should say, and she can't walk without a crutch."

"Oh the poor little thing", exclaimed Marguerite with a thrill of compassion, all her displeasure gone.

"Well, yes it is plum pitiful to see her, and she so bright and pritty like."

"Her sister is a beauty," returned Marguerite with renewed admiration of the dark, sad face.

"They git their good looks from their pa. Their ma aint bad lookin nuther; she was real pritty when she was young, but some folks fade easy you know, and just git washed out and all swishy and slabbery like. She was always a mighty good woman," Martha added with some lingering sense of past favors, in the shape of old clothes and cold victuals, and even pecuniary assistance when it was sorely needed, during those first years in New York. "They got three rooms, and Miss Delphine is such a tasty body, and so handy in fixin' things the place looks real nice: The little one, Kit, Katherine's her name but every body calls her Kit, is jest completely took up with her fiddle, vi'lin I should say."

"Oh does she play the violin? that must be a great comfort to her," put in Marguerite.

"Well it is, and Miss Kit talks all the time about givin' lessons when she gits big and strong, and supportin' her ma and sister, but I recken it wont be a fortune sh'ill ever earn. It takes a pow'rful lot o' money to pay her perfesser for learnin' her, but Miss Delphine she wont hear of her stoppin'; she says that music is the only thing that keeps the child alive, and I recken she's 'bout right. Miss Delphine can play the pianner like a masterhand herself, and she did want to be a teacher, but land sakes, she couldn't git no scholars; pianner teachers is as thick in New York as blackberries in Hilsborough; so she went to the store after her ma failed keepin' boarders; she only got eight dollars at first, but she was quick at figgers and writes a hand like a copy book, so they made her cashier. It's powerful hard on her though; she's got her desk in the basement, and the heat and the air and the noise, and bein' cramped up all day in a pen — it aint as big as a pig-pen in Hillsborough, and never gittin' to set down, and some days not goin to her meals till way late in the afternoon, — she does git that tuckered out—lands! I used ter think she'd jest drop dead when she come home at nights."

The Bienvenues formed a never failing topic of converstation for Martha, and when she had as sympathetic a listener as Marguerite she could talk on indefinitely.

"Poor girl! it is pitiful the lives some people have to lead," said Marguerite more to herself than to Martha, thinking how grateful she ought to be for all her blessings, and how good God had been to her. Poverty, to the great majority of Americans, is too recently removed to seem quite like a foreign condition. Marguerite remembered that only a short twenty years before, not the third of an ordinary lifetime, her own father had been very poor, and the father of this girl in comfortable circumstances; her father had died a many-times millionaire, this girl's father almost a pauper.

In families where wealth is an inherited condition for generations, they may lose that sense of the possibility of poverty ever knocking at their own door; the feeling be engendered that in some mysterious, providential way the possessors of hereditary fortunes are set apart from the common mass of humanity; but with the generality of what are called the New People in America, and there are not many very old ones, in the line of riches and distinction, wealth treads in the footsteps of poverty, in one lucky, enterprising go-ahead generation. Marguerite's children might feel that there was a gulf between themselves and the poor, but not Marguerite herself, so long as she retained her recollections of a childhood passed in mining camps, small towns on the Pacific coast and the home, humble enough compared to the one which followed, in San Francisco. She was naturally a proud girl, but her pride was something entirely apart from money. She had nothing of the littleness of soul of the newly rich snob. Besides, she had a generous girl's natural fondness for other girls, and a very human interest in their lives.

"I recken Miss Delphine aint a mindin' bein' poor so much as she is other things," went on Martha significantly.

"What other things?" asked Marguerite, seeing at once through the evident desire to be asked.

"Well mebbe I hadn't ought ter be tellin' tales out o' school, it's a secret in the fam'ly kinder — but she's been crossed in love."

Martha folded her hands and looked down at the floor.

Marguerite, in the glow of her own great happiness, gave all the sympathy that the most exacting of gossips could require.

"She aint never bin the same girl sence then," continued the old woman. "She went up to Hillsborough, her old home to spend her vacation two year ago, and she met a chap from New York up there; people's got to takin' summer boarders sence times has been hard; pears like they aint never a goin' to git no better; hard times is like the measles, they break out when you don't look fur em, and jest sweep the hull country; money gits scarcer than hen's teeth and some places don't ever seem to git over them kind o' measles. Well, he was boardin' at the same house with Delphine, and they sung together, and played that new fangled game, knockin' a ball over a net, rid' horseback and read' under the trees and all sich; and then they got engaged, leastwise folks thought so; Miz. Taylor from up there told me all about it; and Miss Kit kind o' gave me a hint. I used ter do washin' some for Miss Delphine and her ma."

Marguerite, whilst deeply moved by this homely transcript of the sad little tragedy, one only too common, she dimly guessed, mentally noted that "Miss Delphine" seemed to be the leading spirit in the Bienvenue household.

"They was engaged, as I said, or leastwise that's what every body thought," went on Martha. "They come back to town in the fall, and then purty soon every thing was all broke off. He got to goin' with rich girls, and to way-up parties, and got ashamed of a sweetheart what lived in three rooms and worked fur her livin'. I guess that's about the straight of the matter."

A sudden and startling determination took possession of Marguerite. At the first mention of the cripple she had resolved on doing something for the Bienvenues, paying for Kit's lessons, or perhaps getting them a cosy little flat, but when the full depths of this other girl's cup of sorrow was revealed to her, she instantly resolved on something heroic. In the shadow of a love which had gone wrong all other troubles sank into insignificance. She would take Delphine out of that miserable store, and give her some of the surroundings a sensitive, refined girl would naturally crave. Perhaps then her lover, unworthy as he was, might come back to her. She shuddered to think of the wheel of fortune which might have placed her in Delphine Bienvenue's position. She had been given to vague longings all her life to do something really grand: here was a chance. The queens who had played the good fairy to penniless but highborn maidens, and the bountiful patron of unrecognized brains and unappreciated genius, had always come in for a large share of her admiration. She knew of no navigator to send into unknown waters, no poet starving in a garret, no mighty genius languishing for want of the means to give his work to the world; but here was a chance to make one family, who might be said to have claims on her, inasmuch as it was her father who had been the innocent instrument of their ruin, comfortable, if not happy. Here was a Providential opportunity. To be sure, Mr. Dalton, her guardian, had sternly opposed her wholesale plans of benevolence, and what he called her reckless charity, but surely he would advance the sum she would require out of an income so large as her own.

"How much money did Miss Bienvenue's father invest in those bonds?" asked Marguerite abruptly, when she got this far in her planning.

"Land a living! are you goin' to buy them bonds?" exclaimed the old crone, her eyes beaming with the delight of her soul. To her nebulous ideas of Marguerite's great wealth, a few thousand dollars were the merest trifle. She was simply unable to grasp the limitations of millions, and to her mind two millions or twenty, represented the same inexhaustible storehouse.

"Somethin' like twenty thousand dollars I think; I aint plum sure the exact sum."

Marguerite did not expect to hear so large a figure, but she did not abate any thing of her intention.

"Oh, Miss Marguerite, if the world was made up of folks like you, it would be a happy world, it would," exclaimed Martha in a burst of genuine enthusiasm; and then, as if some spring of feeling had been suddenly loosened, she put up her apron to her eyes, and began to cry.

XIX.

WITH Marguerite to think, was to do, if the doing were possible whilst the mood lasted. She would have liked to drive at once to the Bienvenue abode, and put twenty thousand dollars in the hands of Delphine. The necessity of seeing Mr. Dalton in order to get the money, as well as the skirmish she would probably have before she did get it, made her temper her inclinations.

Early Monday morning she ordered her brougham, and was on her way to Mr. Dalton's office almost as soon as that gentleman himself. The pleasure she took in thinking of the pleasure of the Bienvenues, crowded out of her mind all disagreeable conjectures as to how she was to overcome her astute guardian. She had not yet attained the heights of perfection where she could trample under foot the sensible satisfaction arising from a worthy act. The more she thought of the good fortune she was to carry to the Bienvenues the more enthusiastically happy she became, until she forgot Mr. Dalton altogether. But as she neared the office she reverted to the battle before her; for Mr. Dalton, whilst the most generous of men himself, objected very strenuously to generosity in Marguerite. He took a pride in managing her property to the best advantage, and seemed anxious to have it grow as much as possible under his hands. He had permitted a gift of five thousand dollars to an orphan asylum, only after a hard day's begging, and four times that amount to a single family would certainly be vetoed peremptorily. Still, she had great faith in persistent and oft repeated attacks in carrying a point; and if he remained firm, why there would be no difficulty in anticipating her majority — there were plenty of money lenders who did not scruple to lend to minors — at three percent a month.

"I want to talk to you about something," began Marguerite to her guardian, leading the way into his private office. As a preliminary she pulled up the blinds, to let in the straggling morning sun, and pushed a footstool over by Mr. Dalton's own particular chair. And then without any 'beating around the bush', a process the old gentleman particularly abhorred, she explained her wishes, and her resolve.

"My dear Marguerite, what are you thinking of! Your plan does credit to the goodness of your heart but certainly not to your head. You cannot relieve all the families in New York, even those in one street; and from what you tell me these people are no objects of charity; the young lady has a good position, they are comfortable enough; there are hundreds of other channels for twenty thousand dollars far more worthy than this. Of course, if you want to sell your goods and give the money to the poor when you become of age, I have no serious objection, although I fancy his Honorable Highness, Lord Parkhurst, might have something to say." The honest Democrat could not refrain from a good natured jibe at Marguerite's noble lover, once in a while.

"If you are after some altruistic nonsense about

the greatest good to the greatest number," continued Mr. Dalton, you will have to make smaller piles than twenty thousand dollars. At that rate you would need the Treasury at Washington to portion off one Ward."

"Oh, dear Mr. Dalton, you do love to tease me so," said Marguerite lightly perching herself on the side of his chair. He was the only link that connected her glorious young-ladyhood with the happy, childish days in California. He had been her father's partner and best friend before Marguerite was born, and since the father's death, had looked upon the girl almost as a child of his own. After Marguerite came back from France it seemed natural to return to the old time affectionate ways with which, when a mite in pinnafores, she had successfully inveigled him into some scheme not looked upon favorably by her old nurse, and general care-taker.

"Now my little girl," he went on seriously, the business man again, yet not putting aside altogether his character of foster father, and indulgent friend; "of course you know I am not going to allow you to give your fortune in this reckless way; the law would be after me if I did, and my own conscience would not let me sleep at night. I am glad you have such good intentions, but you must cultivate a better judgment. You always were a generous little thing, giving away your candy or your dolls to any other little girl that happened to be around — so long as it pleased you; if you lost your temper or some one provoked you, you could be as sternly just as the next one, the justice principally in your own favor."

"Was I such a little vixen? but you don't know how much I have reformed," answered the girl gaily.

"I am glad you are resolved on making a good use of your money; I should rather see it going to the orphans and the poor than being squandered in London extravagances." The 'London extravagances' sounded rather tame, considering all that he wanted to say. The astute guardian had made inquiries into Lord Parkhurst's financial affairs, and the investigation had been any thing but satisfactory.

"No body wants to squander it in London extravagances," retorted Marguerite.

"Excuse me, my dear, but I know men, especially lords; and if you come to me when the time arrives, I am going to make the settlements hard and fast. — But that is not to the point now."

"Why Mr. Dalton, I thought you liked Paul!" exclaimed Marguerite, hurt and instantly on the defensive. 'Lord Parkhurst' and 'Miss Clayton' had become 'Paul' and 'Marguerite'.

"Well, not quite as well as you do, but I guess on the whole he'll do. And maybe it is because I do like 'Paul' as you say, although I would never venture on such familiarity — it would seem almost like swearing, or calling my grandmother Jane — that I want to save your fortune for him; from all accounts he has none of his own."

"He is better than rich," said the girl, prepared to do battle on other lines than she had expected, but Mr. Dalton capitulated on that count, and admitted that the Earl of Parkhurst might be neck and shoulders ahead of his class.

Marguerite was shaken intellectually, by his arguments against her scheme for assisting the Bienvenues, but she was just as anxious as ever to help them.

"Well, Guardie, I don't want to make a present of twenty thousand dollars to every needy family in New York, but this is a very particular family. It is strange you don't remember them; I thought you knew all the people that Papa knew."

"Oh, not quite all; there were two or three not down on my list," answered Mr. Dalton with good natured sarcasm. "In this particular case I was out of the country; the Golconda Mines came on deck during the three years I was in South America."

He did not add that he had valued his friendship with her father too much to inquire too closely into the particulars of a transaction which had been characterized in the chance gossip of the street as shady.

"These people seem to cherish some sort of hard feeling towards poor Papa — of course I would not allow them to insinuate any thing like that to me for a moment; yet I feel somehow, that I would rather no living creature thought ill of him. He was such a good papa to me, before he was, — when I was a little girl," she added, with a quiver in her voice. "Then we were not very good friends, you know, and then, — then he died, and I never saw him again."

"Yes, yes, my dear, I know. But he always loved you better than any body in the world, Marguerite," Mr. Dalton interrupted hurriedly. He had his own opinion of a man who could allow himself to be hoodwinked so completely by even the cleverest of women. But then there was no accounting for widows, he had admitted in justification of his lifelong friend, and old partner.

Marguerite lingered on in a fruitless endeavor to win some concession, and only left when the office boy announced that a gentleman was waiting to see Mr. Dalton.

"Yes, in a minute Tom," answered her guardian, and Marguerite feeling that she had been lifted bodily from her chair, and thrust into the publicity of the outer office, arose to go, although Mr. Dalton made a feint of begging her not to hurry. She turned around at the door to add: "I am determined for once, and I am going to say a little prayer that you will change your mind; I promise to be very docile and good and obedient, and I want you to let me have this money as a reward of merit."

A week later she was summoned to the office by a note asking her to come down, as there was an offer for the property in California which she had inherited from her mother. This property consisted of some lots and an old house, purchased at a trifling figure, on the outskirts of the town, and which had suddenly tripled in value, then tripled again, and had kept on rising steadily ever since. She knew all about the history of the property, although it was purchased before she was born. Her mother had taken up a mining claim, or rather her father had taken it in her mother's name, and had sold it for three thousand dollars. With this money he had bought the property in San Francisco, giving the deed to his wife. "In case I die penniless you will have a little something to live on," he had said. "This property is yours absolutely, and I don't want you ever to sign the deed away no matter how much I beg you to do it. The fever of speculation comes over a man and he would sell his shirt, but this I want you to keep. It may be valuable some day."

Marguerite did not know whether her mother had ever been called upon or not to deed away the property; and it had certainly grown in value beyond her father's most sanguine hopes. When she recalled the story, it struck her as a want of moral courage in her father to be unable to control his passion for speculation without putting the property beyond his reach; but she banished the thought with horror, instantly, as a sort of disrespect to the father she remembered so much more vividly than she had the dear, sweet mother, who had saved this property for her child.

"I am offered seventy five thousand dollars for it Marguerite, and I think it will probably not go any higher, at least for some time, and it might fall very considerably," explained Mr. Dalton. "Now I am going to follow your father's example in regard to this property. I want to invest the money in some safe bonds, and I want you to promise me never to dispose of them, if you live to be a hundred years old, without my consent. Or if I am dead, and I daresay I shall be before that time — well the truth is I want you to hold on to this little investment; it will be only a trifle compared with your other possessions, so let it accumulate. It might come in very conveniently for your grandchildren."

After the business, which had brought her to the office, had been disposed of satisfactorily, and she had resisted the temptation to intrude that other business so near her heart, Mr. Dalton remarked casually, as if entirely by the way: "Here is a check for that twenty thousand dollars you want to give to those Bienvenues, and start a socialistic riot on a small scale in a peaceful community. Where a 'woman wills she wills, you may depend upon it, and when she wont she wont, and that's the end on it'; and I like a sensible man, yield to the inevitable."

Even in her joy at getting the money without any further trouble, Marguerite was conscious of a very strong desire to know what had made her guardian change his mind. And, as she gave him a kiss as a part of the exuberance of her gratitude, and of the gratitude the Bienvenues ought to feel, with that complex action of the human mind, especially when the mind is feminine, she was inventing half a dozen causes, every one of which, good sense made her reject.

"Don't you bother about my mind, or I might change it again," said her guardian; "just take this money, buy those Bienvenues' bonds and say nothing about it to any body. I am lending this money to you, and not advancing it out of your income. I have entered it on my private account, and when you are of age you can pay me back, or if I should die you can consider it a legacy from your old friend."

XX.

"That Miss Clayton was down at the store today."

Delphine Bienvenue threw herself wearily on the lounge, which at night did duty as a bed, and stretched her shapely arms over her well poised head in the attitude of utter weariness, and let every muscle relax. It was a trick she had learned at a Working Women's Club, which she some times attended under protest; and at which a certain brilliant and philanthropic woman had given a course of lectures on Physical Culture. She was too tired to care for the effect her words might have on her mother, but her repose of manner seemed the apotheosis of a restrained intensity.

"Well, of all people — what could she have wanted there," exclaimed Mrs. Bienvenue. "I thought ladies like her never condescended to such plebeian counters as Dexter's."

"They don't as a rule," replied Delphine, "but perhaps she is the exception."

"I guess she was buying things to send to some mission or other," put in the mother hypothetically. She was one of those women who can never rest until a motive, probable or at least plausible, has been found for the most trivial of actions.

"They say she is very charitable — and I guess she can afford to be," she went on with a tightening of the lips, which needed no interpretation to Delphine.

"She condescended to bestow a bow, and a very sweet smile on my poor little self; she even started to say something, but the floor walker came around with such a scowl, you know he does not allow talking during business hours, that she fled precipitantly.

Fancy his thinking Miss Clayton a friend of mine," and Delphine laughed, but her laugh lacked the bitterness of her mother's smile.

"Old Martha thinks she is a sort of earthly angel; and I suppose she is not to blame for her father's rascality. I dare say he was not any worse than plenty of other rich men, although poor papa was not knowing enough to save himself. Oh, well! — Is dinner ready?—I am awfully hungry. I was docked ten cents today for being late, so I cut my luncheon down to a cheese sandwich."

"Oh! my child, you must not do that, you will ruin your health," protested the mother with a sigh.

"If I do I can go to Florida, or to the South of France to recuperate," rejoined Delphine.

"Dinner is all ready but the bread; I sent Katherine for a loaf of bread. She wanted to go, and it does her good to get out; she mopes too much." The mother gave another sigh, which was taken up impatiently by the daughter. Mrs. Bienvenue vanished in the tiny apartment, which did duty as a kitchen, general store room, and dining room for breakfast and luncheon. The evening dinner, the principal meal, and almost the only one for Delphine, they made a sort of feast of, and spread in the sittingroom.

The mother had been a handsome woman in her youth, a pronounced blonde, although her children were both dark; but time and care, care more than time, had faded the eyes and the roses from the cheeks, thinned the hair and bent the graceful figure which yet retained some of its girlish curves, and much of its grace. A network of fine wrinkles around the eyes and mouth would have betrayed to a physiognomist the disposition to take trouble, the tendency to worry over trifles. She might have degenerated into a hopeless grumbler and a slattern housekeeper, the outward sign of inward decadence in the poor, had it not been for the mental tonic of her elder daughter. If the rooms were in disorder when Delphine came home in the evening, she would rise from her lounge or rocking chair, no matter how tired she was, and proceed quietly to put things to rights. Mother-love could not stand this, besides she felt the injustice of allowing the girl, who had stood on her feet all day earning their daily bread, to exhaust herself yet more, doing housework. As it was, there was an air of refinement about the place in spite of the very evident poverty. A cracked piano on which Mrs. Bienvenue had played sentimental airs as a girl, and which had been saved from the hammer only because its age and tintinnabulations repelled all buyers, stood in one corner of the sitting room; photographs in cheap but pretty frames relieved the barrenness of the top, that feature of a square piano which refuses to lend itself to harmonious treatment. A bright rug, made of a carpet remnant, covered the middle of the floor; the sides had been stained by Delphine's tired hands after her store duties were over; a camp chair with cushions, and a rocking chair stood near the table, on which rested a little work basked belonging to Katherine, and a lamp; geraniums were in the one window exposed to the sun, swiss curtains were looped back with olive green cords; occupying the place of honor over the mantel was the violin, the very apple of Kit's eye; in fact, the whole household, to a certain extent, revolved around the violin. The mother was sure that her child would one day be a great artist despite her lameness, and in the few bright day dreams she permitted herself, in her usual revery of pessimistic gloom, she could hear the applause which would greet the young musician as she limped on the stage and poured out her soul in Paganini's own impassioned strains. Delphine loved it because her sister loved it, principally, and incidentally because of the pleasure the music afforded them all. There were drawings on the wall, not bad as amateur work goes, done by Delphine in her ambitious school days; a shelf in one corner was filled with books, stray classics of English and American literature, with here and there an old volume of French, all in the garb of beggars, picked up at the dingy book stalls where Delphine had a weakness for stopping. Not even the awful dangers, pictured with startling force at the Physical Culture class, of microbes lurking in the faded covers, could make her forego the delight of spending her noon hour in one of these stalls. "It is better than the theatre for studying human nature, and it does n't cost any thing. With Greek and Latin folios, German and French novels, the Spanish pamphlets and the Italian poets piled all around me, gathered from the four quarters of the Globe, I can construct a drama of my own, with characters from all nations to fill the roles. Why, I bought Moliere in French for ten cents. How is that for the vanity of human greatness?"

Besides her purchases at the second hand stores, Delphine had two library tickets, and always read the new books worth reading, and the magazines. There were few subjects on which she could not have given a very clever opinion, albeit, her time for reading was limited to short evenings in the week, and the twice blessed Sunday, that day designed especially for the poor, and those who do the world's work.

In the kitchen were large chests which contained their last season's clothes and the household linen; in the one small bedroom were two little iron beds occupied by Mrs. Bienvenue and the cripple. Delphine utilized it for purposes of the toilet, but slept on the lounge in the sitting room. Sometimes, when she indulged in wild flights of girlish fancy into the realms of plenty, her most daring dream was of a little room in blue and oak, with a curtained bed, a real bed, and all her own.

The family had not fallen at once to their present state of genteel, but unmistakable poverty; after her husband's death Mrs. Bienvenue had turned to that multitudinous occupation, which has been the refuge and the ruin of so many helpless women, — keeping borders. She rented a furnished house, and for a time really did seem on the high road to prosperity; Delphine and Katherine went to a select and semi-fashionable day school, the elder, with the fixed idea of becoming a teacher, and thus adding to the family exchequer. But boarders proved capricious, and the tide of their patronage fluctuated; an objectionable class of tenants filled up the block in which Mrs. Bienvenue lived; her furniture was discovered to be old fashioned, her cooking behind the times, and her best paying boarders went elsewhere; she fell in arrears with the butcher and the baker, and only kept straight with the milkman because he did a strictly cash business. The inevitable, long delayed by one makeshift or another, at last came, and the auctioneer's flag hung from her door. With the odds and ends of the furniture they moved into a flat, and Delphine left school, resigning her hopes like the brave girl she was, and sought a place in a store. And in the store she remained, as the spring followed winter and the summer changed to fall, for three weary, health-breaking, spirit-crushing years. The terrible illness of the little sister came just at the crisis of their trouble, to add the last drops to their overflowing cup. One of the keenest agonies of the loving Delphine was the thought that had they possessed the means to procure proper medical aid, Katherine, curly headed little Kit, might not have been a cripple. It was too late now to do any thing; the leg was hopelessly shortened.

In spite of her work and their poverty, the humiliations and the little makeshifts of an indigence which refuses to accept its fate, and is constantly reaching out after some of the things of a more fortunate existence, Delphine had not been unhappy. She played duets with Kit, or read or did fancy work in the evenings; occasionally she pocketed her pride and attended the Working Women's Club, where, amidst a crowd of unrefined, ignorant girls and women, she not infrequently met reduced gentlewomen like herself.

Once in a great while she and her mother went to the theatre, taking seats in the gallery, and going closely veiled. Every Sunday she could be seen at the great Cathedral, heroically ignoring the shabby gown, where the fourfold activity of her soul could find an object, the spiritual sense at the altar, the reason and the moral sense in the sermon, the aesthetic sense in the music, the paintings, the sculpture, the architecture. Her body was refreshed by the purer atmosphere of the Avenue, and by the walk.

Then, after three years of work, the supreme agony of a woman's life came to her, — a deep and ardent love went awry.

She had turned her steps towards Hilsborough to spend her month's vacation, and there she met the first refined, well-bred man she had known since her father. Propinquity did its work too surely, both in his case and in hers.

In six weeks they were engaged to be married.

There had never been a time in her life like to those short, rapturous, August days. The drives along the long, cool shaded country lanes; the boating, the walks, the music, the books they read—there would have been delight even in the Anatomy of Melancholy if read under conditions so dear — the talks, or the languorous moments when both were silent, happy just to be together. The sweetest and best that life could offer seemed to have come to her in this quiet, country village. She did not trouble herself to think when the marriage could take place, — not for a long, long time for reasons on both sides. Hers, the dependent mother and sister; his, poverty. To her simple ideas the poverty was purely imaginary, since the man she had promised to marry had a salary of two thousand five hundred dollars a year, besides the rent of the house he had built on installments, and dividends from a few shares of stock in a good company.

"I want my wife to take her place among the best in the land," he had said, looking down into her dark, soulful eyes, with all the fondness of an accepted lover. "Delphine, you were born for a princess, and placed by some mistake in the wrong place; and some day, my darling, I shall restore you to your rightful position. Then the world will do you homage."

But to Delphine, in her youthful simplicity, the homage of the world had no charms. The homage of one was enough. Still, if wealth and honors were necessary for the happiness of her intended husband, then she would pray for wealth and honors with all the fervor of an anchorite.

"Such beauty, such grace, such rare perfection, were not given to be wasted on a poor devil, working for his daily hire; you ought to throw me over and marry a millionaire." The common language of love perhaps, everywhere, and old as the human heart; but new and strange and sweet to the ears learning its first lessons.

Even in the agonies of the after-day, she never quite forgot the rapture of that summer dream.

On his return to town in the autumn, he went to see his betrothed at once.

She had preceded him by two weeks. Although prepared to find his princess in Poverty Quarter, he was not prepared to find her in a tenement house; and Delphine herself, in her worn black gown, her cheeks pale from the bad air of the store, her natural vivacity dulled by the extreme weariness engendered by ten hours on her feet, counting money, — money, money every where and not a cent to spend.—Delphine in New York was not the fascinating creature like the Delphine in cool dainty muslins, rosy, animated, happy, frolicksome, filling the old fashioned house with her songs, her laughter, conquering all before her with the charm of a magnetic personality. And the mother, stitching away on a garment to be worn, perhaps, by a maiden with whom he had danced the german, seemed to intensify the general shabbiness. Even the little sister with her crutches, was not as pathetic as he had been prepared to find. He called again in a few days, then again after a longer interval, and then they had quarreled. The high-spirited girl gave him back his ring and his right to select a wife from the circle of more fortunate maidens, who did not have to spoil the charm of girlhood and fresh beauty by long hours in a dirty, foully ventilated, inexpressively commonplace shop, maidens to whose beautiful homes he would not be ashamed to go. Delphine did not say all this in so many words, but it was implied in her haughty dismissal. He thrust the ring into his waistcoat pocket, not knowing that in the little circlet was congealed the life blood of a woman's heart. He had loved Delphine in his own selfish way; loved her still, and was bitterly angry with her for having read his snobbish soul as she had done, and yet curiously enough, he felt a thrill of pride in her for the spirit she manifested. If he were only rich', was the refrain of his thoughts as he twirled his curling mustache with savage force, then all would be so different. He could lift Delphine to the plane where she and he belonged. With money and Delphine he would have his heart's desire. But poverty, poverty was the millstone that was dragging him down beneath the maelstrom of squalor and obscurity and stunted opportunities. And railing at fate, he went out into the night, once more a free man. On his way up town he stopped in at a theatre to drown his sorrow; the curtain rose on the last act of a melodrama, in which the lowly maiden and the rich lover are united, after unheard of obstacles which crop up with such tropical luxuriance along the pathway of melodramatic heroines. The play made him positively savage.

But Delphine, crushed and suffering, could not afford the diversion of the play, a change of scene, or any of the balms which affluence has for sorrow; for her it was only work, work, work, in the treadmill of her hard lot. She tried to think how contemptible was her lover, how unmanly, how ignoble his soul. He had outraged all her ideals of manhood, of truth, of honor, and yet despite every thing, she had to acknowledge, with angry contempt for herself, that she still loved him. And in the secret communings with her own soul she had to face a future which would be but a sunless path of torturing renunciation. She could not hope to forget — she knew herself too well.

"Is there any limit to the suffering a woman can endure and yet live?" she cried out in the first throes of her pain. She repelled the consolation offered, with a suggestion of hysteria, by her mother. Only when Kit stole in, so fragile in her little print nightdress, for they were too poor to afford the dainty cambrics of more fortunate maidenhood, and pressed a kiss on her sister's hot dry lips, as she lay feverish and nervous on the lounge, and then limped back to her bed again, did Delphine break down into a burst of passionate sobs.

But she did not die, and life went on outwardly the same, but nevermore to be the same. She had learned that when a woman loses faith in the man she loves, a something goes out of her life which can never be replaced. Nature heals the wounds left by death, for the reverent memory of the dead remains and the beautiful hope, but for a dead love there is no resurrection.

And for Delphine there was nothing to give a surcease of her heartache.

The man who had planted the dagger in her heart was always in her thoughts; she hated him, loved him, admired him, despised him by turns. One mood followed another without logical cause or sequence.

She got into the habit of going into some dim

old church on her way home from the store; and when she came out, the first star, just appearing in the far off sky, seemed to be a herald of peace.

"I wonder if God is not sorry for me," she thought sometimes, "if He does not sympathize with me, just because I suffer so much, and He suffered too, when on earth!"

XXI.

IN the impetuosity of her desire to bring prosperity and happiness to this family in whom she had become so absorbingly interested, Marguerite had not stopped to consider in what particular way her object could be effected. She had an intuitive comprehension of the independence of the American character which resents charity as an insult, that warned her not to venture to offer the money as a gift. To buy the bonds, knowing them to be worthless, she was shrewd enough to see, would probably be taken as an act of restitution. And she could not brook such an insult as that would appear, to her father's memory.

"Why should there seem any thing strange in giving a competence to one family instead of doling the sum out to a hundred?" mused the girl. "Why wont those people be reasonable, and understand just why I want to give it — because I feel sorry for them, and because they suffered by accident, through my father."

Should she send for Mrs. Bienvenue and her daughter, or have a lawyer attend to the matter, and thus put it altogether on a business basis; would she call herself, would she go back and ask Mr. Dalton to be her agent,—he had not offered to appear in the affair, — would she send it secretly? She rejected the latter suggestion as childish in the extreme.

The thought of a personal call might have been entertained only that the daughter was away from

home all day, and she did not feel mentally able to
alone cope with the mother, whom she pictured as
commonplace and narrowminded — a woman who
would put the worst construction possible on her
generosity, unable even to understand the filial
affection and the kindness of heart which were the
impelling motives. That she had never seen the
mother and only heard of her through an ignorant
old woman, did not modify her innate prejudice.

She decided at last that the plainest course would
be a letter of explanation, nominally to Mrs. Bienvenue, but which would, of course, be read and
discussed hilariously by the entire household. She
took a renewed delight in picturing the rapture
this missive would bring. She could almost fancy
herself admitted to the little council where the best
of surgical aid for Kid, a new home, trips to the
South, plans for days of ease and nights of contentment, would be talked over with all the zest of
repressed desire at last set free. She had the broad
sympathy of character which could put herself in
another's place, and see with another's eyes, and
from another's point of view. She spent two
mornings in a fruitless attempt to draft a suitable
communication, and was almost tempted to break
through her resolution of secrecy and tell Edith.
She had not thought of telling Lord Parkhurst;
she felt that it was not a step he would heartily
approve. Diplomacy was not a gift of hers — she
was too much accustomed to plain dealing, to a
mental directness analogous to the shortest line in
physics.

After much deliberation she went to a lawyer,

not without a fear that her guardian would not approve of this course, and put the matter in his hands. It took a great deal of explanation to make him understand that there would be any difficulty in persuading a poor family to accept a present of twenty thousand dollars. He was not acquainted with the poor of that class. Nor could he understand that the money was not to be considered as a gift, nor as charity, nor as an equivalent for value received, nor as payment of a debt, nor yet as restitution. It seemed an illogical, crazy sort of proceeding altogether, but he had had during a score of years, a great many feminine clients, and had learned to be cautious in the expression of his opinions. He was a middle-aged man who felt that he ought to know Marguerite better than he really did, because he had known her father, and he wondered why Mr. Dalton, her level-headed guardian, had permitted such a Quixotic scheme.

As Marguerite sat in his private office he quickly drafted a letter to Mrs. Bienvenue, which he read as he went along:

"My dear Madam; I am instructed by Miss Clayton to open negotiations with you for the purchase of the bonds you hold in the Golconda Mining Co., of which the late Mr. Charles Clayton was President. Miss Clayton wishes" — He threw down his pen abruptly. "My dear Miss Clayton; it will never do in the world to put your proposition on paper," exclaimed the lawyer; "the letter would be a sword over your head for the rest of your life. Don't you see that if news of it became public, and every thing becomes public in these days, every bondholder in existence would besiege you to buy his bonds; it might even form the basis of a legal action against your father's estate, for every body knows the company is now extinct and that the bonds are worthless. Law is a terrible power in unscrupulous hands. And we are not always credited with our generous intentions. Not one in a hundred would believe in the noble motive you really have in wanting to relieve this family. You must offer the money as a gift or not at all. I fear it is an ill-placed beneficence, and it certainly would make a bad precedent. I confess I cannot understand myself, why the mere accident of your father having been president of the company in which these Bienvenues lost their little all, makes you feel that they have any claims on you."

"Why I don't feel that they have any claims," answered Marguerite, "but they think that poor papa was to blame, and are cherishing all sorts of dreadful thoughts about him. And I don't like that."

The lawyer laughed, his laugh expressed a large toleration of the idiosyncrasies of humanity.

"My dear child, that has been the experience of the world since business began. Success always seems to the unsuccessful like a personal wrong. It is hard to convince a man who has speculated and lost, that another man who speculated and won is altogether honest. If your father had died poor no question of blame would have entered their minds. The poor in these days are apt to suspect a want of square dealing on the part of the very wealthy, and they look upon their splendid acts of charity as merely a return to the public treasury of some of their ill gotten gains."

He spoke earnestly and convincingly, and Marguerite was half-tempted to tear up the check, or to send it to an orphan asylum.

"I thought it would be such a simple little matter to restore a family to comfort, in whom I happen to take an interest," said the girl, "but somehow I am involved in a whole network of complications. I am accused of encouraging socialism, giving an excuse for discontent, acting rashly, laying myself open to legal action, putting a stain on my father's honesty, and doing all sorts of undreamed of things. Perhaps if you would just call on this Mrs. Bienvenue, if you would be so kind, and proffer my little donation, it might be accepted, and all this bother done away with. You know why I want to give it, so you can patch up something to say to make it all right."

Afterwards, in describing this call to Marguerite, Mr. Dorsey, the lawyer, chose to dwell on the humorous side of the interview in which he was loftily insulted for attempting to do a good action, but in reality he did not think it humorous at all, at the time.

Mrs. Bienvenue insisted, at first, on an acknowledgment that the money rightfully belonged to her, and that her husband had been cheated out of it; but when the lawyer arose quickly from his chair and started towards the door, with the air of tolerating no nonsense, she took a very much less assertive stand, and admitted that of course she understood how the young lady felt about her father.

She said that she would like to consult her daughter, and that together they would call at his office on the following day.

He had divined from the start that Delphine was the head of the house.

For once it was the mother who seemed the more inflexible; she was for holding out firmly against accepting the money in any other guise than as their right, whilst the daughter was for accepting it on any terms.

"It is this way, mamma, the money rightfully belongs to us; of course we would not accept it otherwise, but it does not belong to us legally; Miss Clayton is restoring it to us of her own free will, and therefore in that sense it is a gift, and should be accepted gratefully. You know in your heart that we would no more refuse this money, fortune it is to us, than we would cut off our hands; it means life for each of us, and I — I could get down on the ground and kiss Marguerite Clayton's feet, that is how much I appreciate her generosity," she went on passionately.

"Does the beggar refuse bread, the drowning man a rope because he does not like the way it has been offered to him," Delphine continued. "Why mamma we have been mentally starving all our lives, and now — why it makes me dizzy to think of it. Life might have been so different for every one of us if papa had never heard of Charles Clayton, but Miss Clayton is not to blame for that."

Kit was the most joyous, outwardly, of the three, and with the unselfishness born of that higher spiritual nature which deformity so often, if not usually creates, as a rich compensation for a physical handicap, it was of Delphine she thought first. "Maybe she will not be so miserable now." But the castles which all three built, as they sat grouped around the little table in the same old familiar attitudes, were enchanting enough to have been a delight to Marguerite could she have looked into their souls and seen the airy structures.

Delphine lay awake for hours that night, tossing about, thinking of all that the future now held for her. But the keenest, most concrete sense of joy came with the thought that she would have to return to that hideous store, becoming daily more unbearable, but once, and then to give in her resignation. 'Happiness would never again be for her,' she told herself, 'but life could have many objects besides happiness'. And with all the new visions and possibilities before her, the ache in her heart was almost forgotten. The release from the store was enough, she felt, to atone for much that she had suffered. "God is so good," she thought: "He does not make the burden greater than weak humanity can bear; and life may be rounded into usefulness and contentment without love". She sternly checked the seduction of a revery as to the 'might have been', had the money only come sooner. She hoped *he* would hear of their good fortune; she despised him for his little soul, and he was less than nothing to her, but she viciously wanted to show him the difference between a tenement house background, and the one she meant soon to have, and to challenge comparison with other gentlewomen on his own plane. No psychologist has ever analyzed a woman's heart, with its sublime impulses, its grand depths of love, its pride and its caprices!

Early the next morning the mother and daughter called at the lawyer's office and received a draft for their money.

Although the transaction had been entirely through Mr. Dorsey, Delphine in the glow of her gratitude could be contented with nothing less than seeing Marguerite in person, and voicing as best she could the glad appreciation of her heart.

On the way up to the grand mansion on the Avenue she dramatized her visit, even to the tones of her voice, and the queenly patronage of Marguerite, which she schooled herself not to resent. She would be very dignified, and yet grateful, for after all, it was a visit of thanks to a benefactor.

Marguerite entered so soon after the footman had shown the stranger into the magnificent drawing-room, that the latter was thrown off her guard. She arose awkwardly, a great lump came into her throat — the words, "I want to thank you," sounded like the words of another person. Marguerite came over and kissed her, — this was more than the impressionable Delphine could stand, and her tears fell like rain.

They sat down side by side on the sofa, and chatted like old friends.

"I heard of you from Martha Grigsby, about

your unfortunate speculations in my father's mines. And whilst, of course, you are too sensible a girl, and too good a business woman to blame him in the matter, yet I thought it might please my dear father to know that nobody was suffering, however accidentally, through him. Besides, to be frank, I was struck with you that day at Martha's, and your sister, and—and every thing. You must try now to imagine that the mine has revealed a new vein, that we have 'struck it rich,' as they say out West, and that I have paid over your share of the profits."

They kissed each other again at parting, and Marguerite said she must be allowed to come to see them when they got settled in their new home.

This question of a new home was now the all-absorbing topic for the Bienvenues. Delphine would have liked a cottage in the extreme suburbs, or even over in Jersey, but on account of Kit's music, and the medical skill they intended to invoke for the crippled leg, it was decided to take a flat in the city. Hunting one proved a gold mine of delight to Delphine, and a constant worry to her mother. After a sober calculation as to the value of stocks and bonds and other investments, the twenty thousand dollars went down from a fortune to a very modest competence. Twelve hundred a year, would be all that they could possibly realize from it, and Delphine with her wider knowledge, declared that ten hundred would be nearer their real income. One thousand dollars would have to go for furniture and living expenses until the investments could be made. The rents that were asked for anything like desirable flats seemed simply extortionate. After searching three days they found a flat in an unfashionable neighborhood, which came almost within the limits they had marked out for their rent. It had five little rooms and a bath, and seemed spacious to all three. Delphine's exquisite taste soon transformed it into a home. Stained floors with rugs, a new piano, dainty wicker furniture, a set of china, a new selection of flowers and climbing vines, a canary for Kit, and Delphine's own long dreamed of room, were some of its features. It was not a fine interior, it would have appeared almost common to some; but it was new and immaculately clean, modern and sweet, pretty and cozy and homelike. The pangs which arose in the girl's heart as she thought of the home she had dreamed of making as a happy wife, were crushed by the image of Kit's dear form, and her mother's contented smile.

They had a house-warming at which ice cream and pop-corn and the new piano figured prominently, and Kit threw aside her crutch and kept time with her sound foot to a popular dance.

In the matter of investments they had some trouble. They succeeded in placing fifteen thousand dollars at five percent, and lending four thousand on securities said to be good, but not demonstrativly safe, at seven. Wealth had dwindled to a limited income at the final readjustment. Close economy would be necessary; they would do their own housework, excepting the laundry work which they had always hired, even in their poverty. Washerwomen were cheaper than doctors, Delphine had said, when her mother wanted to do it. They would have in a charwoman once a week, live principally on fruit which was wholesome, and thus save cooking. They would have to practice economy but it would not be a grinding economy. And as a beginning, they would all three have some new frocks.

XXII.

LENT came very late that season; the winter had been an extremely gay one, and every body welcomed the figurative sackcloth and ashes as a relief from pleasures which were becoming a penance instead, if for no other reason. Edith declared that her soul needed recuperation quite as much as her body. To effect this twofold regeneration, the little circle of intimates, Mrs. Kingman, Edith, Lord Parkhurst, Marguerite and John Raymond went to Old Point Comfort for a fortnight. The change from New York and its usual March weather, to the delights of the Point proved enchanting. Lord Parkhurst was beginning to think that in the matter of physical comforts the Europeans could go to school to their American cousins.

Since the engagement had not been publicly announced, Mrs. Kingman saw no objection to his staying at the same hotel with the rest of her party. In the spacious coziness of the Hygeia, opportunities were presented for an ideal wooing denied in town. There were casual meetings almost every hour in the corridors or the verandas; yachting, excursions and nightly hops; explorations of the Fort and of the old historic landmarks. It was imperative that Lord Parkhurst, as a visiting Englishman, be initiated into the military tactics of the Defenders of the Stars and Stripes, and where so good a place to learn as the Point, with its gallant boys in blue, dotting the horizon, both literally and figurativly, of the maidens assembled there for the benefit of their nerves. And who so good a teacher as Marguerite with all her young enthusiasm about her native land, and her beautiful theories unspoiled by gross facts and figures, as to the perfections of her country's government.

There never had been such a period before, she thought; the sky so beautifully, softly, radiantly blue; the sea so calm, so playfully rippling, so gently yielding to the embraces of the pleasure crafts which dotted its blue expanse.

"We have been engaged over a month, and have never had a single quarrel," said Marguerite with childish coquetry, one morning, as she and the earl strolled down by the beach. "Aren't we an exceptional couple?"

"Would you like to quarrel?" responded her lover good naturedly. "I cannot imagine the man so lost to all sense of his own good fortune as to want to quarrel with you, but if you desire it very much, I might try."

"Well, that is what we ought to do according to the story books, and we seem to get our ideas for the proper conduct, — of people from them:" She shrank from saying 'sweethearts,' with her lips, although the old fashioned, caressing word was in her thoughts. "Of course we would make it up again."

"Oh yes, we must be sure about that point before we quarel."

"I would cry and feel miserable in secret," went on Marguerite, "carry my head very high, and flirt desperately with the officers at the fort if I could get any of them to flirt with me; you would look savage, pull your mustache fiercely, but then you have none so we should have to omit that part of it, — you might tear your hair instead. You would go off fishing by yourself, lose your appetite and swear at the waiter — you would not positively have to swear you know, but just say 'Caesar' or 'Great Scott', with the air of uttering something dreadful."

"Why, you are describing the symptoms of a quarrel most beautifully," answered Parkhurst. "I am getting afraid that story books have not been your only teachers. But you have not said how we are to make up and that is the most important point."

"You might get very ill so that I could bribe the nurse to let me take care of you, you would become delirious and call me all sorts of endearing names, upbraid me for a want of trust in you, and explain every thing in your mutterings; then you would get well, and discover that you owed your life to my careful nursing. — That is one way. Another one would be for me to go off in a sailboat, and get caught in a squall, when you, at the imminent peril of your life, would come to my rescue. Or a wild horse might be brought into play; horses are quite popular I assure you, among the *dramatis personae* of a quarrel, in America; on the whole, I think I prefer the horse to the water, for you must save me, you know, before I get hurt, seize the reins, or lift me off the flying steed, or something like that; we might rehearse beforehand so as to do it perfectly. In the water I should get all wet and would look simply horrid as I passed up the hotel steps with my skirts dripping, for I couldn't very well have on a bathing suit, it is too cold for bathing yet. With the horse I should simply look pale and interesting, with my habit just the least bit dusty. Yes, let it be the horse."

Lord Parkhurst entered into the spirit of her badinage readily enough, but at the same time he was carrying on a sub-stratum of wonderment. The longer he knew Marguerite the less he knew her. 'Was this the girl,' he asked himself, 'running on banteringly, quite as Edith Kingman might do, the same who last night, had talked to him so earnestly, about the goodness of God, the grand harmony of nature, life and its duties; and who had seemed almost a goddess in her unconscious beauty as the moonlight, sent a silvery gleam, like an aureole, over her dark hair. But she was his own precious Marguerite, in whatever mood, always charming, to be loved and shielded and adored all his life long.'

There arrived one morning at the hotel a certain weekly periodical, very much effected by cultivated Americans, because it presented gossip in a guise which at first sight did not look like gossip, and because it was a particularly national affair which ought to be supported by all loyal citizens. Every body seemed to have bought a copy, and seated in friendly informality on the broad verandas, the balmy softness of a day in June projected into March, all eagerly scanned its piquant pages.

The leading article of the week, most admirably illustrated, dealt with an American heiress of

'Pork extraction', as a native wit put it, and a prince, impecunious as he was noble, with past debts in plenty, and future troubles imminent. It gave a full account of the rather abrupt termination of the wooing, owing to the refusal of pater familias to make settlements generous enough to satisfy the rather expansive ideas of the prince. It was plain that the sympathies of the paper, as befits the sympathies of an American paper, were all with the young lady. The people of the Hygeia, some of whom would have sacrificed their right hands for an alliance with a real prince, agreed with the paper. As it happened, the prince was an old friend of Parkhurst's, and they had recently spent a month together in Egypt and Algiers.

"I call this a beastly shame," said the earl, biting his lips, a mannerism with him indicative of great displeasure. Every one thought that his words referred to the dastardly conduct of the prince, and instantly gave him flattering attention.

"Your American papers seem to deny the least bit of privacy to a person's most sacred affairs. Why, Von Hillern is no end of a good fellow. I am really very sorry for him."

Lord Parkhurst was betrayed into a greater warmth than he was conscious of, by the remembrance of a certain monetary transaction in which Prince Von Hillern had acted with chivalrous forbearance, considering how poor the earl was known to be.

"Well, you see in America we marry for love," answered an unsophisticated maiden of thirty summers, with just a touch of malice, Edith thought, in her tones.

"It seems quite shocking to our simple ideas that a man who is half a man, would let a consideration of money stand between himself and the woman he wished to marry. But I believe you Europeans think differently."

"In this particular case the young lady seems to have been as mercenary as the prince," answered Parkhurst. "He is a charming fellow, and his title is one of the oldest in Europe. He could have made his wife very happy, and if she cared for him, since you wish to treat it wholly as a question of love, she would have secured the settlements necessary to the marriage which promised so much felicity for both."

Lord Parkhurst chanced to glance up as if impelled by some invisible force, and caught a look on Marguerite's face which boded ill to him, he instinctively felt.

"Oh, why did I speak so hastily!" he thought. "All Americans are sensitive on the marriage question, and Marguerite particularly so. As if a fellow could support a wife on nothing a year."

The little gathering presently dispersed, some to answer the letters just received, others to attend to the mysteries of the toilet, a few to don their tennis suits, and Marguerite went with the crowd.

The earl hovered around hoping she would come back, and give him a chance to make his peace, if peace were really lost. He knew he could explain whatever might need an explanation. Of course Marguerite was not seriously offended, that would be absurd, it was merely a girlish caprice which had chosen to misinterpret his defense of his friend.

He loved her with all the strength of his soul, there could be no question about that, and she loved him. Then why should their love fret and fume over a chance pebble which had been carelessly, thoughtlessly, thrown into its limpid course?

At last she came, walking very straight, her head thrown back, her lips compressed. She made a pretense of surprise at meeting her lover, although she must have seen him as she turned the corner of the veranda, ostensibly in search of that hateful magazine.

Parkhurst advanced to meet her as if nothing were the matter.

"Why, little girl, aren't you coming for a walk this morning? I have been waiting here for an hour. — Im afraid it is too late now before luncheon."

"Ah, you might find a more interesting companion for your walks; I might lose my money before the year is out. American fortunes are very uncertain, you know, and then you would regret so much wasted time."

There was no mistaking the insult of the words, as well as the tone, and the curl of the lips which accompanied them.

Parkhurst's face turned scarlet, for a moment, and then got very white, and he drew back as if a blow had been aimed straight from the shoulder.

"You surely don't know what you are saying, Marguerite. I have not deserved this from you — and I shall not stand it," he concluded hotly.

"You might seek consolation from Prince Von Hillern."

"You surely do not attach any personal meaning

to careless words uttered about a couple whose affairs are public property! Why should you insult me, stab me so cruelly with no cause at all? I asked you to marry me because I loved you, because I thought I had found in you the one perfect woman in all the world, because —" He broke off suddenly, for Marguerite had turned away her head, and there were tears in her eyes. Tenderness mastered his anger.

"Is this the quarrel you wanted, Marguerite? If so you make it too real for me to enjoy. But come, you were surely only jesting. You know that I love you with all my heart, that every hair on your head is inexpressibly dear to me," and then he put out his hand and took her's, forcing her gently, but masterfully to a seat by his side on a rustic bench. One big tear rolled down her cheek, and the quarrel was made up before it progressed beyond a skirmish. Finally, she got her hat and went with him for a stroll along the beach.

"You love me, you say," Marguerite resumed, "and I belief you, I should die if I did not, but would you have loved me if I had not been rich, an heiress as that odious paper puts it?"

This was a hard question — one of the dilemmas that try men's souls, especially when it is the soul of a lover. A less honest man might have evaded it, or taken refuge in a falsehood, but Parkhurst had an Englishman's honesty, and he would not deny the truth, although it might cost him dearly.

He drew himself up, the smile gone instantly from his face, and even in her formless jealousy the girl could not forbear a thrill of admiration in his good looks and his manliness.

"I have never concealed from you my circumstances, Marguerite; I am, and have been for years involved in a network of difficulties which only those who have passed through the like can understand. I have been humiliated, annoyed beyond endurance; my debts have grown bigger, my available resources constantly less, my expenses have kept on just the same; the only relief possible to a man in my position is marriage with some one willing and able to cancel those debts and enable him to face the world a free man, with the means to keep up the style of living his position and rank demand."

Marguerite had it at her tongue's end to say: "An American would get to work and earn the means to pay his debts; he would consider it degradation to go on as you have done, and with such an object in view," but she controled herself, and said nothing.

"My mother has urged this step ever since my father died, and I came into the title. And I might have married — you will not consider me unduly confident if I say so — more than once, but I never was tempted even to think of marrying a woman I could not love, as an Englishman knowns how to love the woman he makes his wife. Then I saw you that week in France, and my fate was settled as far as I was concerned; I loved you almost from the first moment. You were my ideal, and I determined to win you for my wife if the winning were possible. I came to America with that sole intention."

"Or to win some one else equally rich," interposed the girl bitterly.

"I don't think you quite mean that Marguerite. And you are not yourself this morning or you would not so cruelly wound me. The more I saw of you the more I loved you, if I could love you any deeper than I did already; it seemed too good to be true that a girl with every quality to attract love, and with the world to select from, could ever care for me; but Fate was kind, and I won. You are dearer to me than life, I love you with all my soul, with all my heart, can man say more."

Marguerite, in spite of herself, was touched at his vehemence.

"But, since you asked me," he continued, "I never should have allowed myself to love you, had it been impossible that our love could prosper; I should have run away from you before hopelessly in the toils of your fascination, had I not known that you had the means to restore my house to its original status. You do not believe that a man's heart is not under his own control, at least in the first stages of an attachment. I was too poor to think of marriage with a poor girl. It is hard to have to say these things Marguerite, and our love has been so sweet. And now I have come to love you so, that life without you would hardly be worth the living; and poverty with you, had I only myself to think of, would be happiness compared to which, the wealth of the Realm with another, would be as nothing." His truth in essentials made him lenient with himself in little things, and besides, in the heat of his passion, he really thought that his words were true; and perhaps they were.

"Wont you look at me Marguerite, and tell me that you believe me, and trust me, and love me. And be your own dear self again? You don't know how you hurt me, when you look that way."

"I don't want to hurt, you Paul; but I cannot be my old self again, as you say. You have spoiled something that was inexpressibly dear and sweet to me, something has gone out of my life. I did not realize, I could not believe that my money had any thing to do with your love."

He saw that the battle would have to be fought all over again.

"Nor had your money any thing to do with my love. Your money enabled me to win your love, to give you mine. You are my happiness, my life. But I must do my duty, you yourself have said that duty should be our first consideration. I am the eldest son, the bearer of the title, I do not live for myself alone. The honor of my race is in my hands, and I must perform the duties my station imposes. I can give my wife an honorable name, the love, the devotion of a lifetime, the tenderest care a man can have for woman, but I cannot give her wealth."

"You do well to remind me of your title. I had forgotten it, so little did it count with me."

He inwardly writhed at the want of logic which forgot the title and remembered so vividly the fortune, and hurled it at him so pitilessly. He answered humbly enough: "I offer you all that I have, it is not very much I know, — and it seems you do not value my love."

"I do value it, more than all the world."

"Why then Marguerite, my darling, the rest does not matter."

The second breach was thus partially healed.

"Marriages even in America," went on Parkhurst, "are not always solely for love, regardless of all other considerations. I have heard of more than one case—and my chances for hearing have been limited—where a marriage was made for money and position, and love had no place at all. I have also heard of instances of parents disinheriting their children for marrying in a rank beneath their own, although theoretically you claim no class distinctions. If you wish every dollar of your fortune settled on yourself, have it so; I can compromise with my creditors, let Parkhurst to the highest bidder, borrow enough money from my friends to start a sheep ranch in Australia, and try to make enough to pay my debts. Then, at least you cannot say that I loved your money and not you."

Marguerite smiled, and so far descended from her pedestal of wounded dignity as to say: "Oh well, I guess we can manage without your going to Australia; I should be lonely in England by myself, and it would not look well to return to America without my husband."

Parkhurst felt that he was forgiven.

"Now you are my own darling Marguerite once again. We have had our quarrel, suppose we let it be the last one as well as the first. Marguerite cold and cruel, and unjust is not nearly so charming as Marguerite loving, and trusting and kind."

The quarrel was over, but it had left a mark, too faint to be called a scar, on the heart of the girl who had put both her love and her lover on a wonderful height which never yet rose from land nor sea. They had come down to a plane where material considerations had place. Position, appearances, prudence, duty, debts, difficulties, establishments, the tax collector, settlements — all the accompaniments of wealth and its tangible responsibilities, had been suddenly projected into the field of vision, hitherto tinted but with the roseate hues of love.

XXIII.

LORD PARKHURST stayed in New York but for a day or two on his return from the Point, and at the beginning of April sailed for England. He was graciously pleased to admit that his visit to the States had been charming in every way. Raymond suggested that he go home and put that opinion in a book. He said that it would be different in that case, from the books the English usually write about Americans, and that it would be a relief to read one in which our corruption was not held up as an awful example, our ice water and messenger service treated with contumely, our children's fondness for giving advice to their parents, and the parents' willingness to take it, commented upon, a book in short, which would deal with our virtues and be silent as to our faults.

Mrs. Kingman, Edith and Marguerite were to go over in May and take a house in London for six weeks. Marguerite's engagement would be announced in the autumn, she would attain her majority on the thirtieth day of December, — had she been consulted in the matter she would have had her birthday on the first of the new year instead of the last of the old one — and early in January the marriage would take place. So ran the plans as outlined in a little private council before the party broke up at Old Point Comfort.

Although so many years had been spent in Europe, Mrs. Kingman had never seen a London season at its height, so she did not demur greatly when it was proposed to lead her lamblike to the social slaughter.

"A mother is never to have peace until her daughter is married and off her hands," she murmured plaintively.

"And perhaps not then," Edith retorted.

Lord Parkhurst secured a residence for them, not far from his own town house which his sister and her family were occupying, Lady Mortimore welcomed her brother's friends with expansive cordiality, and it was under her chaperonage that they were to be presented at the May Drawing-room, and introduced into London Society. She was large and blonde and very handsome, with laughing blue eyes, not in the least like her brother's, which seemed to reflect her soul, for she appeared always to be taking the best out of life. She was the mother of four sturdy boys, and one little blossom of a girl, and had been married ten years; but despite her inclination to stoutness, which was the one great worry of her existence, she was not at all matronly. She laughed and joked with her brother on his infatuation for America, showing her large white teeth more than was altogether becoming; her tendency was to laugh with everybody, which, on the whole, Marguerite decided, was more pleasant than to laugh at any body. She kissed Marguerite rapturously on their first meeting, and whispered that it was the one dream of her life to have an American for a sister.

Edith and Marguerite were joyous with genuine republican joy at the thought of their presentation to her gracious Majesty. They did not pretend, as loyal Americans sometimes do, that it was because of her 'goodness as a wife and mother.' To a compatriot long self-expatriated, who touched upon this side of the affair, Marguerite replied with her accustomed frankness: "Oh, we do not think so much of that, — good wives and mothers are the rule in America, we do not know much of any other kind of wives and mothers. And it is not because of her goodness as a woman, for we could match that every day at home, but because she is the Queen of England, that I have been going through the paces, and chasing around London to get my presentation gown. Theoretically, we are all queens in America, but practically our royalty is not very apparent."

The day of the Levee was delightful, although Edith had confidently predicted rain, relatively delightful, that is, for they had already had experience of a London fog. Marguerite was radiant as she entered the carriage, and even the tiresome wait at the entrance to the palace did not put a damper on her spirits. The long line of carriages advanced a step, and Lady Mortimore whispered that the first load of people had been discharged at the entrance to Buckingham Palace. From the time it took until their own gorgeously caparisoned steeds made any headway, Edith said she thought all England and a part of Ireland were in line to pay their respects to royalty. And when told the entrance was spacious enough to permit of six carriages drawing up at once, she uttered a distinctly Yankee exclamation. They reached the palace at last, and gathering up their trains, grasping their boquets, and dropping their cards into the hands appointed to receive them, they found themselves in the vast anteroom. Marguerite was getting dizzy; she saw, as in a dream, the crowds of noble women with their shimmering trains, carried like hers, on their arms, their feathers waving like a grenadier's, and wondered if her own were as unbecoming. The throng advanced step by step, and then she was in that inner, august chamber, and in the presence of Royalty; she saw an old woman who looked tired and bored and unwell, men in quantities of gold lace, their breasts a glitter of decorations, the pompous chamberlain in his stiff cloth of gold robes of state, noble attaches, a little semicircle of princesses to whom she would have to make a certain number of obeisances; the hush was so great she could hear it, and then — she was bending her lips to the hand of a queen. And the young American, whose childish memories were of mud pies on a Western frontier, the primitive comforts and discomforts of a mining camp, red letter days when she was allowed to ride a burro down the trail, was as beautiful, as regal in bearing, as daintily cared for, as cultivated and refined, as patrician in every outward way, as any of these stately dames and damsels who traced their pedigrees to William the Conqueror, or straight back to Adam.

Seeing her grace and dignity, the thought had come to Edith that the world is divided into patricians and plebeians after all; and that the patricians are as apt to come from an Eastern farm or a Western ranch, as from a European palace or a New York mansion.

And Marguerite thought, as she passed before the 'Queen of Great Britain and Ireland and Empress of India,' with her satellites of lesser magnitude, not of the historic pageants the scene ought to have recalled, but of — who can control the vagaries of a thought, — of a certain humorist, and one of his absurd skits at the Royal family. She had not realized before, the colossal absurdity of the greeting: "How do you do, Queen, I am very glad to meet you."

"Were you frightened, Edith?" whispered the younger girl, as soon as she felt sure of being beyond the Lord Chamberlain's eye.

"Frightened, not a bit of it. Why should I have been? I have kissed Lady Mortimore's hand so often, as a proxy for the Queen's, that my lips are sore, and as for the rest of the salutes I could do them backwards."

"I am awfully hungry; I would give the feathers off my head for a sandwich," Marguerite exclaimed, when they were once more in their carriage. They were to go on to a Drawing-room Tea, and meet other rapturous maidens who had been presented.

"Oh, I am so tired, I could sleep for forty years," confessed this daughter of California wearily, as she tumbled into bed that night, the eventful day at an end.

Towards the last of July Mrs. Kingman and her charges joined the English colony at the Swiss Lakes. Marguerite wanted to spend a few days with her beloved Madame Florac, but her wish was overruled.

"You can see her frequently when you are living here for good," Mrs. Kingman had argued, "and there is some fear of cholera in Paris."

In the autumn they went as the guests of honor to Parkhurst, the Earl's fine old country place, where a large house party had been assembled by Lady Parkhurst.

"I want you to see something of English country life, for then you see us at our best," Lord Parkhurst had whispered with fond pride, to his betrothed.

Parkhurst was a magnificent old place which had belonged to a cadet branch of the first Lady Parkhurst's family. The long avenues of trees, the wide sweep of lawn, the undulating park, the broad drives and picturesque walks, the ivy covered lodge, the hot houses out of repair, the kennel's, the stables, — every thing was there which Marguerite had learned from books to expect at an ideal English country residence. The house itself, built of massive stone, with an imposing entrance, balconies and bay windows, broad halls and lofty apartments, was of an architecture which might be called eclectic.

"Ah, this is grand," said Edith as she stood a moment on the high stone steps, taking in with cultivated appreciation, the beauty of the rich autumnal scene: "And to think Marguerite, that next year you will be mistress of this perfectly enchanting old place. I am almost tempted to marry an English peer myself."

The two American girls were very popular from the start with the distinguished party assembled at Parkhurst.

"Miss Clayton has more distinction of manner, Miss Kingman more esprit," declared another American who had married an Englishman, a commoner of very old family, in the course of her analysis of her countrywomen.

"Miss Kingman would be immensely popular in the Prince's set. Miss Clayton would not take at all."

After dinner, on the first evening of their arrival, a young lady came over to Marguerite, and sank in a graceful heap on the sofa by her side, introducing herself: "I am Maud Atherton, a cousin of Lord Parkhurst's, indefinitely removed, and I have heard all about you. I have been dying all evening to talk to you." She seemed to be in a very vivacious condition, considering her closing assertion, Marguerite thought.

She was a petite, dainty brunette, exquisitely gowned, decidedly more French than English in appearance, who looked eighteen but honestly confessed to twenty five.

"Lord Parkhurst was my first sweet-heart, ever so long ago, when I was a little girl with a governess tagging after me, and he was an Oxford undergraduate. He was only the Right Honorable Paul Hunter then." And the little Gaellic beauty with the very English name, chatted away of those early days, giving all the details of the earl's boyhood, flattering herself that she was entertaining Marguerite most charmingly. She would have laughed merrily could she have known of the vague emotions she was stirring in the other's heart, a sort of *ex post facto* jealousy, as unformulated as it was unreasoning. Marguerite was not jealous of Miss Atherton, but she was jealous of Miss Atherton's past. She had not realized until then that Parkhurst had lived a life of thirty years in which she had no place. Even as she listened, outwardly smiling and pleased, to her indefinitely removed cousin-to-be, she was gathering in her mind the threads of their separated early lives. She had the impression of being unpleasantly young by comparison, when she recalled herself as a tot of six, holding on with both tiny arms to a burro, about the time when, thousands of miles away, Lord Parkhurst was a youth of twenty, almost grown, playing tennis with pretty English maidens, studying Greek and Latin, riding to hounds and fancying himself a man. And when she was sobbing out the grief of her homesick, desolate little heart in a French convent, he was a man, of twenty five playing the gallant in London, making love to his cousin, dancing and going to parties, and never dreaming that there was such a person in the world as herself. And during all those years that she was studying her verbs, and teasing Edith, and adoring Madame Florac, what was he doing? A man with all a man's interests in life, going here and there and every where, seeing the world, ripening in experience, and meeting scores of those magnificent, beautiful, perfectly-bred English girls, for whom Englishmen think the world has no equal. There was no denying that she was getting distinctly jealous of the past. In that moment she could have wished that Britain's population, during the preceding decade, had consisted of men and boys and women over fifty.

Miss Atherton's confidences were interrupted by the dowager Countess of Parkhurst, who carried Marguerite off to sing a duet with Edith. She had won the girl's heart at once by the sweet welcome she had given her, and by the deep rich tones, the voice for expressing great thoughts in beautiful words, in which she had wished her every happiness.

Marguerite had been rather in dread all along of the ordeal of meeting her prospective mother-in-law. But this gracious matron, with the delicate profile, the clustering snowy curls, the smooth white complexion, almost like a girl's, the winning mien, the proud repose of manner which stamps the inborn consciousness of rank, was all and more than she had ever dared to hope. She could understand why certain matrons from America who had made their way by virtue of their husband's money bags, into the innermost circles of London society, had been considered vulgar and coarse. "But Mrs. Kingman," who had taken willingly enough the secondary place accorded to American mothers, "Could hold her own with the best of any land," she thought with proud satisfaction.

A rapturous five minutes alone with the Earl, in which he assured her ardently that although he had liked many women, he had loved none but her, somewhat restored her peace of mind.

And as she stood at the window in her bedroom that night, looking out on the broad domain one day to be her own, the moonlight touching with a fairy wand, each tree and drive and sloping sward, resting with a burst of radiance on the bosom of the lake, leaving in darkest shadow a distant forest, suggesting rather than revealing the spire of the parish church, a ragged bit of cloud flecking here and there the clear, star-gemmed sky, her heart seemed but a tumultuous thrill of deep, undying happiness. Life was so bright, the future so fraught with every promise to make it full and grand and infinitely sweet. But she would try to be worthy, as worthy as poor human nature can be, of such blessings. She would be a good wife, a good mistress to her tenants, an unfailing friend of the poor. Hand in hand with her manly, idolized, noble husband she would go down life's pathway; together they would lead such an ideal existence, all the charm of beloved companionship, perfect sympathy, absolute congeniality of tastes, would be theirs, each would complement the other as God intended in the perfect marriage; each would be the better, stronger, happier for the other. And then in the great Hereafter, when time would be merged into Eternity, they would come before the throne of God, penitent for human frailties, 'duty bravely performed' inscribed in the Golden Book, and in the Divine Mercy, together to enjoy the Beatific Vision forever.

Even the entrance of Edith, who came in with some nonsense, overflowing from a gay evening, could not quite dispel the exaltation of her mood.

"Marguerite, when you are the Countess of Parkhurst I want you to have the dining-room decorated over again, or I shall have to refuse to visit you: any thing more trying to one's complexion I cannot imagine ; and the heavy oppressive style of the drawing-room draperies can only suit these big, still reposeful English women, and them only after they are forty. But every thing else is simply entrancing."

XXIV.

WHEN Marguerite came back to America from her outing in England, it cannot be denied that the attentions she had received as the prospective Countess of Parkhurst, the deference paid by fashionable and wealthy Americans in particular, had caused a certain girlish elation, not pride exactly, certainly not vanity, but a re-valuation of self, related to both. It was something, after all, to have a title, to belong to the Best of a country, not by virtue of wealth, or of a long struggle for place, but by a hereditary right. Pride of wealth was vulgar, of course, but pride of position was another thing.

She loved her own country with a passionate devotion, and every time the opportunity was presented of defending its glories this love seemed to take on a deeper tinge, akin to the enthusiasm of a fresh discovery; but she had reconciled herself to a future ideally happy, apart from her country and its traditions. She had no notion, in marrying an Englishman, of ceasing to be an American. She did not know that the same resolution had been made by every transplanted daughter of Columbia, and as regularly broken. A wife cannot divide herself if she would, from her husband, and if she loves him as ardently as Marguerite loved Lord Parkhurst, she soon ceases to try. But the girl could not even imagine this stage as yet. There was something grand in being an American. The rush and roar of the nation's traffic, the coming and going, and seeking and finding; the magnificent opportunities, opportunities for every one, the highest and the lowest, the field for talent in every direction, the generous rewards of genius, the manhood, the independence — it was simply intoxicating. No wonder people were leaving Europe in hordes to come into their heritage as men, casting off the shackles of the down-trodden peasants, in the effete monarchies of the Old World. 'Effete monarchies' was a favorite expression of a New York politician whom she had met abroad, and it came unconsciously to her thoughts. Personally, she had no fault to find with the monarchies, if the people were stupid enough to tolerate them.

"My grand, dear country, I love you, I love you," Marguerite cried, as the ship, bringing her home, hove in sight of the Palisades, and the blue outlines of her native land loomed in the distance. In that moment she had wished that her lover were the Earl of Albany, with an ancestral Manor on the Hudson, instead of what he was.

The season of pleasure, glorified by an ideal courtship, had mentally enervated her for the prosaic concerns of business. And it required positive and continued efforts of the will to get herself in a state to listen intelligently to Mr. Dalton's reports as to her affairs, and to receive his suggestions as to the future management of her estate. He had agreed to remain her man of business, and in return she had consented to have half of her estate settled on herself. None of these things could actually be done until she became of age, but in view of her speedy marriage after that date it was thought prudent to have all prelimi naries arranged. She had sense enough to know that the investments which Mr. Dalton had made were better than any thing she could hope for in England. "And you will not be the first one by a long shot to spend honest American dollars in London dissipations," her guardian had said in discussing her dividends.

The formal announcement of the engagement had been made simultaneously in London and in New York the last of October. But considerations of the trousseau had not been postponed. A run over to Paris was at first thought absolutely necessary, but Mrs. Kingman suggested that an agent from the great firm, entrusted with the wedding gown and some others, be sent to London to receive his orders. Marguerite was for having her trousseau prepared entirely on American soil.

"Don't be absurd Marguerite," vetoed Mrs. Kingman, who was taking a mother's interest and trouble in the matter. "Sentiment is all well enough in its place, but its place is not to inflict dowdy frocks on a bride. No body but a Frenchman knows how to make a gown, and you don't want to look like a fright over here for every body to pass remarks about. They are fond enough as it is, of picking Americans to pieces."

So the order was given for the beautiful bridal gown, and for some grand reception and dinner toilettes, but Marguerite insisted that the rest of her outfit must be prepared At Home.

She went almost immediately after her return, to call on the Bienvenues. She pronounced their little flat charming, and after duly admiring all its details and coaxing Katherine to play for her, she carried both sisters off for a spin in the Park.

"Why is it that we never think of inviting one who has no carriage, and to whom a drive would be a real pleasure, and are always asking those who have turnouts equal, if not superior, to our own," she mentally queried, by way of self justification for a kind, but unconventional act. She had no intention of 'taking up socially,' the Bienvenues, and felt that she had done quite enough for them; but she liked and admired Delphine, and recognized no reason why she should not visit her if she chose. Her step-mother was in agonies when she heard about the drive, for she said there never was any telling what Marguerite would do. "And I have enough of impossible people now whom I cannot get rid of, without any new ones on my hands." She did not approve either, of the way Marguerite had of running around the city alone. Her step-daughter believed in the emancipation of the American girl almost too firmly. She herself, as a girl, had carried bundles in a plebeian street car, and gone from Harlem to Brooklyn alone — but that was long ago, and things were different now. When the subject of the Bienvenues was broached, rather hesitatingly, by Mrs. Clayton, Marguerite had answered rather impatiently: "Why should I not go driving with Delphine Bienvenue? why should I not visit her if I like; I know she is not in 'your set'; I would not be in your set either if my father had not made a fortune by hard work, and hard sense. So it is merely a question of accident, after all."

Mrs. Clayton mentally writhed at the fine irony lurking in the pronoun, 'Your'. Marguerite was not above reminding her of her obligations to the Clayton millions. However, the prudent matron sent Delphine and her mother cards to an afternoon tea, which the girl had the good sense to refuse. "I should only be like the proverbial fish out of water," she said.

A few days later Marguerite stopped at the little flat, on her way down town, to leave tickets for an afternoon concert. She had a vague notion of enrolling Kit among her proteges and sending her to Europe to study to be a great virtuoso. In the meantime, she wanted to see if the girl's talent was really great enough to justify the opportunity. Marguerite was not used to the contracted space of the twelve-by-fourteen parlor, and in turning to go, she upset a tiny table on which rested an old fashioned photograph album. Some pictures, which had been laid in between the pages, were scattered on the floor, and her eyes fell on a tintype group of two girls and a young man. One of the girls was Delphine, and the young man — she could hardly trust her eyes, — was Henry Wilson.

"Is he the one," she cried, forgetting, in the warmth of her sympathy and surprise, that she was not supposed to know any thing about that sad little episode in a girl's life. Delphine colored, and answered faintly: "Yes, he is the one. I ought not to have kept it perhaps, but it was in a group, and after all, what difference does it make: It is only a tin-type, and Millie Tabor, the girl sitting on the log, is a very dear friend of mine.

We had some lovely times together." Marguerite recognized the transparent dishonesty of this latter remark, but only pitied the girl the more keenly. She thought she would like to tell Henry Wilson what a contemptible poltroon he was; and resolved to ask him, at the first opportunity, if he had spent the past summer at Hillsborough.

The beautiful weather of October continued into the first weeks of November, and the ozone in the atmosphere, and the ozone in her spirits, gave Marguerite a renewed sense of exhilaration as she read the notes, which now began to arrive, wishing her every happiness. More than the usual number of letters were brought up to her room one forenoon, as she was getting ready to go for a drive, the warm sunshine streaming into the window, wooing her irresistibly from the house. One letter in an unfamiliar hand, had evidently been left by a private messenger, as it had no stamp affixed.

"The man says, as he'ill wait, if you are engaged," the new maid explained, not very intelligibly, indicating with her thumb, the strange letter.

"Why, what man, Sarah?"

"The one what brung this letter, ma'am. Hawkins was a bringin' it up when I come along with the mail, and so he gived it to me."

Marguerite broke the seal hastily, and glanced at the bottom of the closely written pages at the name: Robert Morgan. She was certain she knew nobody by the name of Robert Morgan. Then she read the letter.

Dear Madame: You may remember that I called on you just before your departure for Europe, in regard to the stock my father held, and which is now in my possession, in the Golconda Mining Company.
Like a flash, she remembered. It was the day before she was to sail. He was rather a nice mannered sort of a person, regardless of his shabby coat, just a boy in years although he had assumed a man's place in the working world.

She remembered too, that he had been perfectly respectful to her throughout the interview, despite his absurd demands. It seemed that he had heard through the agent of the Bienvenues' flat, of her generosity to them. How the landlord knew she had never inquired; and Morgan had somehow learned that this generosity was because of the mining venture of her father's in which Mr. Bienvenue had been ruined. Well, his father had lost his all in Golconda mines too, a matter of ten thousand dollars, had died and left his family very poor, the support of whom devolved upon Robert Emmet, the eldest son, then a school boy, with a wild ambition to be a lawyer. Young Robert Emmet had modestly demanded that she pay off his claims also. He was dismissed on short order, for the girl had other things to think of. She recalled at the time, Mr. Dalton's warning that she would have all the bondholders at her heels if her act became known, and resolved to caution the Bienvenues to keep their affairs to themselves. But she had gone to Europe and the matter had passed out of her mind. The letter went on to say: *I was under the impression that if you were made aware of the justice of* my claims you would pay them, as a matter of simple honesty. (The impertinence of the follow!) *I was too poor to have an investigation, although I knew from my father and other bondholders in the mine, that the deal had not been a fair and square one. I clubbed in with three other bondholders whom I knew of here in New York, and employed Mr. Fanshaw, an expert in his line of business, to investigate the matter. He will call on you with this letter, and the result of his investigations, which I am sure, for the sake of your father's memory, you will consent to examine. I hope sincerely, that the necessity of putting the matter in the hands of my attorney may not arise.* (Indeed, your attorney! That is rather a fine phrase, Mr. Robert Morgan, but you forget, I think, that you are addressing Charles Clayton's daughter, and that she is not one to be terrified by your littte scheme of blackmail.)

I beg to subscribe myself, very respectfully yours,
Robert E. Morgan.

Crushing the letter into a heap, and tossing it on her desk, Marguerite went down to the library to hear what Fanshaw, the detective, would have to say. She thought of referring him to Mr. Dalton, but the matter seemed too absurd, besides, Mr. Dalton had strenuously opposed her scheme in regard to the Bienvenues, and he would be more than human to resist the temptation to say: "I told you so."

She found a little man with reddish, closely cropped hair, and a short straight, reddish mustache; he had keen, blue-gray eyes, looking out from reddish eyebrows, shaggy and heavy, as if to afford concealment for the secrets it was his professional duty to ferret. He was dressed with scrupulous neatness in a new fall suit, his hands were small and white, and seemed to grasp firmly any thing confided to their keeping, as if they were a reflex in a material way, of his predominant mentality. He acted like a gentleman, although his manners did not seem to fit him naturally, and arose, with a very deep bow, as Marguerite entered the room. He came at once to the matter in hand, and with an occasional reference to his note book for names and dates, proceeded as calmly and coolly, as if he had been recounting a history of researches in Egypt, to unfold one of the completest schemes of villainy that had ever escaped the penitentiary. The documents laid before Marguerite, sworn affidavits, of people who had lived in the neighborhood of the mine all their lives, copies of freight bills for ore, investigations of mining experts, more than all, the confession of an ignorant accomplice — every thing went to prove, beyond all doubt, that the Golconda Mining Company was one gigantic swindle from the first moment of its organization to the paying of bogus dividends which had been declared. A scheme pure and simple to get money for what was not, and never had been, in existence, for ore that had never been found. It was a perfectly plain case of a 'Salted mine,' a 'Wildcat' speculation. The only thing not plain about it was how the affair had been carried through on such a colossal scale, for millions were at stake, and how the scheme had escaped detection and the relentless clutches of the law. Fanshaw did not seem to notice the increasing faintness of the girl. To him the interview was merely another step in the successful accomplishment of the task assigned him, and professional pride in having succeeded, in spite of great obstacles, apparently overshadowed every other consideration. He was accustomed to sin and shame and suffering in others — they were inalienably associated with his profession, an integral part of it. It did not seem to occur to him that he was speaking to an only child of her dead father, as he went on to show conclusively that the foundations of the fortune which had given her an envied place among the fortunate few of this terrestrial sphere, were laid on a terrible wrong; that in a word, she had been enjoying all her life the reward of stolen gains.

But his satisfaction was purely professional; such as a physician might feel who had successfully probed for a bullet, a historian who had found a precious and long missing document, necessary to complete his immortal work, a sculptor gazing at the finished statue, which had grown to rare proportions under his plastic touch, an artist wrapped in admiration before the picture destined for the Academy. It was not his fault that the materials for his success were so unsavory. In his vocation he lost his character as a man, and became simply the detective. Marguerite, whom he might regard as a beautiful and charming example of American maidenhood, in his moments of relaxation in private life, if by any chance he should meet her there, became simply a part and parcel of his work; no more than the clay or the canvas

to the artist or the sculptor. He unfolded all the
details, dilating on the nicety of the scheme, its
absolute immunity from the law, waxing enthusiastic
over the complications, as having afforded
scope for some fine strokes. In his evident triumph
over a difficult task perfectly accomplished, he
seemed, to Marguerite, a fiend incarnate. Was she
dreaming, or was it a waking nightmare, and this
man a devil in human shape sent to goad her to
desperation. Her hands trembled so that she could
hardly hold the papers he gave her to read; her
lips were getting white with purplish rings around
them, but it was only when she pressed her hand
to her heart to stay its gnawing pain, did he appear
to remember. "Why Miss Clayton, you had nothing
to do with it; and these little things will happen
in business sometimes. You must not mind. I am
employed to lay these proofs before you, but I regret
sincerely, that I have been forced to cause you annoyance."
And he had laid the proofs before her!
There was, there could be no doubt; there they
were, staring at her in all their naked hideousness.

She got up to open a window, the very room
seemed contaminated with something oppressive,
sickening, dreadful. She must have fresh air,
her limbs trembled, and she staggered like a
man intoxicated. What had come over her,
what had happened. The little onyx clock was
ticking away; it was just an hour since she had
entered the room, so happy, confident, secure,
haughty too, at this Morgan's impertinence. The
sun was shining so brightly then, what had happened
to it now, why was she so cold? What was

this terrible burden that was pressing her heart to the very floor, what nightmare had taken possession of her, was she going crazy? She could not stand it.

"This concerns Mrs. Clayton quite as much as it does me. Wait, I will send her to you," and with a springing movement Marguerite dashed out of the room. She went up the stairs two steps at a time, and knocked at her step-mother's door. She found that matron busy over the intricacies of a bill which seemed extortionate, for her eldest darling's fall frocks. The room was elegant, tasteful, supremely luxurious. Money, money was everywhere; it was only saved from the effect of vulgarity which wealth, simply as wealth, conveys, by touches of real artistic genius, purchased along with the carpet and the hangings and the bric-a-brac. As it was, it was beautiful, this boudoir of the ex-widow of Anthony Wall, the caterer.

"I have just come from seeing Fanshaw, a detective; papa has left a terrible debt we must pay," Marguerite panted, sinking into a chair.

Mrs. Clayton could not divest her mind all at once from buttons and silk linings, which cost more than buttons and silk linings had ever cost before, to a consideration of bygone debts.

"Why, what is the matter, Mr. Dalton settled all poor papa's debts; those matters were attended to long ago."

"Oh, but this is someting else: Here you can see for yourself," cried the girl, flinging over the papers Mr. Fanshaw had given her, copies of the originals kept in his own possession.

"And you want me and my children to buy these absurd bonds," exclaimed Mrs. Clayton angrily, forgetting for the moment the habitual sweetness with which she clothed herself, as with a mask, when speaking to her husband's daughter.

"I want you to pay your proportion with me."

At the end of the explanations Mrs. Clayton was angrier than ever.

"What insane folly is this," she exclaimed. "Why, it would take over two million dollars to settle these claims. Shall we beggar ourselves because in a business transaction your father succeeded, and other men went under?"

"But this is something besides business. Papa was human and he yielded to temptation, he was not the first man to fall, but it rests with us to put an end to the suffering as far as we can, which he caused."

"At the cost of untold suffering to ourselves! You must be crazy to think of such a thing," said Mrs. Clayton, then seeing the angry flash in her step-daughter's eyes, she was warned to trim in her sails. Marguerite was not accustomed to being spoken to in just that tone, and Mrs. Clayton had reasons of her own for wishing to remain friends; a family quarrel was always vulgar in the first place, and in the second, she owed not a little of her success with the really nice people to her step daughter's presence. People had come to the house during the past year who had steadily ignored her very existence before, and she was not one to jeopardize her own interests recklessly. And, crowning reason of all, she did not forget that in the angry, aroused girl she saw the future Countess of Parkhurst.

"Why my dear child, you must not think of compromising your interests so recklessly. Mr. Dalton attends to your father's affairs, and he is the best one to decide these business questions. You ought not to have seen the man at all. The whole thing is probably a hoax to extort money from your youth and inexperience. Why did he not come to me?"

Marguerite was struck with the sense of the last question, although she could not think, for one happy instant, that there was any hoax in the matter. Seeing that Marguerite was impressed, Mrs. Clayton continued: "Besides, you surely would not be so wanting in respect to your father's memory as to stigmatize him as a thief, and that is what this fellow's proposal means."

"But papa was a man, fallible and peccable like other men, and if he made a mistake I am sure he would want to rectify it, to atone for whatever error he was lead into by a business transaction. I am sure that we could be showing no greater respect for him than to pay any just claims that might be against him." Marguerite spoke earnestly with the hope of convincing her step-mother without needless delay. "And if Mr. Dalton thinks the debt a just one," she continued, "then will you and your daughters be ready to pay your share of it?"

"Mr. Dalton is not such a fool; he will not listen to such an absurd proceeding for a moment. I wont listen to any thing of the kind. I have no right to beggar my children for a whim."

"It is not a question of beggary, since my father left them two millions each. But they might have been beggars excepting for your bounty, had I consented to contest my father's will, as I could easily have done."

There was no mistaking that both the girl and the woman of the world were now thoroughly aroused. Mrs. Clayton controled herself however, and even simulated a degree of composure, as she left the room to dismiss the waiting detective. She turned back to say mildly: "See Mr. Dalton, Marguerite, and don't do any thing rash."

The advice was not needed for Marguerite had already determined to see Mr. Dalton as speedily as possible.

Her gray, and very level headed guardian, was just pulling on his gloves, preparatory to going out for the hurried luncheon which American millionaires permit themselves in the middle of the day, if business be not too pressing, when the girl swept like a small whirlwind into his private office, and demanded an interview on important business. She clutched desperately to the last straw of hope that Mr. Dalton could dispel in some way this ugly cloud which had gathered so suddenly in the horizon of her young life.

He listened in silence to her story, poured out in a torrent of words, but he made no attempt to discredit it, and Marguerite in her passionate longing, was ready to accuse him of heartlessness, indifference to her interests. He examined the papers, carefully, judicially.

"My dear child, this is an ugly business, an ugly

business. I heard something of it ten years ago, but the matter was hushed, and I had not supposed it was any thing serious. When you came to me about those Bienvenues my mind reverted to the transaction after you were gone, and I made some examinations of old papers and accounts which lead me to believe that the Golconda Mine had — had been slightly misrepresented to the stock holders. There was a suspicion that the mine had been floated on wildcat securities. I did not care to make a full investigation. I had not the chance nor any cause to do so, and it would serve no good purpose. But after studying the matter, I thought if you wanted to make it all right with the Bienvenues, I would not object."

"Oh that was the reason," said Marguerite, under her breath.

"You know, Marguerite, in business, men sometimes forget themselves, and go to lengths in these ventures which promise such stupendous returns, they would not dream of in calmer moments. The times were ripe then for all sorts of speculations. The conditions of the market and of the public mind were peculiarly susceptible to — to," he hesitated for a word, and then compromised on a change of sentence. "Your poor father probably got in deeper than he intended, and was carried along with, the current. I was not here at the time — your father was making money, and big money too, when I went away, and when I came back I found him a millionaire two or three times over. He told me only in a general way that his mining ventures had been dazzlingly successful, and regretted that I had gone out of them when I did go. "But I had been successful too, in a way, in South America, so I did not repine; and I never had your father's head for speculations. He probably intended to make every thing all right with the Golconda stock holders; but death sometimes overtakes us before our resolutions can become accomplished facts. Your father made a great deal of money, an enormous lot of money in deals that were perfectly fair, indeed I never knew him to be engaged in any other kind. And you must not judge him by this one transaction."

"Then you mean to admit that my father was really dishonest — actually cheated all these people who bought Golconda stock. That he really did know all along that the mine was worthless, and that the dividends he paid never came out of the mine. Oh Mr. Dalton, I must be dreaming. This is surely some jest, or else I am really going crazy. Mamma said I was crazy."

"My dear little girl, you must not judge your father hastily. He has gone where justice is meted out to each and every one."

"I am not judging him, but I cannot spend another happy moment until this money is all refunded. The people who gave their money under false pretences must have it back again. You must make my step-mother see this at once, at once."

"I do not think, Marguerite, in fact I am sure that the stock holders cannot do any thing legally against the estate. The matter is outlawed in the first place by the statute of limitations, and in the second, these proofs, whilst convincing enough, would not hold good in any court of law. And I think they realize this fact, or they would not have gone to you. This Morgan's threat is only a bluff, although he might make an ugly scandal."

"The law has nothing to do with it, if the claim be a just one. I don't care for the law, Mr. Dalton," and Marguerite looked up with a mild reproach in her eyes that her guardian could have implied that she did.

"But Mrs. Clayton may. At any rate you had better not say any thing more to her, and I will call this afternoon, and have a talk with her. I do not think she would care to have the matter brought into the courts, merely for the looks of the thing. Your step-mother banks a good deal on appearance."

Marguerite smiled. The old gentleman had studied human nature to some purpose. In his mind he had very serious doubts as to Mrs. Clayton's willingness to part with any of her precious ducats.

"You have nine million among the four of you," he continued, "so you might settle the matter satisfactorily without seriously crippling any one. And I think, Marguerite. that your father, if he could speak from the grave, would wish you to do just what you propose. Of course, it is not a matter which I can settle officially as your guardian, for it is, so far as I can judge, purely a matter of honor, and the law does not take cognizance of affairs of honor in a trustee's report of his trust. But you will be of age in two months, and at liberty to do as you please. I am sometimes troubled in my mind that we did not contest your father's will. As a rule it seems a shameful thing to do, this contesting of wills, although I cannot but believe there was undue influence. Your father never seemed so fond of those Wall girls as far as I knew, and I was at the house constantly. But as I said, I will see Mrs. Clayton this afternoon."

XXV.

MRS. CLAYTON was even more obdurate in her refusal to consider any proposition in regard to the Golconda bondholders than Mr. Dalton, in his moments of thinking worst of her, had expected. He talked more plainly to her than he had to Marguerite, telling her without circumlocution that had the matter been ventilated in the courts at the proper time, and by the right sort of a lawyer, there would have been a fair prospect of her husband's spending a few years in Sing Sing. She was too shrewd and too cool to be moved by a retroactive danger. It had not been taken to the courts, her lawyer told her that it could not be now, at least with any possibility to the bondholders' gaining any thing, and what mattered danger that was past. She was not legally bound, and therefore, not morally so. Mr. Dalton wondered in what particular school of theology she had imbibed her very convenient creed.

"Well, there is nothing to be done, Marguerite," began the faithful guardian. "Neither threats nor entreaties, the law of the land nor the law of heaven can move your father's widow. I do not think there is any danger of the affair's getting to the courts; Morgan realizes that he has no case, and besides he has no money to prosecute it."

Marguerite left Mr. Dalton's office after an interview, in which the fruitless result of his mission had been discussed, feeling a sort of relief. The matter had weighed on her mind, interfering with other considerations more personal and more pleasant. But she had not gone half a block when the terrible thought came to her: If the debt be a just one are you not bound to pay it regardless of your stepmother? "Why of course not; I am bound to pay one fourth, I am willing, nay anxious to do that, and to do it as soon as possible, but the whole — Absurd! Why should I be responsible for all the debts when I received only one fourth of the estate?

"Why has such a horrible thought come over me! Oh! why did not Mr. Dalton force that Wall woman to give up the money which belongs to another?" The girl felt that she disliked her stepmother more than she ever had as a child.

"Why did I fail to insist that Mr. Dalton pay off one fourth of the debt at once; one fourth, half a million, — Paul will not like that, but it must be deducted from the amount to be settled exclusively on myself. I cannot spend another cent in any peace until I have paid my part."

"But what right have you, to any of the money in your possession," said the inner voice. "You did not earn it, it came to you as a gift from your father, and what right had he to make such a gift with his just debts unpaid."

"Am I really going crazy that such hideous fancies come to me!" Marguerite put up her hand as if to ward off some malignant presence pursuing her.

But the presence had come to stay. It haunted her like a spectre, clouding all her days and making the nights a torture. It was in vain that she said her fortune was legally and rightfully her own. She thought indignantly, 'why was the woman, who had wheedled her father into making his most unjust will, left in peace, and the debt placed like a pall over her life, so happy but for that! Why not ask her spiritual director — he would surely tell her that the uneasiness was merely a temptation, that of course she was not bound excepting *pro rata* for her share. But maybe he would not! Better let the matter alone until she was of age. In three weeks after that date she would be married, for the wedding had been fixed for the fourth Wednesday in January, and then she would have the broad shoulders and the cool head of Paul to bear her burdens.'

In a spasm of moral rectitude she wrote to the Earl that her affairs were very much involved, and hinted at great losses and even possible penury. She was like a cat toying with a mouse she meant to let go free.

The letter sent consternation to the heart of the noble lord at the first reading, but on a second perusal he smiled. He had undoubted warrant for believing that Marguerite's millions were about as safe as millions could well be, so he explained away the letter as a joke, or as a test of his affection. He was half disposed to be angry with the girl. Those stupid romances with their nonsense about the world well lost for love, and all that absurdity, were at the bottom of it.

"'I did not think that Marguerite would do any thing of this sort, she has such good taste generally, and she is too clever to be caught in any sentimental, crazy scheme. And Dalton is as honest as the bank of England." So he pigeon-holed the missive with restored complacency. He was tempted for one foolish, tender moment to write a lover's real love letter, filled with all the assurances so dear to the feminine heart, but the mood passed away, and he wrote instead, a spritely epistle, telling her to consult Tanner on fasting, and that gruel was both nourishing and cheap.

Marguerite played with the idea of restitution, but in an abstract, philosophical way. She developed a fondness for the discussion of ethical problems into which she skillfully interwove hypothetical cases analogous to her own, especially with Carroll Kirwin. She shrank from going to one whose mission in life was to settle just such questions, from the same feeling, perhaps, which makes the doomed consumptive defer asking his physician's final verdict. Kirwin gave her an uneasy shock by saying that the person would be morally bound for the whole. She had confidence in him, she thought that his fine legal mind was trained to habits of logical reasoning, and that his high moral rectitude would not permit of his playing with equivocations either professionally or in private life; the dividing line of all questions with him, she was sure, would lie between right and wrong. But she was now disposed to think that she had rated him too highly. It was at an informal little dinner at Mrs. Kingman's that he had given this opinion.

Mrs. Kingman was a capital hostess, and every Saturday evening for many years, she was in the habit of assembling a few congenial spirits around her dainty table. Invitations to these dinners were more prized than those to her formal affairs; for the latter were like the formal affairs of everybody else, but the Saturday dinners to the little coterie of intimates, had a charm all their own.

"I am not just in the right state of mind to discuss these intricate problems of *meum* and *tuum*, Miss Clayton," Carroll had continued. "There are always so many modifying circumstances when these cases occur in real life that no hypothetical statement ever elicits a practical decision."

Marguerite sat, outwardly smiling and nervously tearing a rosebud to pieces, as the young man riddled her rebutting arguments, arguments which she vaguely felt at the uttering, were sophisms. She admitted that she was no match for a lawyer in a discussion.

"A man who obtained money under false pretences—dishonestly, not to beat about the bush,"—continued Kirwin, "is morally bound in conscience to make restitution; his estate is liable for his obligations. His heirs have rights only to the property left from his just debts."

"How about the homestead exemption?" queried Raymond.

"That is another thing. That question has been settled by the law of the land."

"But according to Miss Clayton's statement, the law of the land cannot touch this case. What is fish for one ought not to be fowl for another."

"Really Raymond, I cannot follow more than one question at a time, especially after such a very excellent dinner.

A man must be just before he can be generous. Justice requires him to pay his debts. The heirs have a right to an estate over and above the just debts against it. Of course all the heirs are equally bound, just as all partners in a business firm are equally bound. But as in business, each partner is liable for the debts of the whole firm, so each heir is liable to the debts against the estate to the extent of his inheritance. If a man leaves twenty thousand dollars and owes me one thousand, I am entitled to that one thousand; I have nothing to say about the other nineteen; if he wills the nineteen thousand to one man who leaves the country, with all his wordly goods and cannot be found, and but one thousand to another man who is honest and remains within call, I may be very sorry, but nevertheless I want my money, and as my claim comes ahead of the heir's, the one available thousand belongs to me."

Raymond thought the comparison not a very good one, for the law would have taken charge of the estate, and the debts would have been paid before the legacies.

"There was an *If* all the way through, in both cases," answered Kirwin. "And Miss Clayton's case, if she will pardon me, is more improbable, a great deal, than mine."

The matter was debated warmly, but Carroll was firm in maintaining that the creditors would have first claim.

Raymond thought that an heir would be bound only in proportion to his inheritance. If he inherited but one twentieth of the estate then he would be liable for only one twentieth of the debts. Edith said of course that was the way, and that she was surprised at Carroll Kirwin claiming anything else.

"Well, as my opinion can have no effect one way or another we can all agree to disagree," said Carroll. "I confess that I am beginning to feel quite as if I were in the court-room, or in one of those little boxes in church where all good Catholics take such questions."

"Marguerite, go sing something. We have had enough of law and the catechism and the Ten Commandments," said Mrs. Kingman.

"Yes do," seconded Edith. "Sing us a ballad about hearts and darts, and the deap sad sea and lovers coming to me, something awfully sentimental, in short, to counteract this legal-ethical flavor to our dinner."

Marguerite declined pitifully, said she could not sing, that her head ached, and her voice was husky, but the importunities of the company, of Mrs. Kingman especially, who did not believe much in girlish headaches, prevailed, and she went to the piano.

She complied literally with Edith's suggestion, and as she sang, her voice really sounded like the wail of a broken or breaking heart.

"Mazzini does teach a girl to put more thrills that make for a fellow's heartstrings, to the square inch in a song than any other teacher I know of," said Raymond, as Marguerite left the piano for a picturesque, though unstudied pose by the mantel.

She refused positively to sing again.

"Miss Clayton has left us feeling that a whole shipful of our sweethearts and all our hopes have gone to the bottom; Miss Kingman must be the diver to bring them to the surface again," continued Raymond.

Thus abjured, Edith picked up her banjo and dashed into a lively glee, which brought smiles of appreciation to every one but Marguerite, and her depression was successfully concealed under the convenient plea of a headache.

"Miss Clayton did not seem very well to-night," said Kirwin with a note of concern in his voice, to John Raymond, as they sauntered out into the clear, calm November night.

"She has been dissipating too much perhaps, and she is not very strong. Parkhurst will be coming back soon, and then her spirits will revive," answered Raymond, eyeing his companion rather curiously.

He shared Edith's opinion that Carroll Kirwin was in love with Marguerite, or at least that he ought to have been.

But Carroll spoke calmly enough, when he said that he hoped Parkhurst appreciated his luck; that Miss Clayton was a beautiful girl and deserved the brightest and best that life could offer.

XXVI.

AT times it seemed to Marguerite that her cross was greater than she could bear. She had heard of people going insane or getting dangerously ill under the stress of a great mental agony, and she wondered why it was that she was able to bear so much inwardly, with so few outward marks. She scanned her own face eagerly in the mirror to see if the lines of trouble were forming around mouth and eyes, but beyond a purplish blotch under each eye, and a slight pallor, there was no outward indication of her suffering. She was unable to do any thing, and would be so long as her minority lasted, but beyond that—she shuddered and resolutely refused to think of the future. She sometimes fancied she was the victim of a moral obliquity of vision which prevented her seeing the affair in its true light. She was not responsible, it was only a terrible temptation of of the Power of Darkness which made her think she was. What had she to do with her father's business. There were other men, almost at her very door, who did every day, and over and over again in different forms, just what her father had done; and people called them shrewd, sharp fellows, and envied their luck, and no one but the carping few, thought of blaming them, or calling them dishonest. Why should this hideous thing come to torture her? Then her mind was cleared as the atmosphere is cleared by an electric flash, and she saw herself the possessor of a fortune wrung from unsuspecting victims. She stood horrified at herself, for not being horrified at the association of dishonesty and her father's memory.

"Something must happen! I cannot go on in this way, it is killing me," cried the girl. "I can not stand it. Oh Paul, Paul, why are you not here to shield me, to save me—from I know not what."

When she received Parkhurst's letter, so gay, bantering, teasing, loving in tone, but with no word of the assurance she was longing for with all the fervor of her quivering heart, that loss of money was as nothing to him, that they would manage, somehow, to live and save money on nothing a year, an icy numbness swept over her very soul.

"Oh! why does not Mr. Dalton make my step-mother do what she ought — I cannot give it all. There is no justice in that. Shall I, my father's only child pay his debts and beggar myself, and those women with no claims on him live in luxury and honor? Never." She forgot that one of them had been his wife.

With this decision reiterated almost every hour, in her mental consciousness, she went on with the preparations for her coming wedding, and the daily rounds of the winter's pleasures.

Mrs. Kingman was the first to notice that there was any thing seriously wrong with Marguerite.

"She has not been feeling very well lately, you know she was never very strong, and the excitement and every thing have been too much for her," Edith had said in reply.

"I think, my dear, that it is more than merely not feeling well — a physical indisposition. There is something on her mind if I am not very much deceived. Has she and Lord Parkhurst had a quarrel, or anything like that?"

Edith declared with certainty that the love affair of her friend was running smoothly, all proverbs to the contrary, and laughed at the idea that Marguerite was in trouble.

"She is passionately attached to her own land, and the thought of going away to England to live may have a depressing effect at times, but nothing more serious, I am sure. Or she may be contemplating some grand scheme of charity which Mr. Dalton vetoes, or something of that kind. You never can be certain about Marguerite; she is always doing or thinking the unexpected. But she tells me every thing, and I would be sure to know, right away if she were in trouble about any thing."

And Marguerite had told Edith every thing, until the one Great Trouble came to her, which she did not tell.

She suddenly developed an unusual fondness for seeking out the poor, and contributing every cent she could spare to charities. She would make her money an instrument of good as she had so long dreamed. She went to the Bienvenues and begged, almost implored, to be allowed to defray all the expenses of Kit's musical education, and the bills for the best medical aid the city afforded, for the crippled leg. They finally consented to accept the latter half of her offer, but merely as a loan to be repaid in installments.

By acts of charity she succeeded in lulling her conscience, and was beginning to take some pleasure in her wonted affairs, when in an idle hour, she went to a matinee. It was a sensational play which turned on restitution. The usurper of the estate was an intriguing adventuress; Marguerite was conscious of being the very antipode of this type, but the play left its mark on her, a depressing effect which she tried in vain to shake off. It was a dull gloomy day, and by nightfall it had begun to rain and sleet, not violently, but with a stubborn persistence, and the wind blew just enough to send moans around the eaves, and to rattle, with ghostly ghoulishness, the heavy shutters of the double windows. Although invited to a large reception, the first really Big Affair of the season, she declared her intention of taking a night off, and going to bed for a good sleep.

She tossed about for a while, thinking of the family in the play, not unlike the Bienvenues, who had come into their own only by the death-bed confession of the adventuress; of her father; of Robert Morgan; of the faithful lover in the play, who had a mustache, and was little and fat, and not in the least like her darling; then she gradually lost consciousness and passed out of her own personality into that of the adventuress; then she was the victim, the beautiful brave girl who was the heroine of the play; then her father came, and she was a little girl again back in California; but all the time there was the money and that terrible woman. Divergent images lurking for years in some subtle depths of the brain, had been precipitated by the afternoon's sensations, and were now woven into the fabric of a troubled dream. Her father appeared to her again, not as she had ever known him, but clothed in the habiliments of the ghost which had sent wild shivers racing up and down her spine, the first time she had seen Booth in Hamlet. He looked so sad, so very sad as he seemed to emerge from his grave in beautiful Greenwood; she could see the cemetery plainly in her dream, just as she had seen it in the early autumn days, when she had gone with Edith to pay her accustomed visit. Rising easily from his last narrow bed, despite the tall granite shaft resting on it, he came to her couch, and pointing with one, long, ghostly finger into unknown regions of horror, murmured in the deep sepulchral voice, crystallized forever in Tragedy as the voice of the dead :

"Until the last farthing has been paid."

She awoke with that icy hand clutching at her throat, and her heart beating with frantic madness against her bosom. She sprang out of bed and touched the button which sent a blaze of light through the room.

"What a hideous, horrible, terrible dream. Ugh!" She crouched down by the smouldering embers of the grate, and tried to stir them into life again. Then she looked at the dainty silver timepiece ticking away on the mantel. "Why it is only twelve o'clock. It doesn't agree with me to go to bed so early. I ought to have gone to Mrs. Van Horn's. I suppose Edith is talking to John Raymond, and having a lovely time."

She picked up a book and attempted to read, then she knelt down and tried to say some prayers, and then she crept back to bed, but leaving the light still aglow.

And still that voice kept sounding in her ears: "UNTIL THE LAST FARTHING HAS BEEN PAID."

The next day she took down the Bible and hunted up the fateful passage. She turned the pages at random, reading a text here and there. Certainly, there was not in the Sacred Writings much account made of happiness, as understood in modern times.

"Verily, it is as easy for a camel to pass through the eye of a needle as for a rich man to enter Heaven."

She had heard sermons on that text. It had seemed very clear and simple to her then. It meant that one should not get attached to riches so as to object to leaving them; to love money more than God, more than one's soul. It was not meant literally, of course, and explanations made it very easy. There had never been any thing personal in it, before. But it came to her now with added and most terrible force.

"Was she so attached, not to her money, but to all that her money would bring, to the human love it was securing, the pleasures, the honor, the ease, all that this earthly existence could offer of bliss, as to prefer it to her father's soul, to her own?" She closed the Book.

"Why am I tortured so? Why do I yield to these miserable temptations? I am *not* responsible."

And then that malignant voice:

"UNTIL THE LAST FARTHING HAS BEEN PAID."

She went down to a large bookstore, and bought all the works she could find, bearing on the legal and moral obligations of restitution; on the Rights of the Living; on the Condition of the Dead.

Was her father still lingering in some terrible charnel house, her thoughts took on unconsciously, the Shaksperean language — doomed to stay there for years, centuries, till the end of time, waiting for some one to pay his living debt. The thought was maddening. She would make another appeal to her step-mother. She would threaten her with the law, with a scandal, a great public exposure, any thing to make her yield.

"I never cheated, I would not harm any one for the world. I want only my own. My father repented I know, if there had been any wrong doing." "But remorse is not restitution," whispered that terrible voice. Prudence told her that she could gain nothing by bringing up the matter again, with her step-mother. She bore the conflict as long as she could, in silence, and then went to Mr. Dalton.

He had always said that she possessed a business head worth something when she chose to use it, and that her talents developed in all sorts of unexpected directions when emergencies called for them, despite her whims, and her general girlish helplessness.

She explained to him frankly and without reserve, all her scruples, her upbraidings of conscience in regard to the bonds.

"I know perfectly well that my step-mother will not do any thing unless she is forced. But could you not hunt up this Morgan, and a few more of the bondholders, and have them bring a suit. Of course she knows, and they know, that they could not gain it. But you could go to her with a full account of all the dreadful things that would come out in the trial, and for very shame she might be induced to pay off these claims. I shall never know another moment's peace until they are paid."

"I will think over your plan, my child. But frankly I don't like it," answered Mr. Dalton, after a pause. This woman knows more than you think. And she is prepared to defy every one of us and every thing. Don't say any thing more to her about the matter. And I will do my best, little girl. You know that."

The matron and the maid were still living under this truce when, a few days later, invitations were received to a large reception.

"I am not sure about these Carsons. New York is getting so big, and new people are constantly pushing in, that one never knows who is who," said Mrs. Clayton, toying with the envelope in her hand.

This seemed to Marguerite, who was in one of her bitter moods, the very height of assurance coming from the queen of the Pushers herself; she was perfectly familiar with this well preserved matron's history.

"No body had ever heard of these Carsons five years ago, and one can't be too careful with girls," went on the perplexed mother.

"Well, we can be sure of one thing," answered Marguerite, with the light of a smouldering fire in her eyes. "The house, and the pictures, and the carriage, and even the people, are new, very new as you say, but at least, their things are paid for. Mr. Carson may not be very polished, or used to society ways, the hand which he offers with his old fashioned hospitality, old country if you will, may be hard and large, and not particularly refined looking, but it is an honest hand, a clean hand, the brand of a thief is not on it. His family may not be just as high-bred as some other's, but the money which makes them what they are, is honest money. There are no widows and orphans going hungry, and in want of the necessaries of life, that they may give a banquet to other rich people who do not care for it, and who may perhaps, forget the laws of good-breeding so far as to sneer at them behind their backs, they can offer it with a clear conscience. The tears of victims do not mingle with the wines of their feasts, they do mingle with ours. Who are we that we should be taking airs to ourselves? Twenty years ago my father was a hard-working son of the people, and yours was the same. My father left me a fortune, and you married one. — If we paid the just claims which my father would come back from the grave to pay if he could, if we saved his name from being dragged through the mire of a disgraceful suit, and remembered with curses by hundreds whose money we are spending to-day, we would neither of us be as rich as we are. And don't fancy that because we go every where and are received with kindness, that people have forgotten your father's little grocery store and your husband's oysters; the world has a long memory when it comes to these things. I have not forgotten my father's mining pick and I have no desire to forget it."

Mrs. Clayton listened to this outburst with a

feeling of stupefaction, then a wave of anger came near carrying her off her mental balance, but Marguerite went on without giving her a chance to say any thing. She had often suspected that there were possibilities of temper, hardly dreamed of, in her step-daughter, but the reality exceeded all her calculations. She had steadfastly ignored Marguerite's coolness since the matter of the Golconda bonds had come up for discussion. She did not forget that a quarrel would be a quarrel with the future Countess of Parkhurst, and so she heaped coals of fire on the other's head by being unusually sweet. In the present instance, what ever she might have been tempted to say remained unsaid, for Marguerite, feeling that her tears were coming, the tears of anger, indignation, futile desire, wild longing, — dashed out of the room and went to her own apartment. She remembered Mr. Dalton's injunction too late, and was sorry enough for her outburst.

"Why Marguerite Clayton, did I ever in my life!" exclaimed the widow, surprised into a momentary return to the semi-slang of her youth and obscurity.

The Carsons intended that their party should be one of the Great Functions of the season, and they did not purpose that its influence, operating for their own social advancement, should stop with the season. Their mother, with the adaptability of the American mother to circumstances, especially when the Americanism is of Celtic origin, had determined that her children should go with the best; naturally then the coming function was the subject of their conversation, often recurred to, and never satisfactorily disposed of. It had had the effect of sending Mr. Carson, every evening, to a club which had recently elected him, after the first week of domestic discussions. He could not see that his children were not the best, already. Certainly, the new home had been written about in all the papers, and pictures of his daughters given in a weekly journal devoted to society, just as if they were of the nobility in Europe, or the children of a president; every body in New York knew that he was worth any where from twelve to twenty million dollars.—If his family were not the best, then who were any better ? was what he would like to know.

"I am not sure that we did just right in inviting that Mrs. Clayton and those Wall girls," said the mother; "I heard young Blakely at Mrs. Van Horn's the other night, laughing about her first husband, who it seems, wasn't a bit nice. But of course, it looks as if one could hardly invite that lovely Marguerite without inviting the rest, so long as they all live together."

"Mrs. Clayton goes every where now, and they say that when Marguerite Clayton is married to Lord Parkhurst, she intends going over to London to hunt up titled Englishmen for the Wall girls," interposed the elder Miss Carson languidly. She had been told in the Delsarte class, that the lily was her type.

"And Miss Clayton is just simply exquisite, and with the most distinguished manners of any girl I ever saw," exclaimed Miss Carrie Carson enthusiastically, looking up from a psychological novel it was the fashion just then to read, — a novel in which the author demonstrated his unconscious ignorance of applied psychology, after the manner of the average psychological novelist.

"And they say she is related through her mother to the Westchesters of Virginia, and the La Villiers of Louisiana, and some great family in Ireland" continued Carrie throwing aside her book.

"Oh, it is not a question of Miss Clayton, any body can tell she is an aristocrat, but of those Walls" interrupted the mother tentatively.

"But, mamma, those 'Walls' are regular belles now; why, they have millions of poor Mr. Clayton's money; they will be marrying into the peerage soon, and cutting us."

"Cutting us indeed, the assurance of some people!" retorted Mrs. Carson. And then this good matron, wife and mother, who twenty years before had washed her own dishes and put her half dozen little ones to bed, went on pencilling names on a list which she meant for her secretary, a young lady whose grandfather had been a senator, to copy.

"We simply can't invite every body," said the mother, after a silence. "This house is not half large enough, big as it is, to hold all that I would like to entertain."

"And yet we could put our friends into your little sitting room, mamma, and still have space for a few more," said Carrie, who was unpleasantly frank at times.

"I am almost sorry we did not go to Sherry's and invite all the world, and then have a reception for the heavy swells later in the season, to show the house," said her sister.

The eldest Miss Carson was twelve years old before the family made its first upward move from the obscure little street where she was born, and the language of her early associations sometimes obtruded itself through the veneer of the best finishing schools of New York and Paris; 'heavy swell' was a survival of these early days.

"Leaving out the three Walls wouldn't help along a great deal," pursued Miss Carson, "none of them are very big. — And why Mamma, what are we thinking of ? Don't you know Mrs. Clayton, she is not a Wall any longer, will have the inviting of people to Marguerite's wedding. I wouldn't miss seeing that girl transformed into Lady Parkhurst for the half of Texas."

Thus in homes not many blocks apart decisions complementary to each other were reached. Mrs. Carson, after mature deliberation, decided to invite Mrs. Wall-Clayton, and Mrs. Wall-Clayton, after equally prolonged considerations, had decided to accept the invitation.

And the American Aristocracy, as embodied in plutocratic millions, went serenely on its upward way.

XXVII.

BY the middle of December the winter's pleasure had set in, in its accustomed grooves, and, as an irreverent young reporter phrased it, every thing was in prime running order. There were receptions, balls at Sherry's and Delmonico's, private parties, musicales, dinners and teas galore; potent wealth in one end of the town, hopeless poverty in the other — the poles which have always existed in the social world. The want and the suffering which Marguerite forced herself to see and to relieve as far as she could, exercised a depressing effect. Her heart bled with compassion, although her head in her calmer moments, told her that both suffering and want were often times, if not generally, the result of laziness, improvidence, a prevalent shiftlessness, when not of vice. When she went on a mission of charity after, being stirred to the very core, by some lurid account of the terrible condition of her fellow beings, she often found that a personal effort, at least in the beginning, could have obviated all difficultly. Older and wiser friends smiled tolerantly at her enthusiasm, and assured her that she would learn that neither Dives nor Lazarus was typical to any great extent, of the people in New York. The rich, whatever might or might not be their other faults, were charitable, generously so; and the poor could help themselves to a far greater extent than they did. There were suffering, starving women and children whose husbands and fathers maudled their days and nights in saloons; people were degraded and hopeless, diseased in body and mind, lost both to the desire and the ability to work, who in the beginning, might have made useful men and women of themselves.

"I tell you Marguerite, the virtuous poor in want exist in a mighty small proportion to the vicious poor in want," Mr. Dalton had said earnestly when vetoing some of her expenditures in the field of charity.

Still the girl could not help being moved at the thought of all the suffering whether just or unjust; so she tried not to think. Every thing in her own life was apparently bright and beautiful and good. Every thing around her was conducive to a grand, noble womanhood, admirable and happy. Money was a gift of God to be enjoyed as any of His other gifts. And the station of life to which it had pleased a beneficent Providence to call her, required the society, the manner of living, the amusements, the dress, the surroundings, most suited to her tastes; then why not accept them gratefully and be happy ?

Her friends vied with one another in lavishing attentions upon her, and this, her last winter of maidenhood and American freedom, would have been enjoyed to the utmost but for that terrible spectre standing so direfully in her path. For the most part she closed her eyes and refused to see it.

She was quietly resting at home one afternoon, in anticipation of the miles and miles she was going to dance that evening at the first of a series of subscription parties which were always events. Her maid interrupted her at the most interesting chapter of a new book to hand in a note which she recognized immediately as from Edith.

"I am awfully sorry," it ran, "but I cannot go with you this evening; Grace Farr is feeling quite unwell, and I am going to play sister of Charity on a small scale, and stay with her. Nothing serious, only a bad cold, her lungs always were weak you know."

Marguerite immediately set out for Mrs. Kingman's domicile only a few blocks away, and presuming on her intimacy with Edith as giving her a sort of vicarious relationship with Edith's connections, offered to accompany her to Mrs. Farr's bedside.

After some demur, the offer was accepted.

"You were always the sweetest, most unselfish girl in the world, Marguerite," said Edith, who was given to the use of superlatives. "Even at your worst you have streaks of virtue that leave the rest of us in the shade, and at your best you are simply angelic."

It was a cozy home into which the two were ushered, and where they, with the freedom of kinship and intimacy, went on up stairs to the sick chamber without waiting for a formal invitation. All the belongings of a cultivated taste, with the means for its gratification on a modest scale, were manifest every where. — The drawing-room with its dainty olive and old blue upholstery, its seductive divans, its Venice vases, signed etchings and bits of statuary — Margurite declared to be the most home-like drawing-room in New York.

The girls were rather taken back at finding Mrs.

Farr looking so ghastly; the effects of illness, although one is intellectually prepared for them, always strike the physical vision with something of the shock of a surprise.

Despite her evident suffering Mrs. Farr greeted the girls gaily, and chided Edith affectionately for staying away from the Assembly. "And keeping Marguerite too. There will be one, and I know not how many more disconsolate youths. And I am not very ill. The doctor thinks there is danger of pneumonia; but doctors don't know every thing; besides, I think he only said so to escape being rude to Ed, for he insists that I am very ill."

She was half reclining in bed, propped up by a sea of pillows. Her voice was husky, her temples hot, her hands feverish and dry, and her chest, she confessed, was paining her very much. Still she kept up a cheerful chatter with her visitors. It was a bright, dainty room, with something personal in it, so it seemed to Marguerite. She remembered that some people have the knack of giving this air to the most nondescript surroundings, and as Edith and Mrs. Farr both possessed it, conjectured that it was a hereditary trait, received from the Kingmans, since it was on that side the relationship existed.

There was a clatter on the hard asphalt outside, of carriages passing and repassing in a constant whirl. The noise was enough to set an ordinary invalid wild, but Mrs. Farr did not seem to mind it, and when Marguerite asked if it did not make her nervous, she said she rather liked it. Her bedroom opened into her boudoir, and through the half drawn portiere, Marguerite caught glimpses of a dainty coziness, even more pronounced than that of the rest of the house. It was not a wealthy home exactly, although in any other place than New York it might have been considered as such, but it was a home in every sense of the old fashioned word. Mrs. Farr did not appear to be much older than the girls themselves, and illness which sometimes ages its victims so dreadfully, only had the contrary effect on her. She was young in reality, younger than her boy, five years old — would lead one to imagine, if it were not remembered at the same time how very young some girls get married. Students of human affairs, especially if the affairs be American, would be more apt to concede the rule in the other direction, the preponderance being with the girls who marry late in life, at least late in girlhood; in fact, it is only by a total obliquity of imagination that they can be called girls at all.

In the midst of the chatter Mr. Farr came in walking with a quick, nervous tread, which betokened a solicitude not unmixed with anxiety. He bent over and kissed his wife with a caressing touch of the lips, regardless of the presence of the visitors, which, under ordinary circumstances would have restrained any manifestation of affection.

"And how are you feeling this evening, my darling, what did the doctor say, and have you taken your medicine regularly like a good girl?"

"To answer your questions backwards," began the wife laughingly, clasping her husband's hand, "I took the medicine, every nasty dose of it;

the doctor said hum! ah! ahem! then he shook his head, felt my pulse, examined my tongue, that poor overworked member of my body, and said nothing, like a certain talkative woman you claim to know. I am feeling — well, I am not feeling any worse."

Marguerite had noticed that when he entered the room he carried a box under his arm; he now picked it up from the nearest chair, on which he had deposited it, and with an air half of apology for being so lover-like after seven years of married life, opened it saying: "Here are some flowers Grace, dear; I happened to see some unusually fine roses at Peck's today."

This was his mode of confessing that he had gone out of his route on the way home to call at Peck's, and that he 'had happened to see' the great velvety beauties only after a special inquiry for the best in stock.

"And where is Edward Norrisson, Junior," he asked, having satisfied his anxiety in regard to his wife's condition.

"Poor little June! God bless his brave baby heart! I haven't seen him for three hours," answered the young mother. "He went up to the nursery just after luncheon with Sallie, to play horse."

The fond father left the room quickly, and soon reappeared with his son and heir riding in triumph on his shoulder.

The boy jumped down with the agility of a young monkey, and greeted his mother's guests with all the grace of a little gentleman. He was a handsome, manly boy with his mother's merry, innocent gray eyes, and his father's cast of features.

"He is all papa excepting the eyes, and they belong to me," Grace frankly acknowledged.

He clamored up on the bed and was smothered in his mother's arms.

"Poor little June, you must have been lonely all day, shut up in the nursery. Sallie was too busy to take him walking." Grace's first words were addressed to her son, the second part of the sentence was to her visitors.

"Yes we did Mamma, we went a long way," chimed in the lad. "And I saw Dave Chase on his pony. Papa mayn't I have a pony, a pony with a long mane and tail just like Dave's."

"Oh Grace! why do you persist in that odious name? The idea of calling a boy June, and your only boy at that," cried Edith, who was always objecting to this nickname of the little man of whom she was very fond. "I must call him something to distinguish him from his father. June, is simply an abbreviation, as you ought to know by this time, of Edward Norrisson, Junior."

"Why not call him Norrisson then, or call Ed, Edward, and little Ed simply Ed."

Mrs. Farr broke into a merry laugh, which was stopped by a dry cough.

"Ed, dear, would you know yourself as Edward?"

Her husband thus appealed to, acknowledged that his identity would be extremely doubtful.

"Little Ed, and big Ed," Marguerite suggested humorously.

"Marguerite, please don't say Ed, and Eddie" cried the wife and mother. "I really couldn't stand

Eddie. I had an old sweetheart once, that was before your time Ed, named Eddie, who was quite cherubic; his clothes were simply immaculate, and he had the sweetest smile, just like a girl's at her first party; 'Eddie' revives fond memories, but I want to keep the name for him alone. Come June, what shall your name be, I suppose you are getting too big for a pet name; now remember, darling, that your name for company is Norrisson, but you are mamma's own precious June."

The boy was not worried in the least about his name, and began to chatter of his day's doings with the happy unconcern of childhood as to illness and nerves. Then the father, ever on the alert where Grace was concerned, carried him over to a chair by the window for a regular romp. The boy shrieked with laughter, and the merriment proved infectious, every body laughing from sheer good humor.

When dinner was announced Mr. Farr wanted to stay with his wife, and was excusing himself to the girls for not taking them down, when Grace interrupted him: "Now Ed, like a Christian, I want you to go down stairs and eat your dinner; you had only a light luncheon, and besides, I am not a baby; I shall keep June with me for company, and Harriet wants to make up my bed whilst you are all away."

They did not linger long over the dinner, for the girls knew that their host, with all his high-bred hospitality, was longing to get back to his wife's bedside.

Edward Norrisson, Junior, was just finishing his

supper when they re-entered the room, having taken that repast from his mother's tea table.

"Mamma has been telling me a fairy story papa, and now I want you to tell me a bear story," announced the young man.

"From fairies to bears is rather a long stretch for the imagination of a little chap not six years old," protested the father. "Hadn't we better wait until tomorrow night for the bear?"

"I know Ed is dying for a smoke," cried Edith, who was not unfamiliar with the habits of the little household. "Marguerite does not object, and I am sure I do not. I once took a whiff at a cigar myself, though I never took another."

"Perhaps I had better go to the library," replied Farr with a questioning glance at his wife.

"Oh the girls are so very good, they won't mind," Grace replied. Then turning to Marguerite she said: "You see what it is to be married. Ed never dreamed of smoking in my presence when I was a girl; now he smokes any and everywhere as a matter of course; even my sitting room is not free from his cigars, and I am sure half of my friends think I indulge in cigarettes on the sly. You must begin at the beginning by being very severe." Marguerite blushed, but did not look displeased.

"Oh Marguerite wont have the spirit of a kitten; it takes me to manage a husband," cried Edith.

"Yes, I think you could Edith, you get that from your mother. I can remember very well that Aunt Mary always had her way, but Uncle James never suspected that he was a 'henpecked' husband. You take after your mother, Edith."

"Grace, my dearest little girl, I implore you, don't get started on the subject of heredity; your throat is not equal to the exertion. Why, even Gladstone would succumb under such a flow of ideas," interrupted her husband.

"No, that may be a hereditary trait with me, one never can tell," said Grace. "Edith has the same, she never gets tired talking, so I infer that it is a trait of the Kingmans'.

"You can laugh about heredity all you like, but it is one of the vital considerations in the training of children, and in the governing of ourselves."

"Hear, hear, she is going to govern herself," cried Farr.

"I lie awake at night wondering what sort of a man June is going to make. There are so many influences to be counteracted and characteristics to be studied in the training of American children," continued Grace soberly. "Now with other nations there are certain data to go by; the father and the mother, the grandparents and the great-grandparents, and on back to Adam, or at least to the flood, are of the same race; they have the same environment, the same training, the same conditions to a great extent, — like father like son; but with us — why! we are simply made up of odds and ends, and all sorts of extremes in surroundings and character come down to us. I have often thought that I should like to trace our families back to the very beginning, not that I anxiously yearn for an ancient genealogical tree, for I suspect that some of the branches would be quite rotten, but in the interests of science, and of June's education. When one thinks of atavism and all that, a mother can never be sure of the final outcome with her children. Whenever June does any thing peculiar, something that I never did as a child, and that Ed declares he never did, I straightway, want to look up that ancestor who in some age past, however remote, did do it. The currents and counter-currents of good and ill, not taking into account the effects of Original sin,—and we all believe in Original sin in spite of Darwin,—which a child inherits without any fault of his own, are simply appalling. If we could only trace our dispositions back to their sources it would be most interesting and most important in the training. Now, I get my temper from a Spanish great-grandmother; my looks from my father who was half Scotch, a fourth English and a fourth Irish. My mother was French, English and Scotch, fused into American of five generations. I do not know what I get from her, for she died when I was too small to remember her. Now, political and social economists are fond of attributing the greatness of the American nation to the favorable conditions of our laws and resources, but I am sure heredity has a greater claim than any thing else. Just think of all the different races that have contributed to the making of our country, their marriages and intermarriages. Why, we can expect almost any thing of the Americans of the future when atavism will have had time to get in its work.

To begin with we all have two parents —"

Farr said that he did not think any body would call into question that simple statement.

"Four grandparents, eight great-grandparents, sixteen of the fourth generation, thirty two of the fifth, sixty four of the sixth." — Here Grace called for a pencil and a piece of paper, which were immediately supplied by her husband out of one of the numerous pockets that are at once the envy and the despair of the feminine half of creation.

"One hundred and twenty eight of the seventh; two hundred and fifty six of the eighth; five hundred and twelve of the ninth —"

"That will do Grace; there aren't many of us Americans who can go back to the ninth generation," put in Farr.

"Well, I shall stop there but remember that heredity does not. And nine generations could easily be in two hundred years, and what are two hundred years to the old families in Europe! Why a family of nine generations only would be simply parvenues. But think of five hundred and twelve people who have married and intermarried in the direct line —"

"Please, please, Grace, don't get on the collateral or we shall simply be cycloned in traits and anatomical legacies," interrupted the husband.

"Well I wont, although the collateral line sometimes plays very curious pranks, but here are these hundreds of ancestors in the direct line; German, French, Irish, Scotch, English, Scandinavian —"

"Turk, Hottentot, Gentile, Jew," rattled Farr, in the tone of a waiter in a third class restaurant calling off the bill of fare.

"And likely as not the present generation not taking after any of them."

"That is the purest nonsense you know Ed. Of course they must take after some of them," retorted Grace.

"Well, and what does Miss Clayton say on this grave subject?" asked Farr.

"In the presence of such a vast array of learning I am dumb," answered Marguerite. "I am willing to concede with Grace, though, that it certainly is a very serious question."

"Why of course it is," asseverated the wife. "We can see traces of heredity in all the people we know well enough to judge of their characters, or if we have ever known any thing of their family connections. A thief is not always the result of circumstances and a neglected moral education. It may be because of something inate, inherited from a remote ancestor."

"We call that kleptomania," said Farr.

"No, I don't mean the cessation of will power, which distinguishes a kleptomaniac from a thief; but merely that such a person, in addition to the temptation to steal—the blunted moral sense he may have—has yet to fight against a natural inclination. The men who are making money to-day by dishonest, although not always illegal means, knowing them to be dishonest, are leaving a fearful heritage, along with their millions to their descendants. — Marguerite, you look pale: this room is too hot," broke off Mrs. Farr.

Marguerite straightened up, protesting that she felt very well.

"Why, Grace, would you do away with one stroke, the moral law, and our own individual responsibility?" asked her husband in shocked tones.

"Of course not, heredity only shows the absolute necessity of a moral law to restrain the natural inclinations. Why, it is only because of heredity that we have a moral law, or any necessity for one. If our First Parents had not eaten that apple we should have no conflicting traits and impulses. All our desires would be in harmony with the divine law which antedates the moral law. If Eve's children had been born as pure and perfect as Eve was herself at her creation, we would not have needed a moral law at all."

Edith confessed that this was getting too deep for her.

"There is heredity again. Uncle James never could bear to look below the surface of things," exclaimed Grace, triumphantly.

"If we have a natural love of the beautiful and the true, it shows that somewhere in the ancestral line our fathers lived nobly and to high purpose, while petty, mean traits point the reverse. Heredity explains why it is that, sometimes, good and noble parents have very mean, ugly children, and why on the other hand, we see the most refined, lovable, good children with coarse selfish parents. They may get their traits four or five generations back. Now, if we understood our ancestral line, had a chart of it as a navigator has a chart of the ocean, we would know just how to study our children and how to educate them to develop the good traits and eradicate the bad ones. I want to know about ours Ed, so as to manage June properly."

"But my dear, you must apply the principles of cancellation, and the matter is wonderfully simplified," answered Farr. "One grandfather is selfish, another is the soul of generosity; one grandmother loves music, another cannot distinguish 'Yankee Doodle' from 'God save the Queen,'—there is neutrality as far as their particular grandchildren are concerned: one ancestor likes to smoke, another abominates the weed, neutrality again."

"But cancellation does not cancel in this instance. No child takes after all his ancestors; he may inherit generosity from the one, the weakness for tobacco from another, a love of music from another; the ancestors with the opposing traits simply do not count at all with this particular child."

"Grace, dear, you are getting beyond my depths, too. With your permission I shall try another cigar. Some of my ancestors were perfect slaves to the weed, I have not doubt. I am not to blame for my weakness for it is a question which the moral law does not decide, and I am left a defenseless victim to a hereditary trait."

"I am not sure but that I ought to make you quit smoking. It is too late for June to be benefitted; but some of his great great-grandchildren may seriously impair their health and constitution by over indulgence in smoking," said Grace playfully.

"I am willing to make all reasonable sacrifices for my offspring, but really Grace, when it comes to June's great-grandchildren you must excuse me if my interest is not very keen."

"What are my gwate, gwate gwandchilen,

papa" queried the curly headed laddie, climbing to his father's knee, and jumping up and down to continue his equestrian exercises.

Farr tossed him in the air, and kissed him as he came down.

"Something, my boy, you will never see or hear of. And somebody's boy, not a mile away from here, gets his inquisitiveness from his mamma. No remote ancestor for that."

Just then the nurse came to carry the boy off to bed, much against his will, but after a vain appeal to his mamma and then to his cousin Edith to be allowed to stay untill he got sleepy, he yielded to the inevitable. He bestowed his good night kisses quite impartially until he got to his mother; but the father was not jealous of that deeper love between mother and child.

These glimpses of domestic felicity were taking on an added interest to Marguerite. Somehow, in some way, although the conditions would be so different, she felt vaguely that she was seeing her own future.

She looked at all married people with a peculiar interest, speculating on their years of ups and downs together, their mutual love, their common interests, their little quarrels, their glad reconciliations. In her future there would be no reconciliations because there would be no quarrels.

She thought that if all marriages were as happy as this one appeared to be, and as she was certain it really was, then life would not have so many inequalities after all. "Love is the great leveler," a drawing-room philosopher had said to her once, when she sat with him under an improvised bower of palms, and discussed love in the abstract; and the truth of his words was being emphasized in her own consciousness. "Love and home, husband, wife and children, are the centres, the great conservers of the world's energies, after all. Whether the home be a palace or a cottage, that is an accident," so ran her thoughts.

She walked over to the window, and stood in the shadow of the curtains, looking out into the darkness of the night.

If her idol were only an American instead of an English nobleman, then money could make no difference as to their future. They would have each other; they would be simply themselves, and whether their home had eighty rooms or eight, they need not care, so happy would they be in each other's love.

Soon the carriage was announced for the girls. Mrs. Farr laughed at the idea of any one's sitting up with her. Harriet would remain up, of course, to give her the doctor's horrid doses, and Ed would sleep within call, but she was not going to be persuaded into being seriously ill.

It had been an agreeable evening for Marguerite; it seemed such a sweet, happy home. It formed one of the mental pictures that would be pleasant, she thought, to carry all through her life.

"Theirs was surely a marriage made in Heaven," she said to Edith as they rolled along in Mrs. Kingman's carriage.

"At all events, in a very nice part of earth," replied Edith who was practical.

"Mamma thought Grace was marrying too young, she was nineteen, but the marriage has been so happy that she has withdrawn her objections."

"I wonder why it is that mothers and grandmothers all object to girls marrying young, when they were only eighteen and nineteen themselves when they were married," said Marguerite more as a soliloquy than a question.

"Maybe they speak from experience, although they all declare that marriages were happier in their times than in ours," replied Edith.

"I am glad that I belong to our times," said Marguerite softly, thinking to herself that had she been her own grandmother there would have been no Paul, third Earl of Parkhurst.

XXVIII.

JUST five days afterwards, Marguerite was awakened rather earlier than usual by a tap at the door, which called her out of a troubled dream; her maid was standing at the threshold with a penciled note in her hand. Marguerite recognized Edith's writing at once, and with a sleepy curiosity as to what she could want so early in the morning, broke the seal:

Grace is dead. Half past ten last night.

Edith.

As Mrs. Farr was an orphan, with no nearer relatives in the city than the Kingmans, it devolved on them to perform the last sad offices permitted to the living for the dead. Marguerite was with them almost constantly; her presence seemed a sort of support and comfort for Edith, whose strong practical sense could not keep its wonted tenure under the terrible strain of death.

"And so sudden too," whispered Edith. "Just think Marguerite, not a week ago we were laughing and talking so gaily in this very room, with no thought of death."

They passed softly into Grace's pretty boudoir. There was her work basket with some dainty trifle she was embroidering—that saddest of mementoes—the unfinished work of the dead! A bowl of withered roses was on the table.

"The flowers that poor Ed brought home that night," said Edith.

A mandolin was out of its case with one string broken; a toy of June's lay on the floor, a cigar stump was on the mantel. — Grace had been a fond wife.

The pretty belongings of a refined, womanly taste were scattered around — but it was all too depressing, and the girls went down stairs.

The remains had been laid out in the solemn silence of the front drawing-room; Edith and Marguerite stole in idle helplessness into the little reception room just back of it. The hour for the funeral was near at hand, and Mrs. Kingman was lying down for a few moments' rest up stairs. The portieres of the death chamber were pushed aside, and Farr entered, leading his boy by the hand. Grace had been robed in a clinging white shroud, arranged Grecian wise with a profusion of creamy lace. Her hair was curled in the soft fluffy bang she wore in life, her head was slightly turned on the downy pillow. She had not been ill long enough for the signs to be very pronounced, and so life-like did she look that it needed the icy touch of the sweet lips closed and cold forever, to convince one that it was really death, and not a deep sleep.

The girlish hearts ached for the stricken man, who seemed the very incarnatian of a grief too deep for human consolation to ever reach. Presently his sobs became audible, and Marguerite, always sympathetic, burst into tears.

"I cannot stand this; it is terrible."

Then the little boy began to cry; Edith stole in and led him gently out of the room.

"I wants my mamma," he sobbed. "Why is my mamma so told, Tousin Edith?"

The undertakers came, the lid was screwed down, the plummaged hearse with its sable horses drew up at the door, and the sad procession wended its way to the church. Death, the One Thing which no man can stay, had laid desolate the happy home. It had claimed one who had every thing to live for — husband, child, home; position, money, health, beauty, talents, friends, success — every thing — and here she was, dead. Dead, and only twenty six. Twenty six years in which she had tasted all the joys of mortal existence, in which had come to her the common destiny of womanhood as wife and mother. But it was all over now. She had died with a clear conscience. A sweet pure life had been hers, and a peaceful pure death.

Marguerite kept fancying herself lying in the coffin instead of the bright young mother really there. She could almost see herself in that narrow bed, stiff and cold and powerless forever, with a thousand victims pressing on her coffin lid.

What did it matter after all, ran her thoughts; the world and all it could give; not a happy life, but a happy death was the one great thing. In the presence of death all were slaves. Only God is Master.

The bell tolled the brief years, the sacred edifice was already filled with people, for Mrs. Farr had been very popular, and her death was so sudden that it awakened even a deeper sympathy than was usual. In a lingering illness one is in a measure prepared — but only a week —.

"Why, ten days ago she was at my house for luncheon," one matron whispered to another.

"Only a week ago I saw her down town," said a third.

These whispers of sympathetic, affectionate reminiscence did not seem really like talking.

Marguerite saw and heard as if in a dream. She knelt or stood at the proper times, but all the while her thoughts were on the One Awful Thing, Judgment. She had repeated by rote a hundred times, the Four Last Things to be Remembered: Death, Judgment, Heaven, Hell. But they seemed to be burning into her very soul now. It was not death, not even the General Judgment of the Last Dread day, whose terrors she felt, for the General Judgment would be only the reiteration of a fate already known to the soul, but it was that awful moment, when the spirit seems almost to hover around the body, yet warm, and the Eternal Fiat is pronounced. The body is here, that tenement of clay that will soon be only dust, but the spirit has traversed infinite space. — A soul has stood in the presence of God. The thought was too awful, and Marguerite bent her head in her hands as if to keep out the image.

The ceremonies went on; the clergyman mounted the pulpit to deliver the last tribute permitted to human lips.

"I Am The Resurrection And The Life."

His words fell like a benediction. They sent a strange sweet thrill through Marguerite, and she raised her head. He was a good preacher, with that subtle magnetism which vitalizes mere words, and makes the difference between an orator and a speaker. He paid a glowing tribute, which every one felt to be deserved, to the dead woman, her virtues as a wife, mother and Christian member of Society. But through it all Marguerite kept hearing the words:

"I Am The Resurrection And The Life."

It was a weary, weary journey to the cemetery. The funeral train was not long. It had ceased to be the general custom to attend funerals; but Marguerite, as a dear friend of the dead woman's, and above all as a friend to Edith, would have found it impossible not to go. It seemed heartless not to accompany a dear one on that last, sad, earthly journey. It was a tribute of friendship, of love. But she did not censure those who viewed the matter differently. As she stood for a moment in the crush, as the crowd surged from the church doors, she heard a young lady, an old schoolmate of Mrs. Farr's, ask her companion, if she would be at the Grunewalds' reception that evening.

"And so the world goes on," thought the girl sadly.

Marguerite was low spirited and nervous for a week after the funeral.

And the sight of poor little Norrisson Farr, who was staying with Mrs. Kingman, the sunny June of his mother's June-like existence, brought a gush of hot tears to her eyes. In some vague way he seemed to revive her own orphanage. She saw herself repeated in this motherless child, — for she was only a year or two older than he, when her mother had died in far off California.

The thought of the husband, alone in his desolate home, was simply harrowing. Somehow, she kept identifying herself without any conscious volition, with the dead Grace.

Would Paul grieve so for her!

"Oh, Paul, Paul!"

XXIX.

OUTWARDLY Marguerite's life went on the as same ever. Edith was in temporary retirement and could not accompany her as usual, and that may have been one of the reasons why she found no pleasure, only a momentary forgetfulness, an unhealthy excitement, in her amusements.

Mrs. Farr had been dead a fortnight. The rush and roar of the approaching Holidays were felt in every way and by-way of the city; the main thoroughfares, 'the mighty arteries of a city's life,' — as some one called them before Marguerite's time, but she was fond of the comparison, — were pulsing with the ceaseless streams of a common humanity; the eager, alert prosperous buyers, the timid, economical little housewives, the hollow-eyed, penniless lookers-on.

Marguerite declared that there was no harder work than shopping, and after a day spent in the inevitable, non-transferable task, came home thoroughly tired.

The next morning she slept late, and a general lassitude, which she translated into a real indisposition, afforded her conscience an excuse for the luxury of a forenoon spent in dressing gown and slippers.

Her maid brought a dainty repast, the letters and the morning papers. She sipped her chocolate from a gold spoon, after toying with a bunch of hot house grapes, and read her letters. There was a request from a certain potentate of feminine attire to call and try on her frocks; there were nine, only nine, missives from various charitable institutions asking for a Christmas contribution; there was a sprightly letter, scrawled over three sheets, from her prospective sister, Lady Mortimore; another missive from across the ocean was from Madame Florac, wishing her every Christmas joy, and filled with the tender, loving words of counsel the nun never forgot in writing to her dearest child.

Marguerite kissed the name as she folded the letter tenderly and put it in the envelope. Then she picked up the morning paper, that insatiable, never-resting gatherer of the happenings of a universe, which greets the world and the world's wife every morning, and is old, and useless, and a cast-away at night.

On the first page, staring at her in big capitals Marguerite saw:

ANOTHER CASHIER GONE WRONG.
A young Society Man's Temptation and Fall.
Full Particulars of the Defalcation.
Amount not Known.
Scene of the Arrest.
HENRY ARTHUR WILSON IN JAIL.
"Henry Wilson!"

She sat regarding the name as if in a daze, for a minute, before reading those full particulars.

And they were all there! all the harrowing details, real or manufactured.

The fact of his having been, in popular parlance, "a Society Man," seemed to be dilated upon with a sort of pleasure. The particulars included his looks, hair, eyes, stature, weight, as if to serve for identification in case of an escape; his parentage, education, business success, his mother's divorce, his early years in New York boarding houses, his fondness for horses, a description of his luxurious apartments; even the sad little idyl of his love affair in the Arcadian village was touched upon, but mercifully, for the sake of the girl, no name was given. The mania for speculation was adduced as a probable cause. One journal, nothing if not sensational, had a column about the rejection of his suit by a wealthy merchant's daughter, and her admission that she would marry him if he were rich. But the main facts, unfortunately, were too true.

How the papers get all the particulars they do in three hours after an event occurs, is one of the mysteries of journalism to which the General Public has never been able to find a clue.

Wilson's downfall was more than the nine days' wonder.

Every body was shocked, and not a few were genuinely sorry.

Mrs. Gillette asked, of no one in particular, what could you expect from a man who tried to seem what he was not, and who lived at the rate of ten thousand a year on a three thousand dollar salary. There were a few mothers, cast in the same practical mould as Mrs. Gillette, who said, with a certain retroactive anger, that one might look for any thing in men of that kind. Their daughters, remembering certain dances and promenades and quiet talks on seductive stairways, were more tender and forgiving in their judgments.

Marguerite wondered how Delphine Bienvenue felt about the affair. It must certainly have recalled sad memories, and she speculated as to whether the girl would congratulate herself on a narrow escape. But perhaps he would not have fallen had he married Delphine, he might have been saved from the temptation to which he had yielded. For herself she did not give a great deal for a man who was true only because he had not been tempted. Potential dishonesty was almost as shameful, to her, as the actual. But she chided herself for being narrow in her judgments, as she recalled the words of that universal prayer, given for all ages and all nations and all hearts.

Lead Us Not Into Temptation, was surely a petition framed with a special reference to the weakness of poor human nature.

But Delphine Bienvenue knew of the defalcation and the arrest before Marguerite, before any one, save those immediately concerned, knew of it, in all the world. A special messenger had brought her a note, even the sight of which had power to make her tremble.

No answer was required, the boy said, and with burning hands and a throbbing pulse, she rushed up to her own little room to read the familiar looking lines.

There was no form of address at the top, the lines were scrawled, evidently in nervous haste. It ran:

"In a few hours every newsboy in the city will be crying my disgrace. — I send you the few mementoes I have treasured so fondly of the happiest, the only happy time I have ever known in my life, — that summer with you at Hilsborough. You have ceased to care for me, and I am not worthy I know, of your love, but for the sake of old times think as kindly as you can of me. I do not attempt any excuse, — I sacrificed my honor, took the risk of a felon's cell for the chance to make a fortune, and I lost. You will not be angry if I say that through every thing I always loved you, you represented to me all that was sweet and pure and noble in womanhood. And how many times after our quarrel was I on the point of going to you and imploring you to marry me — have I dreamed of a dear if humble home with you its fireside angel. Forgive me if I caused you pain, and pity me. I write this with an officer at my elbow, and another one examining all my private effects. Even this package must be seen before it goes to you, but the letter is private.

Good by — I dare not say in words, "my darling." Mine nevermore.   HENRY.

The accompanying package contained a tintype group, the counterpart of the one which had revealed her secret to Marguerite; a folio of songs she had sung; a knot of ribbon, some faded flowers, a broken fan. But every article potent with memories! At the touch of those silent mementoes, so mutely eloquent with the voices of the past, even more than the letter, a something seemed to revive, to glow within her heart, — the mists of doubt, disdain, distrust, anger wounded pride—lifted and floated away, leaving only the clear heights of a woman's love. He was hers, —

hers by those subtle bonds forged in heaven to unite human hearts, and she would not desert her own.

Early the next morning the keeper of the jail was sought out by a tall, aristocratic looking girl, faultlessly attired, and admission to Henry Wilson's cell requested. He peered from under a pair of shaggy brows; he had read the fiction of the merchant's daughter in the paper, and he felt sure that the young lady was standing before him. The heroine of the country romance did not occur to him at all—a rustic heroine, of course, in ill fitting clothes and with a timid manner. Certainly there was nothing awkward or unformed in this imperious, dark eyed beauty, wrapped in furs and bearing about her all the evidences of culture, and the indescribable air which he associated peculiarly with New York. He did not know it was the air of good breeding, joined to a proud self-respect, every where.

It was his business, when acting in his official character to curb both curiosity and surprise; he deferentially asked her to be seated for a few moments and hurried away. Presently he returned and told her to follow him, which she did, eagerly enough. He turned a key, — it gave that ominous sound peculiar to prison keys, which caused the girl to shiver, in spite of her furs and the steam heat.

In another moment, for the first time in her life, she was in a cell.

"Delphine!"

"Henry!"

And then they both forgot the cell, and the freedom of an old fashioned village was stretching before them.

After the first outburst of a love which forgets all obstacles, Wilson was man enough to say:

"Delphine, my poor darling, I am not worthy of such devotion. — I have only disgrace and a hopeless future before me. Give me up to my fate, and be happy as you deserve to be and will be."

"We will go where the disgrace cannot reach, and together we will begin life all over. I could not give you up if I would," was the devoted answer.

Then Delphine told him, not without some pride, of the little competence which had come to them. At the end he said passionately, and there were tears in his voice although none in his eyes,—

"Delphine, would you leave all this for me?"

She smiled, for a moment forgetful of the doom hanging over her lover:

"No, we will take some of it with us; and Mamma and Kit too; they wouldn't want to stay in New York without me."

It was a sad setting for the renewal of vows that had been plighted in a cool shady glen with the vault of heaven above, this background of a prison wall.

Marguerite was soon made aware of their strange reunion in the simplest of all ways, by Delphine's telling her.

There was the barest suggestion of defiance in her tone, as if she expected and was prepared for a remonstrance; but Marguerite only said very gently: "I am glad, dear, if it makes you happy," and then she added presently. "But don't make a mistake. Don't confound past love with present pity."

Edith was outspoken in her indignation; she had grown rather to like the girl, and Marguerite had compelled her to be interested.

"I confess that I cannot understand a love of that kind," she said. "I can understand a wife's clinging to her husband from a sense of duty, but a girl free to go, she was not even engaged to him at the time — that is a puzzle. But some girls are such fools."

"But if she really cares for him Edith; and it seems he loved her all the time, she was hasty in quarreling with him."

"How can she love him? where is her self-respect, her pride of womanhood? How can she love a thief? And the idea of marrying him! could she ever think of any thing but his dishonor? Why, it seems to me the vision of that cell, the mental image of him in the stripes of a convict, would make her loathe the very sight of him."

"But he has not worn the prison stripes yet, and maybe he will not."

"Oh, no question about that. He is bound to be convicted; he doesn't even deny his guilt."

"I can admire her for her fidelity, even though I pity her too," said Marguerite.

"I can admire a woman for fidelity to a man in poverty, in trouble, misfortune of every kind, even disgrace if unmerited, but fidelity to a thief, never!" was Edith's indignant answer.

"Is a thief so much worse than any other sinner?"

"Not worse perhaps, but more contemptible; and then to think, only a few paltry thousands too!"

"Would the crime be less had he stolen half a million?"

The question was not deemed worthy of an answer.

"And if the girl were merely a commonplace, milk and water sort of a girl, or even of the pink and blue china doll kind, but she is too superbly beautiful, too *distingue*, to be sacrificed that way."

"Henry Wilson would probably not be in love with a girl of the china doll, commonplace kind," said Marguerite.

"Oh no, the selfish dog; he wants the best always."

"Poor fellow, I feel very sorry for him. And maybe he was tempted more than we can have any idea of. Maybe he did fight against it, and fight until his conscience gradually got deadened."

"I daresay he did consider, but it was not his conscience that troubled him, it was the thought of getting caught."

Marguerite did not agree to this, although she acknowledged that a man who did not believe in either a Heaven or a Hell, a Personal God or a Personal Devil, could not logically have a very tender conscience. She could not free herself from the Faith which was a part of her very being, even in thought, sufficiently to place herself on Wilson's plane.

He must have struggled with his conscience and then deadened it; he must have intended to replace the money; he never had seemed to her like a happy man, perhaps he had fought and struggled, giving way by degrees. She could not believe that he had fallen at once. Or perhaps the chance had come upon him suddenly, and he had yielded before realizing the enormity of his crime. She was surprised at her own charity for him, for her opinions had once been very like Edith's in this regard. She repelled the thought as of an insult, that her dead father was teaching her to *judge not*, even in the case of a thief!

She mentally recurred to an article she had read by a certain catch-penny philosopher, who claimed that the good or evil of an act depends upon the result. Perhaps Henry Wilson thought that way too; and since the consequences of an act could only be known at the end of time, had determined to take the risk. He might have reasoned that with a few thousand dollars he could open the way for making a fortune, marrying Delphine and becoming an influential, wealthy citizen; that the loss to a rich bank would be only a trifle, with no result one way or the other. Then his act would be good because the consequences would be good. And she could but admit that if Right and Wrong as the essence of good and evil, were done away with, together with the proposition that the consequences are but the accidents of a sin, not the measure of its gravity, then he would cease to be a sophist and become a philosopher.

Mrs. Kingman interrupted her train of thought

and Edith's chatter, to say that Carroll Kirwin had gone on Wilson's bond, and that he was at liberty again.

But the torturing idea did not occur to Marguerite until she had gone to bed that night, and was tossing about trying to fall asleep, that her father was responsible, in a way, for Wilson's fall.

If the Bienvenues had never lost their money, or if her father had made restitution, Delphine and Wilson would not have been parted because of poverty; with a devoted, Christian wife, a happy home, and Delphine's share of her father's estate, he might never have been tempted to his own undoing.

She shuddered.

'Was the effect of a sin never to end?' she asked herself wildly.

'Would it go on and on, for ages and generations, was it a contagion which seized every thing in its way?'

She thought of Katherine Bienvenue's leg — had it been attended to properly the child might not be going through life a cripple; she thought of old Martha Grigsby, her years of degradation and suffering, her three dead children who might have grown up into useful men and women, but for the poverty and privations to which her father had reduced them; of Emmet Morgan's struggle against poverty, his regret at leaving school, his hopeless ambition. These were all she knew of the hundreds, perhaps thousands, of the victims of the Golconda Mines, and these had all suffered terribly, and the suffering would not end with one generation. She hoped she would never know the extent of the wretchedness of the rest of the victims. Perhaps there were little children starving, men going to the bad, women dying, others struggling along in poverty and ignorance, all because her father had stooped, only once, in an evil hour, to do a wrong to others.

Would nothing, nothing ever happen to lift this terrible load which was getting heavier than she could bear?

Then the stillness was broken by a voice:

"UNTIL THE LAST FARTHING HAS BEEN PAID."

XXX.

WHEN the time for action came, Marguerite was ready. There never had been really any doubt as to the final result, from the first hour the conviction of her father's guilt was forced upon her. There might have been struggles, temptations, a wild rebellion against the fate that was closing in around her like some malignant, labyrinthic net, but never had she deliberately chosen to keep the money which belonged so manifestly to others. She saw the day of her doom approaching, and figuratively went forth to meet it. She even endured the mockery of a little informal birthday dinner which Edith, all unsuspecting, gave for her. Two weeks before her majority she wrote to Lord Parkhurst, that debts of her father which Mrs. Clayton refused to consider, but which she felt bound in conscience to pay, would leave her entirely penniless excepting for seventy five thousand dollars inherited from her mother. She said she was aware of his financial embarrassments, and offered to release him from his promise to herself. It was not an easy letter to write, and the greater part of three days was given up to the task. Sentences were weighed, and analyzed, one was rejected because it was too cold, another because it showed her poor heart too plainly, with all its depths of love. She wanted to leave him free, but she did not want to believe that he would consent to be free.

She dwelt on his tenderness, his manliness, their happy hours together, and her heart whispered joyously: "He loves me too well to blight both our lives for mere money."

The old, sweet dreams which had come to her, at first timidly, half daringly, were constant visitants, now that the clouds of her fate were more lowering than she could bear without crying out with the weight of their pain.

Paul would give up his title and his estates to his brother, and together they would make a place for themselves in America, her own dear land with its glorious possibilities for every one. They would go West. — The West that was beckoning to her children in the East, with the promises and the prospects she held so alluringly out to them. They would have a ranch; in her day dreams she could see the great herdes of cattle, the cozy commodious home — there would be a profusion of books, a few good pictures on the walls, a piano and a mandolin and maybe a harp, soft, fur rugs would cover the floors, great, old fashioned English fireplaces would throw out their cheery warmth in every room, elk horns, and other trophies of the mountains, would adorn the hall, in a room opening from the library, there would be guns without number, fishing tackle, bows and arrows, and tennis racquets, in the stable there would be two good saddle horses, and perhaps, if the ranch were very successful, a carriage and pair, or at least a cart; in the kennel would be a pack of slender, blooded hounds and a royal mastiff, — she could see the mountains, snow-capped and grand, towering in their eternal grandeur to the West, and the plains, like a vast smooth sea, stretching towards the East.

And far away from the demands of rank and of fashion, the petty concerns of Society, the rush and roar of the city's strife, the struggle for place, the eager, ever-seeking throngs, they would live an ideal life together. She was not certain just where the dream ranch was located. It would be pleasant to have it near an army post, for the army people were always so bright and cultivated, and Paul would be sure to like the officers better than he would civilians who were in trade; there would be other ranches in the neighborhood, and together they would all form a society of their own, at once charming and unconventional. They would have card parties and little dinners, musicales and reading clubs; the mail would bring them the new magazines and books, the papers and letters from their friends in the East; they would have picnics in the spring and autumn; in the long evenings and the cool dewy mornings, she and Paul would take rides over the valleys, or up the canons; their evenings at home would be devoted to music and reading, or talking to each other; they would establish a school for Indian children, and she would give some of her time to teaching them; she naturally associated Indians with the army, but in her musings they were good, peaceful Indians rapidly learning, in her school, the ways of civilization. There would be a little church, ivy covered and gothic, built from native quarries, which she would care for faithfully; the poor, but there would be no poor in the neighborhood, for they would all find work on the ranch, — the laboring classes would bless her as their good angel. It would be desirable not to get too far away from a city; they might like to go to town for a few days change every winter, besides, groceries would have to be shipped to them, and she might want to do some shopping occasionally, although she intended, as a rule, to get her dainty, aesthetic robes from New York. She thought of San Francisco, her old home, but land was so very expensive in that vicinity, besides, California was not exactly typical of the kind of West she wanted. Colorado, as far as she could place her geographical knowledge, came nearer to her ideal; and they could run over to Manitou, beautiful Manitou every summer for a few weeks. She had once gone with a party of friends in a special car, for a flying trip to the Pacific, and she confessed that the Rocky Mountains had bewitched her. Wyoming was said to be enchanting in places. But she would leave the selection of locality to Paul. It would be a rich, full, pure, sweet life they would lead. There would be just enough of society for healthy diversion, and not enough to make wearing demands on one's time.

But perhaps Paul would not care for the West; he might like a place in the neighborhood of New York better. In an instant she had transported her goods and chattels across the continent, and was arranging them in a Queen Anne villa in South Orange, ready the next moment to take them on to a farm on the Hudson, or to a place on Long Island. They could have the delights of the city and the country combined. They ought to be able to invest seventy-five thousand dollars so as to bring them in five or six thousand dollars a year, and with their home, and the farm produce and the poultry, they ought to live nicely on that. The Farrs had not spent much more in New York, and poor Grace had never appeared to be stinted for money. Of course, she had not entertained formally, or worn imported gowns, but she had certainly been happy, and looked very pretty, notwithstanding.

Then Paul might go into business; if he ceased to be an English nobleman, and became an American gentleman, there was no reason why he should not earn some money. Of course, he would not do real work, but he might be a bank president, or a railroad director, or something of that sort. They could not live in New York, for it would be derogatory to Paul's dignity to reside in a place where his means would not permit of the style of living in accordance with his rank, but there were hosts of charming places within easy distance of the Metropolis, where they could live cheaply and well. If Paul really loved her, and she could not doubt his love, he would prefer an obscure life with her, to a royal one without her. The younger brother Herbert, was a handsome winning sort of fellow, and she would take the greatest pleasure in the world in finding him an American wife, with a fortune great enough to redeem the decaying glories of the house of Parkhurst; and so long as the title and the family were kept up it did not make any great difference whether it was the elder or the younger brother who did it. She had never heard of an elder brother's giving up his title excepting to take orders, but there was no reason why it could not be done. They could visit England, every year if they decided not to live on a ranch in the West; house parties at Parkhurst were charming, and Lady Mortimore would certainly be glad to entertain her brother in town.

Her own ambition she put aside as less than nothing. She would have Paul, her heart's idol, and all other considerations were trivial. To be sure, plain Mrs. Paul Hunter did not have the music in its sibilations as did Marguerite, Countess of Parkhurst; and dinner cards which conveyed to certain ones of their chosen friends that Mr. and Mrs. Paul Hunter requested the pleasure, would not confer half the happiness on even her nearest and dearest, that would be conferred by Lord and Lady Parkhurst; she knew enough of republican disregard for rank and titles to know that; but still, what would it matter if only Paul would not care ?

She dared not, from womanly pride, make the suggestion, she could only hope that Paul would make it to her. An American lover might buckle on his armor and go to work, but no one in her sober senses could expect that of an English Peer.

And yet she could do nothing but wait. Yes, there was one thing she could do, she could pray with all the fervor of her trusting faith and her earthly love, that Paul would be won over to this plan. The more she thought of it the more practicable did it seem. Surely her Good Angel had suggested it. She visited some church every day, and spent hours on her knees; perhaps there were earthly images flitting between her supplications, which ought to have been banished in that Holy Temple, but they were not wilful distractions. She slipped alms into aged hands and begged for prayers for her intention. She made a pilgrimage to the narrow, old-fashioned street where dwelt a little community of nuns whose lives were given up to prayer for a sinful world, and sought their intercession with Heaven. She promised heroic acts, on her knees, in honor of the Blessed Virgin and her patron Saint, if her petition were granted. Surely so many prayers, so many vows, the army of good works that would crown her happy life, would not be all in vain. So strong was her faith, so childlike her confidence in the power of prayer, that she grew almost happy, and sang so blithly, and chatted so in her old way, that Edith, the truest, most anxious of friends, was convinced that Marguerite's low spirits were attributable to over exertion, or to scruples—her conscience was tender in some ways,—or to jealousy, perhaps. "Those loving, intense natures feel so keenly — a feather is like a blow, especially when it is a question of the feather being on the heart strings," she thought.

Lord Parkhurst cabled to Marguerite that he would answer her letter in person.

And the day when she was to get control of her property, was flying towards her; as it came nearer, all her beautiful, fairyland dreams vanished into the air, and no amount of will power could call them back again. Then she told herself that maybe this load on her heart was a temptation of the Evil One to make her falter in her duty. She had read somewhere in some old chronicle of the Middle Ages, of a man who yielded to a temptation against faith, and was struck dead immediately afterwards.

As the result of many discussions it was decided to give Mr. Dalton power of attorney, when she became of age, and let him attend to the bonds.

On the day before she was to do this, Lord Parkhurst arrived.

He was looking haggard and ill, and he made no attempt to conceal the terrible blow he had received. He told her frankly and without circumlocution, as he had never done before, of the condition of his affairs.

His debts amounted to over sixty thousand pounds; they had been accumulating at usurious interest ever since his father was a boy; every thing in his possession was mortgaged, the family plate, the horses, the pictures, the furniture; he had been borrowing money at ruinous interest, — he had the grace to blush at this confession, — and the only security given was his coming marriage to an American heiress. If Marguerite persisted in her resolve there was nothing left for him but the bankruptcy court — and perdition.

The last day of the old year, the year which had been so full of events for Marguerite, a year which had been so happy—witnessed the consummation of her sacrifice. She arose early, 'what must be done had best be done quickly,' and ordered her brougham for nine o'clock. She hardly slept the night before, and her eyelids were tired and heavy.

She had been the mistress of over two million dollars for just twenty four hours. As she drove up to Mr. Dalton's office, some street urchins, after the fashion of street urchins every where, began to yell at her coachman, who sat upright in the silence of insulted dignity; then they turned their sarcasm on Marguerite herself.

"Aint she a jim dandy though; ketch on to de feather!

"Don't be a starein' at de lady, Peg, can't you see she's a blarsted 'risterkrat!"

The children were dirty and ragged, their tawny, tangled locks were peeping out of their battered hat crowns; the twinkling blue eyes of the boy, the preternaturally grave, black ones of the girl, had grown accustomed to sights not intended for childish eyes; miserable outcasts they were, yet Marguerite found it in her heart to envy their careless freedom from the gnawing pain that was killing her.

She opened her purse, and with a wan little smile, said, approaching the children: "Here, wont you take this and get yourselves some shoes or something," and pressed two bills into their dirty hands.

They stood with open eyes unable all at once to comprehend their good fortune. The girl was the first to recover herself, as the girl usually is in an emergency.

"Oh Missus, we didn't mean nuthin' by guyin' ye, did we Tom! Thank ye, we thank ye, I knowed you was an angel when you first comed, didn't we Tom?"

She looked as if she would like to lay hold of Marguerite's frock in the exuberance of her gratitude, but its faultlessness and style forbade that demonstration. She bobbed her head, and clutched her money in her left hand, and kept murmuring her thanks.

Tom pulled off his battered old felt hat, and echoed his sister's words, with a shamefaced expression and an attempt at thanks, which somehow stuck in his throat.

Marguerite patted the urchins on the head, and asked them to pray for her. At this extraordinary request they stared with all their eyes, and the boy was inclined to laugh. But Peggy said, "Yes 'um," in a non committal sort of way, as if she did not exactly know to what new and strange thing she was binding herself.

Mr. Dalton came out to meet her, and said something about having a cold which made him husky, and that he did not know young ladies in New York were such early risers. He had evidently determined to pass the matter off as an every-day affair, to save his own feelings as much as Marguerite's.

She followed him into his private office, where she had been so many times before, but it had an unfamilar look.

"Here Girlie, just sign this," he said, pushing a legal, formidable looking document before her.

Marguerite took up the pen, as she did so a vision of Josephine signing the decree of divorce, arose before her. Another woman, now sleeping in her grave almost a hundred years, had signed away hope and happiness, and every thing that made life dear and sweet.

"But her fate was not as unhappy as mine, for she was a middle-aged woman who had drunk deeply of life's joys, whilst I — is it possible that I am only twenty one, and I feel a hundred!

"Why do women suffer so much in the world? is it because of the fateful apple which tempted Eve to her undoing, that the heritage of woe has come to Eve's daughters? The history of men is a history of deeds, of thwarted ambitions, of wrong, perhaps, but the history of women is a history of pain, always!"

She put her name to the paper, and arose from the table; her head was whirling, she thought she was going to faint. She had signed the death-warrant of self, would the executioners come and lead her away to the scaffold!

She sank back into her chair, and Mr. Dalton came quickly to her side.

He supported her head with his arm, and forced a glass of water to her lips.

"I did not know I was so much of a baby," she said, with such a pitiful little ghost of a smile that he felt a lump rising in his own throat.

"A baby, Marguerite, you are the bravest girl I ever knew!" and he stroked her hair as he had done in her hobbledehoy days in San Francisco.

"As long as I live Rita, you shall never want for any thing, and when I die you will find that you have not been forgotten. You have grit, lots of it, and I am proud of you."

Mr. Dalton thought to himself, hotly, that 'if that whipper-snapper of a Lord were the hundredth part of a man he would ask no happier fate than to win such a girl for his wife even though she came to him penniless, let alone a dowry of seventy-five thousand dollars!'

The old gentleman was not partial to Lords.

The deed was done! Marguerite did not want to go home, it was home no longer to her; she did not want to go any place. She told the coachman to drive to Brooklyn.

XXXI.

THERE was one more scene in the tragedy of her life yet to be played; its crowning agony was still before her. After that, Marguerite did not allow herself to think what would follow. The future seemed an utter blank, if a blank could be so dark. In the afternoon Paul was coming to say goodbye. Wearily the day dragged, although she had not returned home until noon. The hour hand of the clock did not seem to move at all, and but for the ticking, she would have thought that its marking of time had been suspended. She took a cup of tea in her own room, and at one she began to get ready for the approaching interview.

The thought of what she would wear interrupted the tense ache of brain, and nerves and heart. She even smiled at herself for thinking of such a thing at such a time, and wondered vaguely if these conventionalities of our social code were given as a mocking essence of life's bitterness, or as a merciful diversion to the soul from the weight of its supreme anguish. She had the half-conscious desire, born of habit, to look her best in the eyes that were the only eyes in the world for her.

An afternoon gown that Paul had admired, she rejected with a shiver, it would seem like making merry over a corpse, the corpse of the old Marguerite, she told herself. A dainty little house frock, the very embodiment of the domestic virtues, the quiet happiness of evenings in a happy home, never to be hers, was put aside; a beautiful tea-gown in which she had received him more than once, was too informal, and the day for that was past; her whole wardrobe was gone through cursorily, for Paul was not coming until four; and then she chose black. There was a sub-consciousness all the time that she would wear black; it was only a make-believe that she had been undecided. There was nothing else she could put on that would not seem a mockery, she thought. Black had been consecrated with oceans of tears, the wailings of broken and breaking hearts, as the garb of woe, and a woman in pain selects a black gown, as naturally as the wounded animal seeks to hide its misery from human eyes. It seems to enfold one as under a protecting mantle, to be a silent appeal to all the world — Respect my Grief.

She recalled, still with that sub-consciousness — her active intelligence was never for a moment free from the thought of the approaching farewell, — that in all the great tragedies at the theatre, in the scene where the apotheosis of suffering or sin is reached, black was always worn; she saw herself during a vividly dramatized moment, in a mental picture gallery with all the unfortunate women whose sorrows had made the history of the world.

She arrayed herself slowly, so that the time would not hang so heavily. She arranged and disarranged her hair, the curls that Paul had said, were like fairy tendrils twining around an ivory column. Her eyes were inflamed under the lids from the hot, soul-blistering tears she had shed, and great purplish rings beneath them accentuated the red. She bathed her face in lavender water, and dabbled on powder to conceal the traces of her tears; it made her look ghastly, for she was already as colorless as chalk, but the mask of death seemed a fitting cover for a dead heart, she told herself in the height of her tragic mood. At last she put on her gown, a trailing clinging robe, made with Grecian lines and effects, with long sleeves suspended from the shoulder, and falling almost to the floor, over under-sleeves of a filmier silk. It had been copied, in a girlish fancy, from the gown of a famous actress. As she looked at herself in the mirror she seemed to be another person gazing at a stage picture. But it was only for a moment that her soul was given a surcease of its pain. Her eyes fell on the ring that must that afternoon be returned, and with a wild cry, as if a knife had been run through her heart, she flung herself on a chair and buried her face in her hands, lying there with low quivering sobs. She slipped from the chair to her knees, but she could not pray, the words seemed to choke in her throat, and she could only murmur: "Strength, strength to bear my Cross."

Half an hour before the appointed time, she took up her station at the window.

"The last time, the very last, I shall ever watch for Paul."

Five minutes before two a brougham drew up at the door, and the earl, never so handsome, so manly, so grand to look upon before, sprang up the steps. She trembled so that she could hardly walk. She paused a moment, to determine to be dignified and womanly, he was her Paul no longer, and went down to meet him. She had already given orders that he was to be shown into the library, that room made sacred by their happy love.

She paused, pushed aside the portieres noiselessly and stood at the threshold; it was a cold, dismal depressing day, and Parkhurst was leaning against the mantel by the fire and gazing into the glowing coals. He looked up, saw her and held out his arms.

"Marguerite!"

"For the last time, the very very last," she whispered, clinging to him as if no force in all the world could ever separate them again.

"Marguerite, my darling, my own, there will be a way for us yet. We love each other too well to be parted forever. I cannot, I will not give you up. Our separation will only be for a little while."

Even as he spoke the ghost of a reproach flitted through his mind that Marguerite had caused him to suffer as he was suffering. He loved her as well as he was capable of loving any one; loved her as his ideal of all that was beautiful and true and sweet in womanhood; loved her almost as well as he loved himself.

He stroked her hair, murmuring all the fond tender names she had been so glad to hear.

Then the deliriously sweet thought came to the girl:

"It is not too late, it is not yet too late. I can speak to Mr. Dalton, and every thing can be undone, can be as it was before. I must have been mad to think that I could live without my idol.

God cannot, does not expect such a sacrifice from me. Death — I could be resigned to die, but to live without Paul? Never!"

The ecstasy of this thought went coursing through her veins, bringing new fire into the eyes so heavy with their suppressed agony a moment before. But the temptation passed, she recognized it as a temptation even whilst it lingered.

"Until the last farthing has been paid," said the voice sorrowfully, and then the great black doors of her heart's dungeon rolled shut and pinioned her to despair again.

She pressed her lips to his cheek, and he, feeling strangely moved at their velvety touch, did not know that it was a kiss of renunciation.

She slipped away from him and sat down nearer the fire.

"Don't leave me Marguerite," he pleaded, coming over to her.

"This is the last time we shall be together for so long."

"It is the last time forever Paul," she answered with a sob rising in her throat.

"Don't, don't say that Marguerite my darling — Don't unman me altogether under the burden before me."

The last moments went flying by, the clock seemed to be racing with her heartbeats. He made a move to rise. She took off his ring, and offered it to him, with a dizzy feeling in her head, and a queer numbness around the lips.

He looked at her in a pained surprise, refusing to take the glittering bauble.

"Why, Marguerite, my dearest, you are surely not in earnest!"

Without a word she held out her finger, and he slipped the ring back in its place again. But she knew better than any outward sign could tell, that their engagement was at an end. The sacrifice was complete.

Little as she knew of men's nature she knew enough to feel that if the witchery of her presence, their love at its purest, sweetest point, had not outweighed the worldly considerations on the other side of the scale, they would never do so in the future when time and separation had dimmed his love and his pain.

Her own love, her own pain would be a burden to carry to the grave. But she accepted the cross. In that hour of her trial when all human consolation, and even Heaven itself, seemed to have deserted her, strength came to nerve her for the final renunciation. She did not pray, she did not even think; but the prayers which had been poured out with such a passionate intensity for all the weary, agonizing weeks that had past, must surely have counted for something in the hour of her temptation and trial.

She did not faint, she did not even cry out with her pain when at last the earl took her in his arms, and pressed his lips to hers in their last parting. In only three short weeks they were to have been all the world to each other, one heart, one soul, inseparably united in the golden bonds which only death,—not even death where the love was as deep as theirs,—could temporarily break. And now he had left her! She flung herself in his chair, her whole frame quivering with tearless moans. And when she heard the street door close, the rattle of the wheels of his carriage, and realized that he was really gone, a something within her seemed to snap. — It was not her heart, for it went on throbbing in its anguish, not her mind, she could recall every incident of her life since she had known Paul, as if it were standing out in bold outline before her; not her faith, she was trying to accept bravely the chalice pressed to her lips; but a something of herself had given way and she knew that she would never be quite the same again.

She dragged herself up the stairs, stopping from sheer exhaustion at every landing; when finally she reached her own room again, the clock was striking three. In another half hour the ship would leave, bearing away her love, her life forever. Then a wild, unreasoning desire rushed upon her to see him, only to see him once more. She could not let him pass out of her life without one last farewell.

She threw on her street gown, seized her cloak and purse, grabbed her hat and gloves, she did not know what she was putting on, and went flying down the stairs, and out into the street. She did not have time to get her carriage, she hoped almost prayed that a cab would be passing. She did not know the way very well on the cars, and time was precious. A hack came up, and she offered the driver ten dollars if he would take her to the dock before the steamer sailed. She gave the impression, without actually saying so, that something had been forgotten by one of the passengers.

There proved to be plenty of time. People were just going on board, and the hurry, and scramble, the crowds, the shouts, the huge ship, the dock itself, every thing — seemed strange and yet so familiar. She closed her eyes and tried to imagine herself a little girl again, going away to France, then the bright, happy Marguerite who had sailed, only a few months before, to England, with Paul on the other side waiting for her. She tried to fancy that the horrible weight crushing her inmost soul was only some ghastly dream. The bell began to jangle, the whistle to blow. She told the hackman to wait for her, and went running down towards the ship. She stopped by a grim, ugly warehouse, crouching against its weather beaten walls, hoping yet fearing that Paul would see her. In another moment his brougham dashed up, she recognized the horses, and Paul got out and hurried up the gangplank. A little later and he would have been left. Marguerite strained her eyes trying to distinguish him in the crowd, clutching at her throat to choke back the lump that was corroding it. He went below immediately, his valet followed closely carrying a traveling rug, valise, steamer chair and the other accoutrements of an ocean voyage. But Marguerite did not stir. It was beginning to mist. The forms on deck came and went like ghosts in the gathering twilight. The ship seemed like a phantom from dreamland. The bell kept up its jangle, then the cable was loosened, the great leviathan began to move. A figure came out, apart from the crowd, and seemed to be gazing intently at the receding land. "That is Paul," Marguerite whispered, she was sure she could not mistake him. She waved her handkerchief, the blinding tears shutting out the sight of every thing material excepting Paul — she saw him as plainly as if he were standing at her side. The splash, splash of the waves, the measured vibrations of the screw came to her as a dying echo.

A curve of the shore loomed up in ghostly outlines in the mist, the ship was ploughing down the narrows, throwing up mountains of beautiful spray in its wake — and Paul was gone.

She walked back to the hack, seeing without knowing that she saw, the great barnlike structures about her, the rough looking people staring curiously at her, the drizzle falling on the stony, jagged streets, the lights beginning to appear at the corners.

She did not want to go home, she only wanted to be alone, to escape from herself, her pain, but she gave the driver her number mechanically.

She was learning that the penalty attached to every good and beautiful gift of soul is that the converse of a quality always goes with it.

Lighter natures would never have loved with such passionate depths, — they would not have suffered with such intensity.

XXXII.

MARGUERITE dismissed the hack at Forty Fifth Street, and walked up the Avenue, now beginning to be lighted for the approaching night. She wanted fresh air — the hack had seemed like a stifling prison.

Presently she came to the great white Cathedral, standing like a refuge in her path. She went in. Only the steady gleams from the sanctuary lamp illumined the lofty aisles, throwing shadows around sculptured saint and chiseled altar. Something of its solemn peace seemed to encompass her. She stole over to a statue of the Blessed Virgin, and sank on her knees.

"Mother in Heaven, I have burnt my ships. The most desolate of all your children comes to you. You who suffered so much, by the memory of your own bitter anguish have pity on me."

She grew calmer and a strange sweetness was stealing over her spirits. Then the church, the altar, the twilight, every thing vanished, and she was kneeling at the feet of the All Kind Mother. A hand of caressing softness rested on her head, and a voice said, oh so gently, "My child, I do pity you. Though all the world turn, I am true. You are my child, I am your Mother. I am the Refuge of the sorrowful. You suffer now, but only for a little time, in Heaven there are no tears."

On the beautiful face there was no look of reproach for the year in which an earthly love had been enthroned as an idol in her heart, but only a

Mother's tenderness. Marguerite felt herself being lead by the hand over a dark, rough road through a black forest to the seashore. The great angry waves were dashing against a frail craft creaking and straining in a mighty wind, the Twelve Fishermen of Galilee were crouching in fear and trembling, looking with strained, eager eyes toward a common Focus.

"Lord Save us ere we perish!"

A Form of surpassing benignity and loveliness arose slowly from the raging waters, the majestic figure of the Saviour of the World was with them. Every detail was vivid, the look of fear changing to confidence on the face of the Apostles, the rocky shore, the angry waves towering up with the force of the mighty wind: It was one of her favorite pictures in the galleries of the Louvre,— The Stilling of the Waters,—and she had spent hours and hours before it, entranced at its subtle, grandly beautiful sublimity.

And now she could hear the very words of Divinity: "Peace, Be still!" The boat passed on, the Dear Saviour, clothed in His robes of white was ascending into Heaven, but He was taking her with Him. She was kneeling at those Sacred Feet; pain, every thing was forgotten — nothing seemed worth considering but the privilege of kneeling there forever.

A sudden noise, as of something falling, sounded through the great silent temple.

"Have I been to Heaven, or have I been dreaming," said Marguerite, recalled to herself. Nothing like this had filled her soul since she was a little girl at the convent in dear old France.

She looked around with a startled gaze; the sexton had lit the gas, people were coming in, a clergyman was in the sanctuary. Then she remembered that to-morrow would be the New Year, this day, which had been so fateful for her, was the last of the year, the old year, the year which would ever stand apart from all the other years of her life. These people more pious than she, were coming to cast off the burden of their sins, to begin with a clean score on the morrow.

"My God, my Saviour my All, I am sorry for my sins, I cannot recall them now, but I am sorry, sorry with all my heart. Forgive us our trespasses as we forgive those —" a vision of her step mother came before her. "No, no I cannot forgive her, she has ruined all my life, but for her I would be happy oh, so happy! Forgive her!—I hate her, I hate her with all my soul!"

Again she saw the Fishermen's boat and the Saviour rising from the waters, but blood was streaming from Hands and Feet, and a crown of cruel thorns was pressing into His Sacred Brow.

"No, no, I did not mean that, my God — dear Jesus, I do not hate any body, I forgive her as I hope to be forgiven. I do not wish her any harm, I hope she may be happy! Through the merits of Thy Precious Blood shed for us all on the Cross, forgive me my sins."

A figure shrouded in the long crepe veil which is only assumed for death, not the death of a life's hopes, but the death which is covered from mortal sight in the grave, came over to the altar and knelt beside Marguerite. She was young too, a mere girl, although she wore widow's weeds, and Marguerite felt her heart go out to this stranger in a wave of deepest pity. Other hearts ached beside her own, other lives, too, had been made desolate! Not far away a workingman with his little dinner basket at his side, was praying with all the fervor which characterizes the Christian poor.

"We are all children of the same God," she thought; "whether we are poor or rich, high or low, does not matter much, will not matter at all when the last dread hour comes. And the Good God who made us all, and who loves us in spite of our sins, must feel sorry for us, divinely compassionate for the sufferings He cannot, without destroying His own laws, avert."

The clouds were rolling back again, but they had lost something of their weight. She closed her eyes, and tried to feel again the sweetness of that waking dream, but she was conscious only of the altar, the long aisles of the church, the people, and that it must be getting very late. It seemed agony to tear herself away. She was like a child who fears to let go its mother's hand, to cross a bridge alone. She dreaded lest her burden would be waiting for her just outside the church door. Every thing now was unreal, as if it had happened in some far off time. But she must say a prayer before going, for Paul, that he would be happy, find the means to settle with his creditors, that he would have a safe journey home — ah, she must pray every day, every hour of her life, that no harm would come to Paul. And with the thought of Paul, even as she prayed for him with passionate fervor, her pain came back.

She turned again to the Universal Mother for a last petition for herself. *"Remember, oh, most compassionate Virgin Mother* — I do not deserve compassion, but you are my mother and you will not forget your sorrowful child, God must be a just God as well as merciful, but a Mother is always compassionate — *that it has never been heard in any age, that those who implored thy aid or sought thy protection, were ever abandoned by thee.* In all the ages you have been a mother to all the world; be a mother to me now, I know that I am not worthy, but I can bear no more, have pity. — *Inspired with this confidence I cast myself at thy sacred feet, and do most humbly beseech thee, oh, Mother of the Eternal Word, to adopt me as thy child, to take upon thyself the cares of my eternal salvation, and to watch over me at the hour of my death.* Oh, let it not be said, my dearest Mother, that I have perished where no one ever found aught but grace and salvation. *Amen."*

She had learned to lisp the Memorare at her mother's knee in far off California, and every day of her life she had recited its glowing petitions. Love for the Blessed Virgin who was the Mother of the World's Redeemer, and therefore above all other earthly creatures, was as much a part of her life as the air she breathed or the sunshine. She had early been taught that this tender Mother was especially the mother of orphans, and she went to her in her little, childish troubles with all the confidence of a child. She had always cherished a very tender devotion to the memory of her own mother, and she reasoned with the simple logic of a child, that if she loved her mother so well whom she scarcely remembered, then the dear Jesus must love His with an infinitely deeper love, and that if the Blessed Mother asked Him any thing no matter what, He could not refuse.

She was accustomed to praying for any thing that she wanted. To her trusting faith there was nothing irreverent or unusual in the petition: "Dear Mother, we are going to have our picnic to-morrow; please ask God not to let it rain."

And now that she had come to womanhood, with a woman's sorrow crushing her, she turned instinctively to this protecting, if unseen Mother.

She was startled, and not a little frightened to find, when she was once again outside the church door, that it was so late, and that the darkness was so very dark. She had forgotten the drizzle and the clouds of the twilight. She had never been out at this hour alone before, and a natural timidity as well as the sense of doing something unusual, made her wish to be at home. There was no way to get a carriage or a cab, but it was not very far to walk. As she turned up the street she met Carroll Kirwin walking down. He gave a start on seeing her, and was about to stop to speak to her, when she pulled down her veil as if to avoid recognition; but not soon enough to prevent his seeing her tear stained face, and the look of unutterable woe marked in its every lineament. He had just heard from Edith Kingman the evening before, that the marriage of Marguerite to Lord Parkhurst had been indefinitely postponed, and that the announcement to that effect would be made public on the next day. She had not told him why, but one glimpse of Marguerite conveyed the assurance that a cooled affection on her part had nothing to do with it.

He turned and followed her, keeping well in the rear, to see that she reached home in safety.

A fierce indignation filled his breast at the man who had caused her such grief. And yet whilst he pitied her with all his generous heart, and would have done a great deal to remove her trouble, he was conscious of a certain gladness that she was free. He despised himself for the feeling, and never for a moment consented to being glad.

He said, under his breath, but with manly sincerity, as he walked along behind her in the drizzle, "Marguerite, little girl, I would give a great deal if I could make you as happy tonight as I saw you a year ago."

He watched her enter the house, saw the great door swing to, and then turned and went on his way.

He was not in love with Marguerite, he told himself, but it was only by a strong effort of the will that he was not.

The girl went noiselessly up to her room. It was dinner time, but she could not meet the family; she did not want to see a living soul, her one desire was to be alone. Alone with her terrible grief. It all came back to her the moment she entered the house. She passed the library, the door was still open just as she had left it, the fateful room where the happiness and the sorrow of her life had come. She remembered, as if it were but yesterday, the evening when her father had sent for her in this room to tell her of the new mother he was going to give her; how she had stormed, how her childish heart had ached. Was her grief, she asked herself, but a prescience of the evil that was coming to her with that marriage? Had her father not come within the toils of an unscrupulous woman she would still be happy, rich, loving and loved, instead of the desolate creature she was. She saw the familiar easy chair, a favorite of Paul's and almost expected to see him rise from its depths.

She changed her mind about going to her own apartment, and kept on, instead, to a tiny room in the tower of the house fitted up as an observatory. Her maid would be coming to her room, perhaps even her step-mother, who had refused to quarrel. If she was not there, they would think that she had gone to Edith's for the night. She was thirsty, and her throat was burning, but she wanted nothing to eat. She stopped at a stationary washstand, pressed her lips to the faucet, and then went up to the tower and locked the door. She recalled with a shudder, that the last time she had been there had been with Paul to show him the view. Its pitch darkness sent a shock through her nerves. She crouched down by the window; the lights of the city were twinkling fitfully through the mist and utter blackness of the night. No stars were to be seen any where. Stretched out before her were myriads of roofs: There were lights and warmth in happy homes, with love and peace and plenty; there were homes where death had invaded; homes where victims were struggling with disease; homes where the wailings of sorrow, of sin perhaps, vibrated; homes in which were enacted all the silent tragedies of human life and human passions; but in all the two cities united in wedlock by the bridge, she wondered if there was any one as desolate as herself. The peace which had come to her in the church had not left her, but it only gave her grace to bear, it did not alleviate her anguish. As she knelt by the window she told herself that she was keeping a vigil with the corpse of her life's dead hopes; that the blackness of the night but typified the blackness of her future.

She strained her gaze towards the sea; in fancy she could see the huge ship ploughing the waves. What was Paul doing? Standing on the deck thinking of her!

The thought sent a thrill of tenderness through her heart. For one dangerous moment she pictured a reunion. He would resign his title and his estates with his debts and difficulties, to his brother, and return. The grand new West was again beckoning to them. "Come to me, and find name and fame and a career. I have all good gifts and am crying for my children."

But she banished it as a temptation.

For hours and hours she crouched by the window until her limbs were stiff and numb. Then she walked across the room with a quick nervous tread, to restore the circulation. She was thirsty again, but she was afraid to venture down for water lest some one might hear her. The walking made her tired, and she resumed her watch by the window. The lights in the neighboring windows were going out. A clock struck eleven; she was surprised that it was so early. A star came out and struggled fitfully with the clouds and was swallowed up in the general blackness. It seemed a good omen.

"Take a message to my darling from me. You are shining on him too. Oh, what is he doing? has he but a tithe of my pain this night?"

She began to feel cold in spite of her cloak. She walked again to dispel the chill. The darkness was terrible. Ghosts came out of the tower. Up and down, up and down she paced, trying to project her life into the future. She pictured herself living in loneliness, but the guardian angel of the poor. She would retire to a distant village and devote her little fortune to works of charity. Then she fancied herself in her grave; surely she could not live long and endure such pain. God was merciful — she had restored the money, that was enough! She was so weary, so utterly weary, she longed for rest. God was good, and he would take her to Himself.

She pictured herself in the coffin, cold and still and shrouded in white. She saw Paul hurry into the room; she stopped there in her thoughts, to place the room; it would not be in her stepmother's house, the home for one short year of her childhood, and again in her joyous womanhood, which she meant to leave as soon as possible; she thought of the convent but rejected that for fear that Paul would not be admitted, and at last, placed it in a strange, beautiful home which would be Edith's after her marriage. Edith was there weeping when Paul arrived, but she only pressed his hand in sympathy and left him alone with the dead. He was careworn and pale, torn with regrets, now that it was too late, that he had not counted every thing well lost for her sake. Then his tears and his kisses were falling on her marble lips, and he was weeping as strong men weep. She was feeling pity for him, and longing to comfort him, although lying there, still and cold, in the coffin. It would only be for a little while, and then they would be united forever in Heaven.

Her fur boa fell to the floor, and she realized that she was not in her coffin, but in the tower room, and that it was getting very cold.

Then her thoughts went out again to the ship sailing away to England. They were changing the watch now; now a boat was passing, the fog horn was sounding. Then all was quiet, every one had retired but Paul. He was standing on the deck looking with sad eyes towards New York.

More lights went out; the watchman passed by with his slow measured tread, like a sentinel on duty. She was glad he was there, if she got frightened she would throw something down on the pavement. She was beginning to be sleepy; a tired sensation was creeping over her eyelids, and pressing them down over sad eyes that had wept so much, and were still so heavy with the weight of unshed tears. There was a little sofa in the room — she would cover herself as best she could with her cloak and go to sleep. She slipped her muff under her head for a pillow, but she was cold, and her throat was getting very sore; it seemed to be closing with a big lump; she tried to say 'Paul' softly, but only a hoarse whisper came. Then she remembered that just outside the door was a big rug, she turned the key gently, she did not want any one to hear and come tearing up there in search of burglars. Not a sound was to be heard, the stillness was ghostly; she clutched the rug in terror and got back into the room.

The clock was striking twelve : suddenly the air was vibrating with the bomb, bomb, of a cannon, and then all the bells began to ring, the signal gun went off, and more cannons. Ah! she had forgotten, the old year was dead, and the New Year was being welcomed to his throne.

The dear old Year! She would never forget, — the New Year was nothing to her! Then she stretched herself on the sofa, covered with the big warm rug, and went to sleep, the sleep of exhaustion.

XXXIII.

MARGUERITE turned in the hour of her greatest need to the friend, the counsellor, the mother of her childhood — Madame Florac. She wanted to get away from herself, from her surroundings, from the scene of her brief happiness, her little triumphs, her defeat. She wanted to go where there would be no prying eyes to speculate over the outbursts of her woe, or note the tenseness of its restraint. And yet she wanted sympathy, counsel, love. Edith was all that a tried and true friend could be, but she was too happy, too bright too much of the world in which Marguerite felt that she herself would have a place no more forever.

She had written to Madame Florac a full account of her troubles, and the probable breaking off of her engagement to Lord Parkhurst, a fortnight before their culmination, and by return steamer she received all the comfort that a tender letter could give, and the assurance that an asylum would always be awaiting her in her old convent home. This letter, received the day after the departure of the earl, when she was prostrated on a sick bed with a sore throat, and every indication of pneumonia, roused her to the necessary physical exertion to resist the threatened attack. A sudden resolution flashed through her brain even as she read the loving, kind words; she would go back to the convent and stay there, indefinitely. She had plenty of means to admit of this course, and there, at least, was one true heart on which she could depend. Edith also was true and loving and loyal, but Madame Florac was all that and more, for Madame Florac was above the world, and worldly standards. She raised up on her pillow, called for a pencil and a piece of paper, and scrawled a cablegram: "I am coming. Marguerite."

Edith with a protest on her lips, sent this message immediately, and when, half an hour later, the physician whom Mrs. Kingman had summoned, called on his rounds, he was surprised and gratified to see such a marked change in his patient. After her night in the tower room Marguerite had gone to Edith's early the next morning, and by that young lady had been forthwith put to bed.

Two days later a steamer bound for France numbered among its passengers Marguerite Clayton and her maid. The maid would return on the same ship, Marguerite feeling that her reduced circumstances would not permit the luxury of an attendant, not yet grown so indispensable to American maidens as to their transatlantic cousins; besides, in the retired life she intended to lead and the simple garb she meant to assume, a maid would have no place.

Madame Florac, looking just as she did when Marguerite entered the convent eleven years before, and as she looked when the girl left it, unchanged, and unchangeable, it almost seemed, welcomed her child at the portals, folding her in a long embrace, which conveyed as words could not have done, affection, sympathy, protection, and strength, so far as it is given one human soul to be strength for another in its sorest straits.

Even Mother Salette herself had come out in the wide hall to welcome the returning lamb.

How familiar, how much the same was every thing, and how vitally changed herself! was Marguerite's first thought. She was taken immediately to a bright warm room at the extreme end of the corridor into which her old room opened.

Mother Salette was for giving the girl her former quarters, but Madame Florac wisely decided that there would be too many memories revived and too many regrets in that room. The girls who had been Juniors in short frocks, and were now graduates-elect, whom Marguerite remembered, came in little groups to call on her, and in listening to the convent chronicles and their girlish plans, she was forced into a temporary forgetfulness of her own troubles. She could almost imagine herself a school girl again, and all this load on her heart a dream, or the pathetic history of some one she had read about in a chance biography.

Although no one could have told who started the report, it gradually became known that Marguerite had lost her fortune and that her noble English lover, like Ulysses, had sailed away.

Marguerite felt, or fancied she felt, that there was a change towards her. Every body was most kind, unfailingly kind, but their very kindness was an intimation that she needed it as she had never done in the old days. But she told herself that she was not surprised; she did not expect a miracle to be worked, and the world would not be the world, human nature, human, but angelic, especially foreign human nature, circumscribed and limited by generations of cast distinctions, if there had been no change. An inclination to pride had been fostered by a certain consideration which she had grown to regard as her right, and in its stead she now received kindness and compassion. She could bear this from nuns and from school girls, but compassion from her friends in the gay world would have been beyond her strength.

But Madame Florac had changed only in being more loving, heroically patient with the girl's moods, and infinitely tender.

"Ah! those Americans, you never know what to make of them," sighed Madame Duval with a shake of her head; "rich to-day, poor to-morrow. America must be a strange country!"

And she chatted away in broken English to a maiden from Scotland who had heard Marguerite's history from some of the older girls. The little nun was still wrestling with the intricacies of the English pronunciation which audaciously refused to be governed by any rules, and was as impatient of restraint as the old fashioned American girl, rapidly dying out, who had invaded the country a decade before, and given the staid dowagers a shock some of them never got over. But in spite of her thoughtless gossip her compassion for Marguerite was genuine and without a tinge of malice.

Perhaps, in nothing was the change in her position more manifest to the girl than this changed attitude in Madame Duval.

The nun stopped to speak to her in Gaellic-English, and to ask how she felt, every day. Marguerite wanted to tell her that she need not practice self denial in such a heroic degree; it always seemed to her that Madame was enacting a chapter out of a painfully good story book where inclination and duty were perpetually at war. In the gigantic battle she herself had waged on the same lines, she had not adverted to the story books at all. As in all heroic acts, the grandeur of the act overshadowed every other consideration; there was no attempt even to view it as an act. A general does not stop in the middle of a charge to exult that his name will go down in history; and the soul in its greatest suffering does not analyze its anguish, or think of the degree of sanctity it may attain through its weary way towards Calvary.

In New York Marguerite's affairs were talked of much more than they were at the convent; how they became known in less than a week after her departure, was one of the mysteries which only an expert in gossip could solve.

Mrs. Kingman said, petulantly that, one of the mistakes people were constandly making was to imagine that any thing could be kept secret.

"The world is such a little world after all," she continued, "in spite of the continents and the vast expanse of seas we are always talking about, that we are constantly touching at points where least expected.

"Make up your mind that every thing you ever did, or said, or thought of in your whole life, that you would wish concealed, is known, and to the very ones you would most wish to be kept in ignorance of it; and be equally certain that the things you would wish known and remembered, are buried in hopeless oblivion. The bad in gossip is a gas that rises, and passes through key holes, and registers, and closed windows; the good is a solid which falls to the ground by the force of its own gravitation, so if you want it to spread you must take it up bodily and send it forth well supported.

"Why, a family secret of a family not ten blocks from here, came into my possession not so very long ago, in the most circuitous way imaginable. The housekeeper, in the famly in question, told it, in strict confidence to a friend of hers, who told it to a friend of hers who keeps a boardinghouse, who told it to one of the boarders, a seamstress, who told it to a friend of hers, visiting her from another city, who told it to her friend, who told it to my maid, who told it to me. I was curious, knowing the family very well, so I traced the story to its origin. Of course, I do not believe in allowing gossip in servants, but Leonie has been with me so long, beside it is stupid to say nothing at all when you are having your hair brushed.

"So the best way, my dear, is to make up your mind to have no secrets; for if you do, you are bound to tell them unless you are an exceptionally sensible woman, and when they are once told to one you might as well tell the world. The tale is sure to go from one to another until, at last, some ill natured tongue betrays you. Or it may not be an ill natured, merely a thoughtless tongue. If you cannot keep a secret yourself do not expect any body else to keep it for you."

Everywhere Edith denied the story that Marguerite was penniless, and asserted that her friend had a handsome fortune left. She was careful not to give the amount.

She denied also that Marguerite's engagement to LordParkhurst was at an end, declaring the wedding had merely been postponed. She claimed that Marguerite was not feeling well, and had gone to France, the climate in which she was raised, to recuperate physically, and that she would return in due time to New York.

Edith meant that Marguerite should return, although she was not sure of the means she would employ to bring her back when the proper time came.

She did not believe at all that Marguerite's life was wrecked, or that the future had nothing in store for her. It had a very charming home and a very noble man for a husband if she knew any thing about human nature, and she thought she knew a great deal.

But to Marguerite she would not have dared even to hint at such a future. And Marguerite herself, whilst she struggled bravely to be resigned, had no thought of a future which held any thing else but a cross as heavy as she could bear.

She was realizing, too, as she had not done in the first days of her trouble, that an American heiress, and an American comparatively, if not positively poor, were two very different people. But she bore every thing sweetly as a part of her changed conditions.

Madame Florac spent as much time with Marguerite as she could spare from her school room duties and her prayers. The girl looked so pale, so wan, so sad, there was such a pathetic attempt to seem natural when in company, to show an interest in ordinary affairs where no interest was felt, that the calmest, most phlegmatic hearts were stirred with generous pity. But the compassion was all for the loss of her fortune. The good religieuse talked to her about resignation to the will of God, and the great responsibilities of wealth. It would not have seemed possible to them that a girl could grieve so for a mere fiancé. That the loss of her money was as nothing compared with the loss of her lover, would have been an enigma to these pious, French souls. To them there would have appeared something very strange in a girl's loving a man to whom she was not married; a wife must love her husband, of course, that was right and proper, but a maiden — the most she could do was to submit to being loved.

The past seemed unreal to Marguerite, and yet its pain never left her. She wondered, half-whimsically, at times if she where not under some strange, terrible spell. She was fond of going over all the old familiar scenes: she saw Paris in the distance, as she had seen it on the day Madame Flaubert's invitation began the first link in the chain of her fate; she wandered into the room which had been Edith's and latter on her own, recalling their innocent dreams their girlish enthusiasm; the grove of trees denuded of their leaves, the beeches and maples which lined the great drive, the flower beds well kept and geometrical laid off, where the hardy geraniums bloomed all winter; the summer house with its dead vines, the court where for years and years she had taken exercise,—every familiar nook and corner, hall or corridor was eloquent with the voice of the past, the syren song of her youth's bright hopes.

Madame Florac gently insisted on Marguerite's resuming her musical studies which had ever been her delight, so she devoted hours and hours every day to the piano and the harp, and even took up a new instrument, to occupy her days; she got her sketch book and worked assiduously at sketches of the old scenes. She pleased herself by saying that she was making them to fill a portfolio for Edith, but in the moments of unsparing honesty which she demanded of herself as well as of others, she acknowledged that she was doing them as an occupation for her mind and hands, as a relief from torturing memories.

She spent a great deal of time in the chapel.

"I must be very very wicked," she said to Madame Florac; "I do not feel that holy resignation, that submission to the Will of God that we read about in the lives of the saints."

"Ah! my dear, perhaps that is because in the lives of the saints sufficient stress is not laid on the merely human side of their natures; their biographers are too anxious to get to the heroic stage to dwell with much force on the time of struggle. St. Jane de Chantel was inconsolable after the loss of her husband, her friends even feared for her health if not for her mind; yet we are left to imagine the lonely vigils, the passionate outbursts, the struggle with human grief, before she attained the calm of sanctity, the peace of the religious life.

You must not be scrupulous, that was never a fault of yours in the old days. You did your duty nobly, and God, in His own good time, will give you strength to bear your cross with patience. You may not bear it willingly now, but, at least, you can will to be willing, and that is something."

Again, her whole soul rose up in bitter rebellion. In her dreams the past all came back again. Memory was always busy at night, more than in the day, when constant occupation left no time for brooding. She suffered from insomnia, and seldom went to sleep without first spending hours tossing about from one side of the little bed to the other. When physically worn out, her eye-lids gradually relaxed, sleep would steal over them, and then some good fairy, she said gratefully that it was her Guardian Angel, would lead her sweetly into the enchanted realm of dreams. Again she wandered with Paul down by the seashore at Old Point Comfort, or talked to him in the library at home, or they were together at a reception or ball, at Edith's or in London, or at Parkhurst, but always together. His tones lingered in her ears, his words of endearment, his laugh. Sometimes the spirit of evil hovered near, and in her dreams the agony of the parting was gone through with again. Once she dreamed she was in England at Castle Parkhurst on her honeymoon. She could see the moonlight on the lake, the shadows on forest and glen, and falling athwart the long graveled drives. She awoke to find a stray moonbeam streaming in at a half closed shutter, and it took a moment to realize that she was in a white draped little bed in a Franch

Convent, and not in a lordly English manor. She got up and went to the window, pulling aside the curtain and gazing dreamily at the calm scene. Where was Paul and what was he doing? Was he sleeping calmly, or was he dreaming of her? For a frantic, jealous moment she pictured Maud Atherton at Parkhurst in the place that was to have been hers. Then the silent, majestic beauty of the night filled her soul, she went back to bed, and was soon sleeping peacefully, a dreamless sleep.

A month after Marguerite's return to Paris Madeleine, now the Countess of Clermonde, called in response to a note of explanation and invitation from Madame Florac, and begged and insisted that her old friend go home with her for a long visit.

Madame Florac had decided that a change of scene would be the best thing for Marguerite. She thought that the girl had nursed her grief long enough, and that there was danger of her getting morbid; although Marguerite had refused persistently to see any one outside of the convent, Madame Florac insisted that she must see Madeleine.

"She needs to be where she will be compelled to control her emotions," said Madame Florac, who believed that the ability to do a thing came with the doing; she reasoned that Marguerite, by being forced to appear resigned and contented, would eventually become so, that she could not remain detached from all surrounding objects, but would certainly become interested in something and be in a way, lifted out of herself.

Nor could she see why Marguerite might not in

time get married and be a happy woman. Loss of fortune was no obstacle she was told, to matrimony in America. She knew that her pupil had been deeply attached to Lord Parkhurst, but she had no conception of the real depth of the attachment. She could understand, if the girl had been widowed, how she might remain faithful forever to the memory of her husband, because that was her nature; but that she could or would remain true to a lover who had given her up, one who would probably form other ties, so that her love would cease to be a folly and become a sin, was an enigma in which Madame Florac did not believe.

The best medicine in this case, she thought, would be the society of the cultivated and brilliant men the girl would meet as Madeleine's guest in Paris.

Madeleine was a great lady on her own account, and not merely her mother's daughter; Marguerite noticed the change at once, despite the pre-occupation of her grief, and great grief is always selfish in its first throes: it is only afterwards that suffering makes the heart tender for the sufferings of others, and considerate of their interests.

Madeleine was now the rose which Marguerite had seen before only as a bud; a promising bud perhaps, but still a bud, with no suggestion in its modest petals of the brilliant blossom. Marguerite did not know that it is a constantly recurring surprise to Americans, no matter how much they reside abroad, this change which marriage makes in a French girl's life.

Madeleine was wrapped in rich furs, and wore a gown which fitted as only Parisian gowns ever fit; she had an air of command, of assurance of herself and her own position, which seemed to foreignize the demure little school-girl Marguerite remembered. But the change was all on the surface; at heart she was as simple, as affectionate, as sweetly true as in the convent days. The fondness with which she greated her old schoolmate made Marguerite half-ashamed of her own lack of ardor; her affection for Madeleine had not become less, but it had less vitality; in the glow of the master passion of her heart other affections had not been overthrown, but they had been put aside or absorbed.

Madeleine did not understand her friend's changed conditions, and it would have made no difference had she understood.

She could not conceive of a position resting on money. Money was useful, indispensable sometimes, but only as a means. It enabled one to discharge the duties of one's station, it did not make the station itself. She was too familiar with rank in poverty to feel any thing but the liveliest compassion for Marguerite's losses.

She did not know any thing of that deeper anguish gnawing at the exile's heart. She knew, of course, that Marguerite's engagement to Lord Parkhurst had been broken off; that was public news. It had been cabled across to the London dailies as soon as it became known in New York, and had found its way into half a dozen of the great papers of Europe. It had been freely commented upon in Paris where the earl was very well known, and Marguerite, also, by reputation. The American colony had been especially interested, and Madeleine was exceedingly popular with the American residents of her capital city. But it did not enter into her calculations that a girl could have any deep attachment for a man who was not her husband.

Although Marguerite declined her friend's invitation with tears in her eyes, and tears in her voice, she consented, in the end, to go for a few days. When she was at last in the carriage and rolling towards Paris, she was conscious of a certain desire to see Madeleine's husband and Madeleine's home, and the thought even of Paris itself was not unpleasant.

XXXIV.

THE few days lengthened into a fortnight, and at the end of that time Marguerite consented, with very little persuasion, to spend the remainder of the winter with Madeleine.

Madeleine's home, whilst not luxurious, she made no secret of being only moderately well off, — was pleasant and bright, and spacious enough to prevent a guest's feeling in the way. Her husband was simply delightful. He affected to be a man of affairs, but in reality he was only a big boy. He was so deferential, so considerate, so genuinely good, so honorable, that it would have been impossible not to like him. And his friends, whose number was legion, did not stop to consider if he were very learned, or very deep, or a great genius for any thing but French geneaology and French cooking. Even these things he seemed to know well, simply because such knowledge was required of a French gentleman. He was manifestly so fond of his wife that Marguerite liked him from the first. Although their modest domicile was overshadowed by stately and magnificent houses all around it, the Clermonds entertained in their little drawing-room the denizens of the Faubourg St. Germaine who had never been prevailed upon to see the new palaces, or recognize the newer people. On Madeleine's day crested carriages stood at her door, which envious, and less blue blooded neighbors would have given their little fingers to see at their own. The Americans came to a knowledge of Madeleine's charms through her aunt, Madame Gaston. The defection of this lady from immemorial traditions was secretly mourned by her more conservative friends. She boldly asserted that she preferred to talk broken English, and listen to impossible French in an American drawing-room to any society a native Parisian could offer. But when she openly declared that the time for laziness was past, and that she did not see why Frenchmen, who were as poor as an orphan asylum, should not learn wisdom from the Americans and go to work, even her husband thought it was time to protest against her radical views. Madame Gaston came to see Marguerite as soon as she heard of her presence in Paris, and in less than half an hour had mapped out a course of amusement and social rounds which the girl received in dismay. Only her plea of physical indisposition, confirmed by Madeleine, secured any remission of these well-intentioned plans.

However, Marguerite could not refuse all the invitations sent to her, and she soon began to take even a certain pleasure in the old rounds.

She remembered, with a smile, one of Edith's sayings: "Life may be a desert, but there are a good many oases in it."

She would have been less than human had she not reverted, in the sight of Madeleine's happiness, to the might-have-been, for herself.

"Tell me about your marriage, Madeleine," she said one day, as they sat chatting together after luncheon. The Count rarely came home for luncheon, although Marguerite often wondered what a man without any business, could be doing down town so much of the time.

"In the old days there was no Count Clermond. Did you know him a long time ?"

"His mother was an old friend of Mamma's," answered Madeleine, "but they had not seen each other for years, when Madame Clermond wrote to Mamma that she had heard about me." — The young Countess blushed a little at this point, for the letter had been very flattering to herself.

"She was anxious for her son to get married and settle down, and she thought an alliance between us, the families being such old friends, might be arranged. Several letters were written, and then Mamma and I came to Paris to make a little visit to Aunt Berthe; Madame Clermond and Pierre also came on to Paris, and we saw each other. He was very nice and very devoted to me, and every body likes Pierre. We were both willing for the marriage, and then there was some trouble about the dowry, and the negotiations were broken off."

Marguerite felt a responsive thrill of sympathy at this.

"You poor girl, so you have suffered too," she exclaimed more to herself than to her friend.

Madeleine seemed slightly puzzled at this. "Yes about the dowry," she hazarded. "It was awkward. It takes such a big dowry these days, for living is so expensive; quite different, Mamma says, from what it used to be just after we lost our kings. Then Andre married and made every thing right about the dowry; and so Pierre and I were married."

"But tell me about your wooing, your courtship, as we say in English," continued Marguerite.

"Oh, I saw him a great deal; at Aunt Berthe's reception, and at the betrothal dinner, and afterwards in the mornings when he came to call on Mamma; and we danced together at parties."

"Madeleine, would it have broken your heart to have had to give him up. Suppose your brother had not married as he did, and Pierre had married somebody else?"

"Why, I should have wished him every happiness; he deserves a good wife, much better than I can make; of course, I liked Pierre, but you know we were not betrothed."

"Ah, then it was not a case of love at first sight! I don't believe, exactly, in love at first sight, and not always at second sight, either. But how did you know that you would ever love him — that is as a good wife should love the man she marries?"

"Why, how does one know any thing? I knew he was to be my husband, and of course we would naturally care for each other. If I had disliked him Mamma would not have made me marry him. She says she does not believe in that kind of thing." Madeleine used slang, at times, with pretty unconsciousness, in speaking English.

"Suppose you had loved somebody else," persisted Marguerite. "One who would have wanted a bigger dowry. Could you have given him up and married the Count?"

"There couldn't have been any body else. You surely do not think that I could care for a man to whom I was not betrothed," said Madeleine, her eyes demanding an explanation of such a strange supposition, if her lips did not.

"French girls give their love only to their husbands," she added a little proudly.

Later, pondering over the matter, Marguerite could almost find it in her heart to regret the absence ot the French way in her own dear land. Not long afterwards, the question of the French and the American customs in regard to marriage came up in the drawing-room of a leader in the American colony.

Marguerite surprised every body, and shocked not a few by taking up for the French idea.

"I do not believe altogether in the rigor of the French way, neither do I believe in the laxity of our own. We talk about our progress in America, the emancipation of the weaker sex — God pity our emancipation. But the French really take better care of their girls than we."

"I agree with Miss Clayton," exclaimed a middle-aged matron, too lovely and sweet ever to be old in heart.

"I certainly think, and have thought for a long time, that there was something deplorably wrong in the liberty of intercourse allowed our young people, in America. If I had my way, a girl would never be alone with a young man five minutes until after she was engaged to him. Not because of any danger or imprudence, for the well brought up American girl can be depended upon to take care of herself, but merely as a preventive of needless suffering. Flirtations end too sadly for the chance to flirt to be allowed.

A girl is thrown with a man, and imagines she loves him. He may be unsuitable in every way, but she is not old enough, or sensible enough to see that; if opposed, she elopes with him and is miserable for the rest of her days. Or again, a man pays marked attentions to a girl, meaning nothing beyond a pleasant time. The girl accepts them seriously, and weary years of pain may be the result. Many a heartache might have been spared youth and ignorance, if not always innocence, had we followed more strictly the French way with girls."

"But how are people ever to find out that they care for each other well enough to become engaged, if they are never allowed to be together?" combated a younger matron.

"Ah, now I did not say that they were not to be together, but only that the presence of a third person ought to be there to prevent love-making, or a flirtation. I would favor a modification of our own method and the French way. One is too strict, the other too lax."

A bright girl, just nineteen, said that she thought the idea of a chaperon was carried quite far enough in America; and that she herself did not enjoy a tithe of the liberty which had fallen to the portion of an elder sister, who married happily and well, at the end of her second season.

Despite the pleasures which were so freely given to Marguerite, there were still periods of passionate rebellion, of frantic anguish, of sleepless nights, of long black days; but these grew farther and farther apart as the winter wore away. It is one of the beneficent provisions of nature that the burden pressing on human hearts is lifted at times; it enables the crushed fibres to recuperate, the rays of sunlight to drive away the fogs before they become a permanent shadow. Marguerite would not have believed, a year before, that the heart is elastic, and capable in its deepest throes, of finding a brief respite from its keenest pain.

As the spring days approached, with their magnetic impetus to hope and joy, she took long walks in the parks and the boulevardes; went shopping with Madeleine, or some of her American friends, and even forced herself to wear the gowns which had been prepared for her trousseau.

She went out to the convent very frequently, but Madame Florac discouraged any wish to return to live, and Marguerite herself soon ceased to desire it. She had outgrown a school-girl's life, and as well try to wear her childish frocks as to live her childhood's life again, and be happy.

In the summer she took a house, with an American of limited means like herself, at Fontainebleau. The place had always possessed a strong fascination for her, and a summer there, with its freedom from conventional demands of dress and society, appeared simply ideal to her present state of mind. She never tired of dilating on its attractions to visiting Americans.

The groves, the big forest which had witnessed so much of the intrigues, the jealousies, the amusements, that had gone into the history of France; the stately palace, the bed, a ponderous affair, which had belonged to the First Napoleon, the table on which he signed his abdication, the room of hapless Marie Antoinette, — all the usual objects shown tourists, never lost their interest for Marguerite. Every thing spoke eloquently, when she was in a philosophical mood, of the vanity of human greatness.

Kings, and queens, and nobles, had not been exempt from the heritage of pain which comes to nearly all. She liked to wander, with only a big mastiff for companion, along the beautiful meadows, the smooth clover fields, like vast, well kept lawns, or dream under the hoary trees, their dense shadows making twilight of noon across the long, broad roads.

Some American friends of hers, won over by her enthusiastic praise of Fontainebleau, had succeeded in getting the veritable house of Madame de Pompadour, an old fashioned, ideally charming place, with its memories of sin, of suffering too, of intrigue, of mad pleasures. Marguerite was there almost daily, drank tea in the old garden, drowsed evenings in the drawing-room, invested with a historic interest by much of the original furniture, and indited notes on a dainty little desk where the soulless, brilliant syren had penned her letters, and a king bent over to read them.

She was seated on the Pompadour lawn watching a game of tennis, when a letter was brought to her announcing the engagement of Edith Kingman. She did not have to look at the name to know that the happy man was John Raymond.

"I am very, very glad," she said. "He is a noble, manly sort of a man; I suppose one does not get married to please one's friends, but Edith's choice could not have suited me better had I selected her husband myself."

A passing thought of Carroll Kirwin came to her, but she rejected it, instantly. Intuitively she felt that he and Edith would never have been suited to each other.

It was to the famous Pompadour desk that she ran to pen a few lines of congratulations and good wishes to Edith.

In a long letter which she wrote the next day she gave her reasons for declining the invitation to be bridesmaid. She felt that she was acting selfishly, all the while. Edith had been such a true, tried friend to her, the least she might do in return would be to sacrifice her own feelings and go back to America for the wedding. But oh, she could not! she could not! Edith would understand.

By autumn, Marguerite and Mrs. Webb, her chaperon for the summer, had grown so congenial that they decided to continue the dual housekeeping in Paris. Economy was a consideration for both, and the arrangement had other advantages, besides, especially for Marguerite, who, as an unmarried girl, could not live alone.

They took a nest of a house in the fashionable quarter, announced their Day, and sank naturally into their little niche as resident Americans whom it was desirable to know.

Edith's wedding was set for November, and Marguerite had so far yielded to her friend's indignant protests as to consent to return for the event, when an attack of tonsilitis gave her a valid excuse for breaking the promise. The thought of going back to New York was hateful to her; besides, she would have no place to go, but to

Edith's home,—she had ceased to have any intercourse with her step-mother — and the preparations for the wedding, the love-making, which some one has called the egotism of two, the joyous plans, would be too vivid a reminder of the past. The re-opening of the wounds not yet healed, would be more than she could stand. Again, the expense was to be considered. She was living very well up to her income, for she had not learned the art of saving. It would take time for ideas expanded on a basis of millions to come down to the limitations of a very few thousand. Altogether, there were so many reasons, and a number of little good reasons, make one big good reason, she told herself.

She was glad, very glad in Edith's gladness; and yet down in her heart there was a pang that she would henceforth occupy but a secondary place in her friend's regard. Although Edith was not a person to become wholly absorbed in any one, she was yet woman enough to follow the general rule of her sex in the absorption of marriage.

Marguerite took up the threads of her life in Paris, and interwove them with constantly recurring new ones. She had her little pleasures, little cares, little charities. Every thing seemed petty compared with the dreams of her youth. Every thing but her suffering. That was big enough to be sublime in its pathos.

XXXV.

MR. DALTON had lived in the world over sixty years; he had seen a great many of its phases, and he thought that he knew human nature very well, but he acknowledged to himself that he still had much to learn, before he had proceeded very far towards a settlement of the Golconda bonds.

He received innumerable letters after he had advertised for the stock, asking if the mine was to be opened; he was even approached by financiers, who suspected a new deal in the mining world, but he kept his own counsel. He wanted to buy all the Golconda bonds, at their par value, he could get; if a person had any for sale, very well, if not, there was nothing more to be said. Why he wanted them, what he was going to do with them, whether the mine had suddenly proved to be of untold value, these were questions which concerned none but himself.

It seemed strange to him that the revived story of Mr. Clayton's rascality in "salting" the mine originally, and other shady transactions in regard to it, and the loss of Marguerite's fortune, so much and so widely talked of, were not associated into a coherent whole, and the clue to the purchase thus obtained, but no one hit upon so simple a solution as a daughter's making restitution for a father's dishonesty. Nature and grace had become too largely divorced, in the general estimate of human nature, for this to occur to any one.

Mr. Dalton purchased the bonds, and paid four per cent interest on them for fifteen years, and after a little parleying the holders were usually glad to sell on these terms; however, every one was wildly curious to know what was to be done with the mine.

But there were a few exceptions.

One day a tall, loosely put together fellow, in trousers that were too short for him, and a coat that was too long; with reddish sandy hair, a reddish beard, a reddish complexion, and the pale eyes which naturally go with such hair, and beard and complexion, came shuffling into the office.

To Mr. Dalton's polite and conventional query as to his business, he replied in a phrase neither polite nor conventional, but doubtless very well meant:

"Be you the man that's wantin' Goncondy stock ?"

Mr. Dalton acknowledged that he was.

"Well, I 've got a clean two thousand wuth; it b'longed to my wife, my fust wife, that is to say; 'Mandy H. Jenks that was; she got 'em from her pa. We never nuther of us 'lowed they'd mount to a row o' beans; we hweard the mine wuz a swindle; I wuz plum minded to burn the hull bizness, but Mandy, she said 'better not. They don't take up a great might o' room in the cab'net, and we might as well keep 'em fer luck.' Then a feller does hate mighty, ever lastin bad to burn up a thing what cost a cool two thousan' and so the upshot wuz I kep' em. Mandy alway was a master hand at managin' and projectin'. When I seed your advertizement sez I to my self, 'that's a sell,' but I wuz comin,' to Jersey any how; I live in Pensylvany now, but I allus lived in Arkansaw till Mandy died.''

Mr. Dalton had been trying to place the man, or rather his type, ever since he entered the office, and it now flashed on him that twenty-five years before in the backwoods of Arkansas, he had met him. He was surprised that the species was so little changed.

"So I thought as I'd come and see you.

"Well, now to bizness; I aint a green un, I aint as green as I look, by a long shot. It stan's to reason that if you want them bonds at par val'e, them blasted mines is a goin' to pan out rich, after all. Now I'm square; I aint a goin' to let them bonds go fer no two thousan', nor intrust nuther, but I'll sell for five.''

The stock-holder from the Arkansas swamps, by way of the Pennsylvania mountains, looked knowingly at Mr. Dalton as if expecting that gentleman to recognize a brother in intelligent scheming, and to act accordingly.

"Very well, my good man, do I understand you to say that you refuse to sell your bonds?" responded Mr. Dalton quietly.

"That's about it, but not quite," said the man with a broad grin.

"I aint a goin' to be cheated arter waitin' all these years for them bonds to mount to somethin' or nuther.

I want to make my pile too. Five thousoun 's my figger."

"Then there is nothing more to be said, Sir, and I wish you good morning."

Mr. Dalton stood up, and looked as if he expected his visitor to follow his example.

But the man was slightly abashed. He did not expect nor desire so abrupt a termination to the interview.

"See here, Jedge. I'm on the make, I am, and I recken you be too. I'm willin' to let you have them there bonds at a reasonable figger."

"If you wish to sell your bonds on the terms I offer you, I am willing to buy, if not we are merely wasting time."

The man still remained seated, and was evidently bent on a prolonged discussion. Mr. Dalton was getting impatient, although the grim humor of the situation struck him forcibly.

"Come, my good man, I am very busy this morning, and I must ask you to excuse me."

He walked into the outer office, leaving the door open for the man to follow.

There was nothing more to be done, so the discomfited bondholder took his departure, muttering to himself:

"Them city sharpers can't git ahead o' me! I'm on to their little game."

XXXVI.

THERE was no event in the winter's calendar worthy of note for Marguerite. The season had been unusually gay, even for Paris, and that may have been why there was such a willingness to don figuratively, the sackcloth and ashes, and do penance during Lent.

A certain famous preacher gave the Lenten lectures at a celebrated church much frequented by Americans who spoke French, or thought they spoke it, and Marguerite was among the most eager of the auditors.

After a thrilling discourse on the Littleness of Human Greatness, she again presented herself at the convent gate: this time to ask admission into the Order.

Madame Florac looked grave when the girl announced her wish.

"Ah! this is rather sudden is it not?" she asked soberly.

Marguerite admitted that it was.

It was a warm spring day, more like June than March, and Madame suggested that they go into the garden.

As they passed through the long familiar corridors, the years seemed to drop away from Marguerite like a discarded mantle, and she could almost feel herself a child again. The hyacinths and crocuses were peeping up, a bird was chirping in the trees, the sunlight lay in playful shadows over the walks, and something of the gladness of spring was filling her heart.

They sat down on a rustic bench in the south walk where the sun was shining brightly. Both Madame Florac and Marguerite were sensitive to cold — physical and metaphysical.

"Now Marguerite, my dear," began the nun, "I need not say that it would be the one desire of my heart to see you in the cloister if you really have a vocation.

Perhaps God in His goodness has given you one, but we must not be hasty in deciding. You must weigh well the step you wish to take and its consequences. You must ponder over the hardships of the religious life as well as its consolations. It is a life of utter self abnegation. You were always strong-willed, Marguerite, passionate, impulsive, fond of your own way. Here your will must be relinquished, extinguished would be the better word.

As you are now situated you regulate your life to suit yourself, your own inclinations, your own convenience. You go and come as you please. There is no one to say you nay; if you want fresh air and exercise, you go driving in the parks, or walking on the boulevardes; you feel lonely, there is a score of delightful homes in which you are more than welcome; you love beauty and that love is gratified in the art galleries, in travel in your surroundings; your heart is restless, you wish to be lifted out of yourself, so to speak, and you go to the theatre where every fibre is thrilled by the tragic power of some great actress, — you told me only a month ago that the theatre and the opera were your greatest material pleasures; the flash of the lights, the brilliant toilets, the hush of a vast crowd, are exhilarating to one of your temperament; you are tired or sleepy in the morning, you turn over for another nap, or call for your chocolate in bed; you vary your occupations as you please; you have change of climate, of scene, of faces, when and where you like. You have the world and the world's pleasures. —"

"Oh, but Mother mine, I am weary, utterly weary of it all."

"Ah, my child, utter weariness is not a motive for entering the convent.

God does not want a heart that is utterly weary.

Time heals many wounds, Marguerite; Nature repairs her ravages; you may get married and make a noble, useful Christian woman in the world. And even if you remain as you are, there are many interests in the world besides love. That may be a great factor in life, perhaps the greatest, but it is not the only one. And I am told that there are many maiden ladies in America who are most highly respected, and who exert a great influence on society."

Marguerite rejected, almost with impatience, any suggestion that she could ever again think of marriage. And she insisted that she was tired of the world. The nun continued, interrupted now and then by Marguerite:

"Besides the things that you must give up, have you thought of the things that you must do ?

You rise in the morning at the tap of the bell; you may be sleepy, tired, but unless positively ill you must get up; no maid assists you to dress, no refreshing bath awaits you, no dainty gown to put on, no dallying in making your simple toilet; you don your coarse habit in silence, you repair to the chapel for morning prayers, for meditation for Mass; not until these are over do you break your fast, and with only a roll and a cup of thin chocolate. After that you begin your day's work; teaching the multiplication table to one, the intricacies of crochet to another, not as you will, but as the will of your superior bids you; a frugal dinner and a short recreation at noon, then work again. When the school hours are over and the children go to their play, their exercise, you go to your prayers; the rosary, the office, vespers, all must be said. A slight collation is your portion, instead of one of Madame Gaston's state dinners, with an orchestra and lights and flowers, and the tempting dishes of a chef; then you have the long examination of conscience, another meditation, a spiritual reading — the 'Following of Christ' or the 'Lives of the Saints', — instead of the last new novel—; night prayers, and then in silence you go to your narrow iron bed for a few hours of rest and sleep.

This is not for one day or for two; for a week or a month or a year, but for always — as long as you live; when a change comes it will be the last change when you are laid in your coffin.

But if you feel a vocation for this life, if you have made up your mind to it, then there is a peace and a happiness in the convent which no worldly life can ever give. On the other hand, I can imagine no greater torture than being forced into it against your own inclination, or the bent of your own temperament.

By a vocation I do not mean that you must feel that God has specially called you, created you for the cloister; but I do mean that you must have a fitness for the life, you must be able to see beyond the hardships to the grand object in view, and to count all temporal things as trivial in obtaining that object. If you can school your will so as to have no will, in other words, to be able to put your own inclinations aside to follow as obedience calls, if you can rise superior to the charms of the world, the allurements of society, so as to find that higher pleasure in doing your work, leading the self-denying life of the convent, then come to us. I do not believe in any one's entering the convent with too great a natural repugnance to be overcome; I think that a nun should be happy in her convent, happy in the life, happy in the work which must be her portion. If she cannot be this, no matter how great her piety, her heroic desire for self sacrifice, I would say — keep out of the convent. I know that all do not share my views, and many girls have gone to the convent, and some remained there, who would have been better off in the world. Happiness and contentment are the normal conditions of the human heart, and unless these conditions can be had in the convent then, by all means, keep out of it. And I tell you frankly, Marguerite, I do not think you would be happy as a nun. I need not say how tenderly I love you, my child; and if I could see you in the convent, and know that you were happy, I would ask no greater consolation. If I hesitate in giving my approval to your desire, it is for your happiness I do so."

But Marguerite was determined. She consulted her spiritual director, not because she meant to be influenced by his opinion, but because Madame Florac insisted upon this point.

To precipitate the step, Mrs. Webb was to return to Chicago, just after Easter, and Marguerite would have no place to go.

She was therefore received almost immediately, on a sort of preliminary trial, before really becoming a postulant.

She was assigned some light duties, and a course of spiritual reading and religious exercise was mapped out for her. She herself wanted a more rigorous order of life, but Madame Florac told her she must learn to walk before she could run.

The weeks wore away uneventfully enough. Marguerite was apparently contented if not positively happy. She was listless at times, but she did not fail in her duties. She even received a reprimand, which was hardly merited, in silence. This, more than any thing else, made Madame Florac hopeful of her perseverance.

On a bright morning in June the convent chapel was decorated with unusual magnificence, in honor of the Feast of the Sacred Heart. Hundreds of tapers were ablaze on the altars, and trailing vines and a profusion of flowers added their perfume and their beauty to the charm of the scene. The statue of the Blessed Virgin was draped in a filmy lace veil which had been the bridal veil of an old pupil, now widowed and living in retirement.

All the nuns, their pupils, Marguerite, every one in the house, from the Mother Superior to the porter, approached Holy Communion; the day was beautiful and exhilarating, the music, furnished by the best voices of school and cloister, was inspiring, and Marguerite was feeling some of the glow of devotion, the enthusiasm which had nerved the martyrs of old, and sent missionaries in all ages to heathen climes.

The ceremonies were over, all were still kneeling in the chapel when a new acolyte, unaccustomed to his cassock, stumbled in extinguishing the candles and overturned one nearest the Madonna's veil.

Like a flash Madame Florac, who was kneeling near by, had mounted the shrine and extinguished the flame just as it was beginning to blaze.

No one could tell just how the accident happened; she must have grown dizzy or have been blinded by the smoke — she swayed a moment and then fell.

She was carried out insensible, but it was thought she had merely fainted from the shock. At sunset the news spread through the silent cloister that Madame Florac was dead.

And Marguerite!

In the passionate throes of her grief she wailed, "I cannot stand it, I cannot! My cross is greater than I can bear. Oh my sweet mother, my friend, my all that I had, you cannot, cannot be gone from me forever!" She looked at the beautiful dead face, so cold, so white, so youthful, but blinding human tears shut out the sight of ineffable peace it wore.

The shapely, firm hands were clasped over the crucifix, the emblem alike of her life and her faith. The lips that would never again open in words of reproach or counsel or love, seemed almost smiling.

For the first time Marguerite called, and there was no response; her tears fell like rain, and there was no hand to wipe them away; her heart ached wearily, wearily, and there was no soft touch to comfort her.

But as she looked on her friend, it seemed worth a lifetime of self-abnegation to win in death such peace, such a look of deep happiness, as if, in the soul's passage from time to eternity, heaven had opened, giving a fleeting glimpse of the bliss awaiting it, in its everlasting home. She had long known how a nun could live, she now saw how a nun could die. But for herself, all consolation failed.

As she stood by the grave and heard the dull thud of the sod falling on the coffin, she wished, with the anguish of a soul at bay, that they were falling on her heart as well.

She prayed with all the fervor she could command, but her prayers seemed to be forced by some invisible weight, back to earth again.

She cried, in the bitterness of her grief, as she had done once before when in sore distress: "Why am I so punished!"

The convent suddenly became unbearable; her duties hung like millstones around her neck; the very atmosphere was oppressive.

In the changes which followed Madame Florac's death, Madame Duval was placed in an office in which she came directly in contact with Marguerite. There was an antipathy on both sides, striven against honestly, but never overcome.

It was this, more than any thing else perhaps, which decided Marguerite as to her lack of a religious vocation.

Having settled this question she was for leaving at once.

She went up to the chapel, still draped in black for Madame Florac.

The image of that dear face came before her, as it looked on the morning in the garden when they had talked of convent life; she seemed to be smiling in approval of the decision.

"I cannot stay in the convent," cried Marguerite, "but whither shall I go?"

The answer seemed to come back:

"Life is short, it will soon be passed. Live for eternity."

Suddenly the thought of Grace Farr came to the girl.

The Christian matron, and the consecrated nun had both gone to the same God. Both had done their duties according to their stations in life, both had cast off the mask of time, both had received the rewards of eternity, each according to the measure of her works.

As she arose from her knees, a voice seemed to thrill through every fibre of her being:

"I am the resurrection and the Life."

She did not know what she would do, where she would stay, or what would be her future life, but the peace of that voice rested like a benediction on her soul.

XXXVII.

THROUGH the kindness of Madame Gaston and Madeleine, Marguerite found another elderly lady of unlimited respectability and limited income, who wished to keep house 'on the shares' as people made apple butter in the pioneer days, in South Missouri.

This lady was very conservative, and very French, and very decided in her opinions, which were not at all the opinions of Marguerite, but she afforded the nominal protection which the girl was compelled, by the usages of the society of which she was a unit, to have.

Marguerite regretted Mrs. Webb very keenly, but soon came to class her along with the other joys of her life, which were hers no more.

She sometimes asked herself if she was fated to sacrifice every thing in the world, near, and dear, and pleasant, and sweet.

She spent the summer, just beginning when she left the convent, with Madame Gaston at Homburg, where she was forced to go a great deal in society, when her own inclinations were for solitude and retirement.

In the autumn she returned to Paris and continued her second venture at co-operative housekeeping.

Edith wrote indignant letters railing at Marguerite's self-expatriation, and asking if she had no heart at all, that she could treat her old friends as she did.

Only when a cablegram arrived, announcing the advent in Edith's household, of a cherub to be named Marguerite, did she acknowledge a desire to return to New York. She really would like to see Edith's baby.

As the godmother by proxy, she sent the most beautiful christening cup to be found in all Paris, and spent a forenoon praying in a big, dim, historic old church that the little stranger might grow up to be as sweet and sunny as its mother, and be spared the terrible woes which had made desolate her own life.

Winter came, and life went on very much as life goes on everywhere with the rich and prosperous. Although Marguerite would not have classed herself with either the rich or the prosperous, she yet outwardly belonged to both. There was a certain charm about her defined by none, but recognized by nearly all, which made her very popular, although she used no effort to be so. In fact, she was utterly indifferent, but the air of being slightly bored was just then much affected by young ladies, and Marguerite's spells of languor and abstraction passed for the perfection of good form. Again, she would be so bright, so animated, so interested in all that was interesting to another, that she won all those in quest of sympathy and appreciation. Young men especially, who could not divine how very, very young they appeared to her, found her uniformly charming.

It seemed to be generally understood that, although she had lost a great deal of money, she still had a great deal remaining. She was naturally distinguished looking, and she wore her gowns with a certain style which enabled her to make a better appearance than many other women who spent ten times as much as she, on clothes.

It was whispered that Marguerite was very charitable, and that she preferred to put her money into bread for the poor, rather than in champagne for the rich, as a reason why she did not entertain.

The months wore away, and it was June again when a card was brought up to Marguerite's little sitting room, littered with the late American magazines, bearing the name of Carroll Kirwin.

She greeted him with the joy she really felt at seeing him, both on his own account, and because of the nation he represented. America was home, no matter how long she might elect to remain away from its shores.

He was looking older than she remembered him, and handsomer, too. But on the matter of his looks she had not, in the old days, formulated any decided opinion. There had been only one man for her then, the others were very much alike, excepting that some were old and some were young; some were agreeable, and some were not.

An hour passed in eager questionings about Edith, the baby, New York, about people she did not really care for at all, but who were acquiring a sort of value because they were Americans. The happiness of her life had come to her in America, and there were a hundred thousand other reasons why America must always be home.

A clock struck somewhere, Marguerite had ever

indulged in a fondness for clocks — Carroll shifted uneasily on his chair, straightened up with an air of determination, and changed his tone and his expression so suddenly that Marguerite straightened up too, as if to meet something, she knew not what.

"Miss Clayton," he began, "I have come to Paris but for one purpose — to see you. You must know why. Three years ago when you first came home from the convent, I loved you, and I dreamed for a day that you might be my wife, but I soon discovered that my dream was vain. I have loved you all these years, and I have come to beg you to try to care for me in return."

He spoke earnestly, the light of a grand passion was in his eyes, and Marguerite was touched, although the thought of marrying Carroll Kirwin was as foreign to her mind as any thing could well be. It simply had never occured to her.

But as he spoke, and a vision came before her of all that love might mean, she could almost regret that she did not love him. There was something so noble, so manly in him, he was a man any woman might care for, and be proud of her affection. She thought, with a wave of shame, of that other one who had given her up, the man whose love had not been equal to the sacrifice of rank and title. But she banished the comparison, almost as a sacrilege to love; the other man was the prince of her dreams, the idol of her life. The Paul she had loved, and worshipped, and revered, was hers forever, living, always the same, in her memory and in her heart. The Paul, wearing his mask, might forget her, but the real Paul never could.

By that strange duplex action of the mind she was thinking of Parkhurst, and yet thinking, too, of what life might be with Carroll Kirwin. The thought of his silent devotion ever since he had known her, had something beautiful and touching in it. He was naturally an eloquent speaker, and he pleaded his own cause with the girl he loved, with something of the fire, as well as the trained directness of his speeches at the bar. He was a lawyer by nature as well as by profession.

He begged her not to give an answer then, but to think over her decision, and to try to be kind to him.

She told him that she had no thought of marriage, that she had loved once, as he and all the world knew, and she could never love again. She said she appreciated his regard, but was not worthy of it. That he deserved a fresh, unspoiled affection, and that she had suffered too much to ever think again of that kind of happiness.

Even as she spoke the thought of her life as Carroll Kirwin's wife came back to her. She admired him, liked him very much; they had common tastes, common interests, a common Faith. He loved her devotedly, there was no doubt about that, and some one had said, a writer she affected in her cynical moods, that it was better to be the loved than the lover. Her ideals of marriage had all called for a mutual love, she could not understand marriage at all on any other basis, but an experience wider than hers had pronounced differently. A wave of home-sickness stirred her heart at the sight of Carroll. This unsettled, uncertain Parisian life was unsatisfying, utterly hateful at times. Why not go back and be the centre of a home of her own, the gracious presence which might make the happiness of a noble man, an influence for good to those around her ?

She might grow to care for him in time. Love begets love, was an old adage. It might be true in her case as it had been in the case of others. Her life would then have an object. It was not as if she had a grand talent for literature, or music, or art, or charity — something to occupy her time, to give value to her life. The Paul she had loved so passionately was dead to her in this world, and a living husband ought not to be jealous of an ideal.

She liked Carroll so much that she was genuinely sorry to have him leave her, and she was thinking, as he arose to go, after having been there nearly three hours, that it would be pleasant to have him live in Paris, and drop in informally for five o'clock tea in her drawing-room. He was simply perfect as a friend, and she was a great believer in friendships between men and women, but as a husband, — ah! that was another question. Could she ever be sure that her heart was not already wedded, and that indissolubly, as hearts in all marriage must be !

She refused at first, but finally consented to think seriously of the matter, and weigh well a decision which would mean so much to a good man.

Carroll Kirwin remained a week in Paris, and then went on to Rome. As he told Marguerite goodbye she was unmistakably glad that he was coming back again — so many goodbyes in her life had been final, or for an indefinite period — but still she could not think of marriage. She almost doubted either the wisdom or the kindness in trying to do so. But he was coming back, time enough then to think, and she could have even more time if she wanted it.

The house seemed quiet, almost lonely after Carroll had gone, and she took her maid, who also performed the duties of an American second girl, and went for a stroll in the park. It was a bright, balmy spring morning, and Marguerite had always been peculiarly susceptible to atmospheric conditions. She was walking along leisurely, thinking of America and Carroll Kirwin, whe she was startled out of her revery by a familiar voice: "Miss Clayton! how lucky, I was just going to hunt you up," and in a moment she was shaking hands warmly with Mr. Farr.

After the usual greetings, and half coherent questionings, and bubbling laughter, from the mere gladness of two compatriots meeting each other in a foreign land, Farr exclaimed in joyous tones, but as if he had forgotten for the moment:

"I want you to meet my wife, I am over on my wedding tour, you know."

Indeed she did not know! Marguerite wanted to say; nor could she altogether repress the astonishment she felt, as she responded:

"I did not know you were married."

She was wondering why Carroll had not told her, or Edith, in some of her letters, — the marriage must have been very sudden.

"Perhaps you knew my wife as Miss Carson, Carrie Carson," he went on in the same joyousness of tone.

"Why certainly I know Miss Carson, but I am forgetting to congratulate you, in my own selfish joy on seeing a friend from America," Marguerite answered, with the conventional smile of pleasure society demands, and sincerity permits, on such occasions.

She really knew very little of Carrie Carson, and that little she did not like.

But she had liked Mr. Farr in the old days, and she gave no sign of how immeasurably he had fallen in her regard since the announcement of his marriage.

"And how is poor little June," she asked with the vision of a hapless, forsaken childhood surging through her brain.

"Oh, June is with Aunt Mary, Mrs. Kingman, you know, — and Edith. He divides his time quite impartially between them, Aunt Mary's dog and Edith's baby being the rival attractions. You would hardly know June now, Miss Clayton, he has grown so, and he makes my life miserable begging for a gun, a real gun that shoots bullets. He wanted to come with us whether or not, and we had to slip away at last. I daresay he raised an awful howl, poor little chap, when he found that we were really gone."

Marguerite was glad to see that the joy of a bridegroom had not obliterated his fondness as a father. She almost forgave him for marrying again when he spoke with so much affection of his boy.

He gave the address of his hotel, and she promised to call immediately on Mrs. Farr, Number Two.

But there was a scornful little curl of her lips as she went on her way, the mood of the morning completely changed.

She recalled, as if it had happened but yesterday, his grief, his burst of sobs by the coffin of his dead wife. She remembered her pity for him then, and how many times since she had thought of him, picturing his loneliness, his vigils with grief in the desolate home. And all the while he was consoling himself in the presence of Miss Carrie Carson!

"So much for a man's love," she thought scornfully. "It is a poor thing at best, after all.

Dead to-day, forgotten to-morrow!

Poor Grace!

And it seemed such an ideal union, too."

She did not understand an affection which could enshrine another woman in the heart, and after but two short years. If Farr had told her that he still loved Grace, and cherished her memory with all tenderness, she would not have believed him. She had one ideal, she did not know that there could be many others, and she made the mistake of trying to fit all temperaments to her own theories.

She invited the Farrs to a little dinner at which the Count and Countess of Clermond and two Americans were the other guests, and the next day she wrote a letter, which was forwarded to Carroll Kirwin by his Paris bankers.

She said that it would be cruel to keep him in suspense any longer. She liked and admired him very much, but she could never love him as a wife should love her husband. She hoped to retain his friendship which she valued very, very much, wished him every happiness, and a wife who would appreciate him as he deserved. For herself she had no heart to give in marriage to any one. Her own life must ever be lone and lonely.

She signed herself his sincere friend, Marguerite Clayton, and even dropped a tear as she affixed her seal. It was a tear of sympathy for herself, a tear of regret for the things gone wrong in the world. She wondered, as she had so often wondered before, why it is that there are so many discords, so many broken strings in Nature's grand symphony of human love.

XXXVIII.

AFTER an exile of four years Marguerite suddenly returned to New York. In one mood it seemed as if whole cycles had elapsed since her departure, in another, as if it had been but a day.

Edith was at the dock to meet her, looking not in the least matronly or mature. As a girl she had appeared older than she was, now she seemed younger. Marguerite noted on landing, the same eager, alert throngs, the same noise and roar, the same hurry, the same beautiful sky, the same exhilarating atmosphere which had struck her on her first home coming, an ignorant enthusiastic school girl, so long, so very long ago. Life was so short and yet so long.

Marguerite herself was much changed. Edith could not define in what the change consisted, she could only be sure that it was there.

There was a different light in her eyes, she told her husband in an exchange of connubial confidences, after Marguerite had gone to her own room.

A calmer deeper light, as if a volcano had smouldered, burnt fiercely and gone out, and a beacon taken its place.

"You were always vividly imaginative, my dear. There is nothing the matter with Marguerite's eyes that I can see, excepting a loss of sleep," said John Raymond, who wanted to read the evening paper.

Marguerite begged Edith not to celebrate her return in any way; declared she did not care for society, and only wanted to see a few of her old friends.

She spent a great deal of time with the baby, the little Marguerite who was beginning to be most enchanting in her infantile graces and wiles. The fond father declared that no boy was ever born who could be so irresistible at so early an age, and declared himself a convert to the theory of feminine instincts. A boy would yell with all the power of his lungs for what he wanted, where this cherubic prodigy simply put out her dimpled hands, and smiled.

Edith took it to be a dispensation of Providence that Mrs. Clayton — the insufferable old cat, and the two young cats, kittens would be entirely too euphonious a term for people she so cordially detested — were out of the country.

They were in London when last heard from, Edith said, and had actually had the sublime assurance to take the very house she and her mother and Marguerite had occupied during that memorable London season.

But she was simply struck dumb, she informed the long suffering John, when Marguerite asked to be kindly remembered to them when they returned.

"I looked closely to see if there was no halo around her head. Such heroic forgiveness and Marguerite Clayton are unreconcilable terms," concluded the happy young wife.

Marguerite had announced in her letter that she would be in New York for a few weeks only, but beyond that gave no hint of her plans.

Edith had determined that the few weeks should be prolonged into months.

Carroll Kirwin was still unmarried, and she was bent on giving him a fair chance with Marguerite.

"I feel like shaking her," Edith confided to her husband.

Marguerite received Carroll when he called, with unmistakable friendliness; she went out a great deal, there were many invitations impossible to refuse, for her old friends seemed anxious to show that she had not been forgotten, the more so since her loss of fortune was very well known. She was almost her old charming self again. A sweeter, nobler edition of Marguerite the schoolgirl. Edith was weaving some very pretty fancies in which Marguerite played the leading part, when they were rudely torn to pieces by the heroine of them announcing very calmly that she was going to Wyoming to become a nun.

"To Wyoming to become a nun!" Edith almost shrieked. The idea could not be grasped at once.

Yes, Marguerite replied; she had returned to America with that intention. She had read months before in a stray newspaper, which she chanced to pick up in a friend's boudoir, of a struggling little colony of nuns trying to maintain an Indian school, in the face of extreme poverty, in Wyoming. It seemed like a special messenger telling her that there was a chance for her life to amount to something. The West had always possessed a strange attraction for her. There was a fascination about its mountains, wild cañons, its untrodden soil, she could not explain. She had tried to put the thought from her as a mere fancy, but again and again it came back, until at last her decision was made.

Edith wanted to know how she could think of the convent after her failure in Paris.

"I do not know unless it be that some fruit ripens slowly. There are apples in June, and apples in November, you know. And perhaps it is the same with the soul. I tried to pluck a religious vocation three years ago in Paris before it was ripe. It is ripe now. But to carry out the metaphor, I also think that it requires the conditions as they exist in Wyoming, to keep. I have a little money, not enough to count for much in a wealthy community, but enough to do a great deal whither I am going. It will build a school, and support it for those Indian girls, and in teaching them the way to be civilized, to become Christian wives and mothers, and a leaven for their tribe, I shall feel that my life has not been lived altogether in vain.

God cannot bless our country so long as the wrongs of the Indians are crying to heaven for redress."

The week before her departure Marguerite was the sole witness, excepting the little sister, now little no longer, of a wedding which afforded her much happiness and some misgivings.

It was the marriage of Delphine Bienvenue and Henry Wilson. The mother had died two years before, and the two sisters had continued to live in their little flat with Martha Grigsby, who had left the "Home" at their solicitation, and had proved the extent of her reformation by making a good housekeeper and a wise protector for the orphans.

Henry Wilson had been pardoned, after serving four years, through the exertions of Carroll Kirwin, coupled with the good reports given of him by the warden. All during those four years a beautiful girl and a gray haired old woman, the latter protesting much at such romantic folly, made their way to the prison on the days when visitors were allowed, carrying books and the things permitted to the convicts by the stern rules of the institution.

The prisoner was now free, and with the girl who had been so loyal to him, was to begin a new life under new conditions.

They too were going West, but Mr. and Mrs. 'Arthur Wilton' were the names marked on their baggage, and checked for far off Seattle. He was going into business with Delphine's little capital; Kit was to fulfil her long dream of studying abroad.

Delphine wore white for her bridal, and looked regally beautiful; too beautiful and too sweet and too good to be wasted on an ex-convict, Marguerite thought sadly. But a glance into the dark eyes made glorious with the light of a great happiness, told the old, old story of the power of love. Carroll Kirwin had hopes of Wilson, and on his opinion Marguerite rested her faith in the future happiness of the pair.

"Delphine may not find happiness with her husband," mused the girl, "but she would have been miserable without him, and who can tell what the future may have in store for each and every one of us?"

Quietly Marguerite had come back to New York,

and quietly she went on her way. There were no figurative trumpets, no goodbyes, excepting to intimate friends, and even they did not know whither she was going. She shed a few tears on parting from Edith, and as the long vestibuled train rolled out of the station, she stood on the platform and watched until the mighty city was swallowed up in the general haze.

Then she went back to her compartment, littered with the ordinary accompaniments to luxurious travel. Edith, with her usual thoughtfulness, had seen to these things. There were the magazines, the last new novel, a box of Huyler's candy, and another box from a well known florist. This had come to the train by a messenger, and Marguerite opened it to find a boquet of exquisite white orchids, and the card of Carroll Kirwin. Orchids, beautiful, and costly and rare, symbolic of the world and its pleasures she was leaving! Symbolic too, of the ambition for wealth, which had been the ruin of her earthly happiness, and the ruin of so many lives!

It was late in the afternoon of a cold raw day in the middle of February, when the train bound for the Pacific slope, stopped for a few moments at a little way station. The only evidences of civilization were a telegraph office, and a waiting room in a low one story log house, and one other similar domicile, with a long board nailed across its front, giving the intelligence to way-farers, that food and lodging could be had within. The smoke was curling sluggishly out of the chimneys as if too cold to escape into the air.

A middle-aged matron with furs and hot water bottles, and salts and down pillows, and all the other belongings of opulent and interesting invalidism, wondered languidly what that tall, distinguished looking girl could be wanting in such an uncivilized, perfectly impossible place.

Her curiosity deepened as she noted the big trunk, of the kind which only wealth can afford to buy, being tumbled on to the platform.

She wondered still more to see the girl standing there alone. Why was there no one to meet her? what could she be doing there, any way? The semi-invalid was almost impatient with the conductor because he could not satisfy her curiosity.

"St. Catherine's" was a few miles from the railroad, and Marguerite had not apprised any one of the date of her coming, preferring to have no witnesses to the first wave of home-sickness for the home she had never known, the tears of natural desolation, of loneliness for Edith, the baby, for the laughter and joy and affection of Edith's home, — of the great world.

She stood on the deserted platform, watching the train, the last link between herself and the old life, rushing on its journey across the plains.

The mountains not far away, snow-capped and beautiful, loomed in solemn grandeur; the few trees were bent with icicles, the ground was bare and brown and hard, heaps of snow had drifted in the gullies and under the eaves of the station; the clouds were massed in sullen immobility in the West, but rolled in majestic, if mournful grandeur to the East, — the East with its light and its life and its warmth. The wind from the great West came whistling about the lonely figure as a reminder and a call to a waiting field of work.

"Look not back, but forward," it said.

"The East is rich in work accomplished, my destiny is before me."

A clump of dwarfed evergreens banded into unity by a canopy of ice, reminded Marguerite of a wigwam, and in the association of ideas, the greatness of her aim came back to her. The aim which had lured her thousands of miles across the ocean itself, from beautiful pleasure-loving Paris to a lonely mountain fastness in her own native West. She was to bring Christianity, hope, a new life to a few, at least, of a down-trodden race; and as the thought of this work filled her heart she forgot the cold, the loneliness, every thing.

Life was rich in its possibilities for good. And the money which had seemed so little in the great world, the world of modern civilization with all its complex wants, its artificial demands, would be a powerful motor in this struggling mission school in the Mountains.

Marguerite looked around her, read the sign on the very primitive inn, and walked over to the door, to find if she could secure any sort of conveyance to take her on to her destination. She had the good sense not to ask for a carriage or a hack when she saw the kind of place in which she had alighted.

The landlord eyed her curiously, and allowed between puffs at a cob pipe, that a wagon might be had, but he did not know whether it could carry that big trunk.

He was not at all ashamed of a curiosity supposed to be feminine, which made him the observer of every thing that came to the little station.

It was nightfall when Marguerite reached the convent, a rude, one story house built partly of logs, partly of unhewn stone. It was immediately at the foot of a mountain peak, and was fenced in by branches of trees on which the dead leaves were still clinging; big boulders made natural mounds to break up the surface; a few evergreens were the only signs of vegetation. A modest cross over the entrance was the sole indication visible, of the character of the edifice as the wagon, drawn by weary and ancient mules, drew up at the gate.

A light gleamed through one window at the side, but all was darkness in front, and Marguerite had as much as she could do to keep back the tears, as she waited, shivering, at the door. It was noiselessly opened by a nun holding a candle in her hand.

"I am Miss Clayton, Marguerite Clayton, Mother is expecting me —" began the girl. Her sentence was not finished, the little Sister threw down the candle, and caught her in a warm embrace, calling and laughing at the same time. The rest of the small community came running into the hall, and such rejoicing had never been surpassed at the advent of a queen.

There were expostulations from the nuns that she had not let them know, so that their chaplain could have met her, mingled with warmest words of welcome, and tenderest inquiries as to her fatigue and cold and hunger.

A blazing fire was in the little sitting room, skins were on the rough board floor, pictures of saints and crayons of the Ecce Homo and the Mater Dolorosa, adorned the whitewashed, log walls.

The Mother Superior, a cultivated charming woman of gracious presence and magnetic personality, stroked her hair, and rubbed her cold hands, and told her that the community regarded her as their delivering angel, and had made a novena of thanksgiving for her coming.

Marguerite felt her heart touched with a strange gladness at these words. She had already conceived a liking for the graceful sweet-faced nun; in a faint way, she recalled Madame Florac; the eager postulant believed that in her she would find a real spiritual Mother, a wise, true friend.

A little table was spread for Marguerite before the fire, and her supper of brown bread, rice cakes and maple syrup was prepared by joyful hands. The nuns were so sorry they had no milk for her tea, but they had sugar. A kind lady from a neighboring ranch, had sent them twenty pounds of sugar. Ah! yes, they were very poor, but God had always taken care of them, the good God who gave them so much more than He Himself had had on earth!

Such simple gratitude appeared sublime to Marguerite.

The Mother Superior insisted on putting a bed for the night in the sitting room, for Marguerite. There was no fire in the dormitory, and she must not take a cold to begin with in her mountain home.

The Sisters prolonged their evening recreation in honor of their new member's arrival, and when finally the signal was given for night prayers, Marguerite went with them to the chapel, taking the orchids which she laid tenderly on the altar. The chapel was poor and rude, but it contained the secret and the centre of the devotion which had brought the little band of women, some of them mere girls, away from home and the delights of a beautiful world, to minister to an alien race.

Marguerite sat long over the burning logs, indulging in her old fondness for revery. Her thoughts reverted to a woman and a little child she had seen that day, waving frantically from a cart drawn by burros, as the train went dashing out of a wild looking station. They had been just a minute too late. The girl wondered whimsically what effect the missing of that train would have on their future lives, and perhaps on the lives of generations yet unborn. She suspected herself of being almost morbidly superstitious about little things. "There are no little things in this world," she exclaimed half audibly. "Has not my whole life been but a chain of little things, the absence of any one of which might have changed it! Had I not gone to Chateau Flaubert I might have married Carroll Kirwin, probably would never have even laid eyes on Paul — on Lord Parkhurst. Had I not gone to the theatre on that fateful night I might still be a rich woman — had a new actress not appeared, had Edith had another engagement for that evening, had that girl not gone on the stage, had any of the things which lead to her going on the stage been different — Martha Grigsby might never have crossed my path. Had I resisted that impulse to go to the station house; had I not gone that Sunday to call on Martha and there saw Delphine Bienvenue; and back of all that, had my poor father never married again, had he died without a will, or to look only to my own life, had I been educated differently, had my disposition been different, the disposition that was determined, perhaps, a generation or a century before I was born, had any one of a thousand, or of ten thousand little things been different, how different might have been my life! Ah! humanly speaking there are no little things. They are boundless because they are but the instruments of the Infinite God." She glanced at the image of the Ecce Homo on the wall. "Jesus, my Saviour, in you are all my hope and all my trust. Ages ago, centuries almost it seems to me, when I was a happy little girl making my daily visits to the dear old chapel at the convent, you saw my future, you took care of me through every thing. The eternal decrees of right and of wrong must work their way, but out from the evil of a violated law Your tender compassion has brought good; after weary years of pain You have given me peace."

Marguerite went to bed but she could not sleep, the very silence was oppressive; she missed the rumble of the engine, the shaking of the car. She got up, stole to the window and pulled aside the scant muslin curtain. There was the mountain towering thousands of feet above her, the moonbeams playing in fantastic shadows over its rugged slope. She could see another log house, the school-rooms no doubt, of the Indian children.

"Here is your work, here is your mission," the voice of the wind whispered to her as it came from the Mountain.

It was getting cold and she crept back to her little bed. But sleep would not come; continuing her revery, she built a large substantial stone convent, beautiful grounds were laid off around it, flowers bloomed, an orchard and vineyards were planted, school-rooms with the latest appliances, dormitories for hundreds of Indian girls, took form.

Mr. Dalton would help her build this edifice, he had told her at parting to let him know if she needed, or wanted for any thing. Carroll Kirwin, who knew all the politicians and influential men at Washington, might get a government appropriation for the school. Edith would interest her friends in furnishing the building and founding scholarships. The girls would go back to their people noble Christian women — but her eyelids were getting heavy. She threw her braids of soft dark hair over the pillow, sighed drowsily, and went to sleep.

XXXIX.

"I CONFESS I do not understand Marguerite," Edith said, in talking over her friend, for the hundredth time, with her husband.

"I am glad there is something or somebody in the world you do not understand," jocosely replied John Raymond.

"Whether she has entirely gotten over her feeling for Lord Parkhurst, whether she has buried it under a higher ideal, I could not tell. She is not a girl to forget, or to change. I do not know whether she is happy, or whether she has drained the very quintessence of despair of all human happiness. She seemed to me to have died and come to life a different person. Or rather, to have died a light-hearted girl, and come to life a woman."

Raymond suggested that becoming a woman was a feat which might safely be left to nature, there was no need of dying about the matter.

Mrs. Farr, whom Edith liked in spite of an early prejudice against her for having taken poor Grace's place, was among the first to find out Marguerite's destination. In discussing the motives which lead girls to become nuns, she said:

"Now, in the case of Marguerite Clayton every body knows it was disappointed love, we all knew about Lord Parkhurst. But there is Nina Markham, only nineteen, rich and popular, the idol of her parents, especially of her father. I went with Mrs. Markham to see her the other day, and what do you think she was doing? washing dishes, as I live! Her mother nearly fainted, but Nina only laughed, and declared that she was perfectly happy. It takes all sorts of people to make a world."

Edith denied indignantly that Marguerite cared for Lord Parkhurst. What ever might be her own opinion, she did not purpose that any body else should analyze her friend.

When it became generally known that Marguerite had entered the convent, and such a convent too, and in such a place, — to say that her friends and acquaintances, whose number was legion, experienced a psychological thunder storm, would be characterizing their emotions very mildly.

This surprise was definitely expressed at a little dinner party which Mr. and Mrs. John Raymond gave, a fortnight after her departure.

"It seems like a desecration to be eating and drinking and making merry, and Marguerite gone forever, almost like rejoicing at a funeral," Edith remarked plaintively, when her husband first broached the subject of the dinner to some old friends of his then visiting in the city.

"We would soon be going to our own funerals, my dear, without eating, and a certain amount of drinking. Under the circumstances I think that Marguerite will forgive us for breaking our fast, and taking the crape from the door."

In reality Raymond's regret for Marguerite was almost as great as his wife's.

"It certainly was a most extraordinary step," said Mrs. Overbeck, "but then they say Miss Clayton always was rather — ah, given to fancies and all that."

Mrs. Overbeck did not know, being strange to New York, and admitted to dinner parties on the merits of her husband's great grandfather, and not on her own, how nearly she was criticizing her hostess in criticizing Marguerite.

Mr. Overbeck, who was usually a ditto to his wife's opinions, from force of habit and as a strategem to keep the connubial peace, interposed with the assertion that the law ought to abolish sisterhoods as "obsolete and behind the age."

"Isn't that rather a heretical idea? that is, admitting the Bible as a canon of conduct and belief," said Mr. Dalton who had been invited to meet the Overbecks.

"Isn't there something in the Scriptures about a man's leaving his wife and all his wordly goods to follow our Saviour, and I suppose a woman is included in its spirit."

Mrs. Overbeck admitted that such things might have been well enough in those times when the Saviour was on the earth, but it seemed a pity for a bright, pretty girl to sacrifice her life for a lot of savages who would just as lief take her scalp as not.

Mr. Farr said that all sweet, pretty girls could not get married, for the simple reason that there were not enough men to go round, and he did not think any body would advocate polygamy.

"Isn't there something else in the Scriptures about a reward of a hundred-fold for leaving all these things," he continued. "According to that standard, Miss Clayton has made a good investment."

Even John Raymond was rather shocked at this

cold-blooded business term used in such a connection, but he only laughed and said:

"A second Daniel come to judgment. Since when Farr, did you get to be a Biblical scholar?"

"Oh, I am too modest to claim to be a scholar, I am merely culling texts from the storehouse of my youth."

"And what does St. Paul say about the man who gives his daughter in marriage doing well, but he who gives her not, doing better? Is St. Paul obsolete too, Mr. Overbeck?" queried Mrs. Farr with a smile lurking around the corners of her very pretty mouth.

After her guests had gone Edith stole into a little den opening from the library, which she had fitted up cozily as a smoking room.

Leaning over her husband's chair she said half wistfully, "I wish, I wish Marguerite could have cared for Carroll. He is such a noble fellow, and Marguerite is fitted in every way to make a man happy. More than I ever was, and I make you happy do I not?" she continued with her hand resting on his hair, where it was beginning to turn prematurely gray.

"Yes, measurably," answered Raymond, clasping her hand in his big, soft palm.

"You are the dearest little girl in the world, Edith. You have the peculiar knack of making a home what it should be. I verily believe you could transform a wigwam so that a man would find it more attractive six days out of seven, than the best club in town."

"And it is just because Marguerite had this

genius for homemaking that I cannot help regretting that she is forever debarred from using it."

"She may have had your genius, Edith, but she did not have your strong common sense."

"Her sense is better than common, if is uncommon," retorted Edith. "And you speak in the past tense, just as if the girl were dead."

"Ah well, she is a Mary and you are a dear little Martha."

The young wife went back into the drawing-room to put out the gas. She was economical by spells.

She had made a restful, homelike home. Her husband's praise was deserved. There were quaint furnishings, artistic draperies, books, etchings, paintings, flowers — all the appliances that comfort could demand, and beautiful things to gratify a cultivated taste. The elegancies of a ripened civilization were visible everywhere. A charming, beautiful woman was the presiding genius, whose life was rounded and given its mission by husband, home and child.

She returned to the smoking room.

"I wish Carroll would get married; he makes me feel guilty every time I see him, as if I were in some way to blame for his failure with Marguerite. If we had never gone on that ill-fated visit! It was only because Parkhurst was the first man she ever saw that Marguerite cared for him so ardently. And loving him, she could never love any body else."

Her husband was trying to read his paper, and so she lapsed into silence.

A bright wood fire was burning on the polished brass andirons, and as she settled herself in an easy chair before it, many pictures formed themselves in the glowing coals. Edith, too, could have her reveries at times.

"Nothing can bring back the past. We are advancing whether we will or not, onward to the great future. We can make our lives what we will, to a certain extent, but beyond that we are powerless.

We are the victims, or the tools of circumstances. Age, death, change, we cannot stay."

And in thinking of these things, her usually sunny soul was clouded, for the while, a smile died from her lips, the sparkle from her eyes. She murmured softly, feeling how impossible it would be for her to imitate:

"After all, Marguerite has chosen the better part."

In London the Countess of Arlington's party was at its height.

The picture gallery, lined with ancestral portraits, and the masterpieces of artists of many climes, had been waxed and embowered in a wilderness of palms and trailing vines, and transformed, for the night, into a spacious ballroom.

A fair English girl with a beautiful, patrician face was talking eagerly to an American who had just arrived in London. They were old friends, and in the pleasure of meeting, forgot the joys of the dance in the interchange of small conversational coin, denominated generally as news.

"Marguerite Clayton, — why haven't you heard? She has gone to Wyoming, quite out of the world, to be a nun in one of those Indian Mission schools."

Lord Parkhurst, standing on the opposite side of a waving palm but screened from view, learned in these chance words, of the fate of the girl who had once been everything to him.

He made his way through the crowds into the conservatory, and out into the silent night.

When he returned, half an hour later, his cousin Maud thought that he was not looking quite well. However, he gave no sign of any emotion.

He was the same handsome, distinguished looking Earl of Parkhurst, with the same manly bearing, the same clear-cut face, like a mosaic, the same magnetic personality, as on the night he had first crossed the path of an innocent, happy little schoolgirl in sunny France.

The perfume of dying flowers was borne on the furnace-heated air; the flash of lights, the gleam of jewels, the vision of beautiful women, made a changeing picture more brilliant than any on the walls.

The Hungarian band was tearing away at its weird, rhymthic harmonies as if each string had a thousand souls.

Marguerite Clayton had loved so well that kind of music!

But the Earl of Parkhurst had certain duties to perform, which did not permit of sentiment or regrets in a ballroom. Making his way to a sofa where rested a dowager and her pretty daughter, he paused a moment and said: "This is our dance Lady Helen."

www.ingramcontent.com/pod-product-compliance
Lightning Source LLC
Chambersburg PA
CBHW051741300426
44115CB00007B/651